The Beauty of Holiness

Other titles in the *Canterbury Studies in Spiritual Theology* series

Law and Revelation: Richard Hooker and His Writings
Edited by Raymond Chapman

Heaven in Ordinary: George Herbert and His Writings
Edited by Philip Sheldrake

Before the King's Majesty: Lancelot Andrewes and His Writings
Edited by Raymond Chapman

Christ Alive and at Large: The Unpublished Writings of C. F. D. Moule
Edited and introduced by Robert Morgan and Patrick Moule

Happiness and Holiness: Selected Writings of Thomas Traherne
Edited by Denise Inge

The Sacramental Life: Gregory Dix and His Writings
Edited and introduced by Simon Jones

To Build Christ's Kingdom: F. D. Maurice and His Writings
Edited and introduced by Jeremy Morris

Firmly I Believe: An Oxford Movement Reader
Edited by Raymond Chapman

The Truth-Seeking Heart: Austin Farrer and His Writings
Edited by Ann Loades and Robert MacSwain

God Truly Worshipped: Thomas Cranmer and His Writings
Edited by Jonathan Dean

Christ in All Things: William Temple and His Writings
Edited by Stephen Spencer

CANTERBURY STUDIES IN SPIRITUAL
THEOLOGY

The Beauty of Holiness

The Caroline Divines and Their Writings

Edited by
Benjamin Guyer

CANTERBURY PRESS
Norwich

© in this compilation Benjamin Guyer 2012

First published in 2012 by the Canterbury Press Norwich
Editorial office
13–17 Long Lane,
London, EC1A 9PN, UK

Canterbury Press is an imprint of Hymns Ancient & Modern Ltd
(a registered charity)
13A Hellesdon Park Road, Norwich,
Norfolk, NR6 5DR, UK

www.canterburypress.co.uk

All rights reserved. No part of this publication may be reproduced,
stored in a retrieval system, or transmitted,
in any form or by any means, electronic, mechanical,
photocopying or otherwise, without the prior permission of
the publisher, Canterbury Press.

The Author has asserted his right under the Copyright, Designs and
Patents Act, 1988,
to be identified as the Author of this Work

British Library Cataloguing in Publication data

A catalogue record for this book is available
from the British Library

978-1-84825-098-7

Originated by the Manila Typesetting Company
Printed and bound in Great Britain by
Lightning Source UK

Contents

Acknowledgements		ix
Notes on the Transcriptions		x
Introduction		1
1	Roots	27
2	Developments and Convergence	39
3	Civil War	54
4	The Cult of King Charles the Martyr	66
5	Interregnum	79
6	Restoration	93
7	Literary Devotion	114
8	Liturgical Devotion	128
9	The Book of Nature	153
10	Christian Ethics	166
11	The Kingdom	179
12	The Church	189
13	From Dust to Dust	203
Conclusion		215
Recommended Reading		217

Acknowledgements

I would like to thank several people for their role in the production of this volume. First, I thank Natalie Watson of SCM-Canterbury Press for giving me this opportunity. Katherine Clark, Sarah Irving and Ephraim Radner offered helpful suggestions early on. Holly Murphy graciously checked over my translations of Andrewes, Crashaw and Laud. I thank Benjamin T. G. Mayes for helping me better understand the influence of Johann Gerhard. I am grateful to Darrick N. Taylor and J. C. D. Clark for sustained discussion on Caroline England and their helpful comments on an earlier draft of this text. The British Library granted me kind permission to reprint several items. Finally, I thank Rachel for her enthusiastic patience and consistent encouragement.

This volume is dedicated to my parents, Robert and Laura Guyer.

Notes on the Transcriptions

In reproducing prose, I have not altered punctuation although in a small number of cases I have modernized spelling. Poetry has been untouched, although I have footnoted words whose meanings may not be known today. The best way to figure out unfamiliar words is to sound them out. Marginalia in the original editions has been [bracketed] in footnotes; my own additional references have only been footnoted. When an author does not provide a Latin translation, I have provided it too in a footnote.

Introduction

Give unto the LORD the glory due unto his name;
Worship the LORD in the beauty of holiness.
Psalm 29.2 (AV)

The Beauty of Holiness is an introduction to the Caroline divines, the major Anglican theologians and devotional writers who flourished under Charles I (1625–49) and Charles II (1649–85). 'Caroline' comes from *Carolus*, the Latin name for Charles. The present volume, however, is somewhat unconventional in its approach. The Caroline divines have long been portrayed as precursors of Anglo-Catholicism, a nineteenth-century reform movement which redefined the Anglican tradition by reviving medieval devotional practices, emphasizing the theological importance of the Church Fathers, and restoring ancient liturgical rites. Many readers will be familiar with the view of John Henry Newman, that 'there have ever been three principal parties in the Church of England, the Apostolical, the Latitudinarian and the Puritan, the two latter have been shown to be but modifications of Socinianism and Calvinism by their respective histories when allowed to act freely, whereas the first, when it had the opportunity of running into Romanism, did not coalesce with it'.[1] As a polemic this is certainly interesting, but as a description of history it is very wrong. In the mid-nineteenth century, distinct church parties began forming within the Church of England such that the whole of Anglican history was eventually viewed through the distorting prism of nineteenth-century ecclesiastical factions and conflicts. This approach persisted for more than a century and, to a large extent, still exists among Anglicans today.

The Caroline divines came to be associated with Anglo-Catholicism principally through the Library of Anglo-Catholic Theology (hereafter, LACT). This was an ambitious publishing effort by young Anglicans affiliated with the Oxford Movement, which began in 1833 as an attempt

---

[1] John Henry Newman, *Lectures on the Prophetical Office of the Church*, second ed. (Oxford, 1838), p. 23.

to shore up traditional theological principles in the Church of England. The Oxford Movement, in many ways unintentionally, became foundational for the development of Anglo-Catholicism. Due to their affiliation with the Oxford Movement *via* the LACT, the Caroline divines were soon seen as forerunners of Anglo-Catholicism itself. But there are good historical reasons for seeking a different perspective. First, and for reasons that remain unclear, the LACT was never completed. An 1840 advertisement for the series in London's *Ecclesiastical Gazette* indicates that 57 authors, ranging from Joseph Hall and Edward Stillingfleet to Lancelot Andrewes and William Laud, were originally slated for inclusion.[2] Only 20 were published, but some of these, such as Mark Frank and Richard Crakanthorp, were not included in the 1840 list. Second, the LACT did not claim to be a comprehensive introduction to the Caroline divines – although some later took it as such. Many of the LACT volumes remain standard reference works, but an incomplete and unfinished body of work, however important and influential, should not determine our own approach to the seventeenth century. *The Beauty of Holiness* is offered as a work of retrieval, re-presenting forgotten and even abandoned writers and concerns. By its offer of a new perspective on Caroline divinity, Anglicans will be better equipped to understand not only their past, but their present.

The sixteenth century

Although we are concerned with religion in the central half of the seventeenth century, we need to understand some of the key religious developments of the century that preceded it. The Council of Trent, which was called by Pope Paul III in 1545 to deal with matters of church reform, ended in 1563. This was the most important religious development of the sixteenth century, for unlike the Lutheran reform movement, which began in 1517 in a small German town, the Council of Trent was concerned with all of Europe. In the words of one modern historian, the fundamental purpose of Trent was 'delineating clearly the Catholic stance *vis-à-vis* the Protestants'.[3] With theological battle lines clearly drawn at the close of Trent between Rome and non-Roman reformers, the churches of Europe embarked upon an extended

---

2 *The Ecclesiastical Gazette*, 23 (2) (Tuesday 12 May, 1840), p. 240.
3 Robert Birely, *The Refashioning of Catholicism, 1450–1700* (Catholic University of America Press, 1999), p. 49.

process of confessionalization. Confessions themselves were not new to the post-Tridentine period; the early Christian creeds were confessions of faith, and successive ecumenical councils promulgated definitions and decrees on theological matters.[4] After Trent, confessionalization facilitated the creation of both ecclesiastical and regional political identities among Roman Catholic, Eastern Orthodox and Protestant churches.

It must be emphasized that *every* church confessionalized in the late-sixteenth and early-seventeenth centuries. The Council of Trent produced canons, decrees and the Profession of Tridentine Faith in 1564; Lutherans gathered their confessional documents into the Book of Concord in 1580; the Reformed produced, among other documents, the Belgic Confession in 1561 and the Canons of the Synod of Dort in 1618–19; the early Uniates composed confessional articles at the Union of Brest in 1596; in 1625 and 1642, the Orthodox produced the Confession of Faith by Metrophanes Kritopoulos and then revised the Orthodox Confession of Peter Moghila.[5] Confessionalization was hardly a 'Protestant' phenomenon. Furthermore, confessionalization was as concerned with liturgy and catechesis as it was about taking a documented stand on theological issues. This is too often forgotten. Tridentine reforms were taught in the Roman Catechism of 1566; the Book of Concord contained not only the Augsburg Confession but Luther's two catechisms; the Reformed produced the Heidelberg Catechism in 1563, and John Calvin spent more time preparing catechisms than the Gallican Confession which he helped compose in 1559; and, when the Church of England revised the Book of Common Prayer in 1662, it included the traditional catechism and the Articles of Religion. Confessionalization was about developing, securing and sustaining a particular way of life, complete with its own rituals and beliefs. Sometimes these overlapped with the rituals and beliefs of other European religious communities, and sometimes they did not.

---

4 There is no finer discussion than Jaroslav Pelikan, *Credo: Historical and Theological Guide to Creeds and Confessions of Faith in the Christian Tradition* (Yale University Press, 2003), Chs 2–4.

5 For Roman Catholicism, Birely, *Refashioning*, Ch. 2, and John O'Malley, *Trent and all That: Renaming Catholicism in the Early Modern Era* (Harvard University Press, 2002), pp. 85–91; for Uniates, Barbara Skinner, *The Western Front of the Eastern Church: Uniate and Orthodox Conflict in 18th-century Poland, Ukraine, Belarus, and Russia* (Northern Illinois University Press, 2009), pp. 3–41; standard Orthodox confessions are listed in Timothy Ware, *The Orthodox Church*, new ed. (Penguin, 1997), p. 203.

The best place to begin a study of seventeenth-century religious conflict is with the confessions, catechisms and liturgies that were already written and promulgated. On the one hand, these were the most widely disseminated texts in reforming Europe. Germans learned about the Evangelical (re: Lutheran) way of life not through the tomes of Luther, Melanchthon or later figures, but through the liturgy and Luther's catechisms. Devout Reformed parents taught their children about thankfulness and prayer by reading to them from the Heidelberg Catechism, rather than John Calvin's more difficult *Institutes*. Pious English peasants did not spend their evenings reading the latest work of high theological controversy, but used their Prayer Books, the devotional material found in almanacs, and the catechetical material approved by royal authority. The simplest ideas were the most widespread and usually touched the most personal elements of faith, such as the meaning of baptism and the nature of public worship. On the other hand, once we recognize that confessional texts such as catechisms were most influential, we need not follow a 'great man' approach to history. History concerns far more than 'great men' like Luther and Calvin, and the writings of these two men simply do not tell us all that we need to know about the religious movements that bear their names today. The Book of Concord is a good example of this: of its eight documents, only the two catechisms were written by Luther alone. Similarly, neither the Gallican Confession nor the catechisms of John Calvin ever became primary in the Reformed tradition. History is not about what great men think or do, but about the development of the whole. We must be sensitive to the ways that peasants, for example, received, revised and rejected the ideas of reformers. This is certainly true of the Church of England, where use of the Prayer Book often led to the mixing of traditional and reformed practices.[6] No one had a monopoly on the direction of reform in the sixteenth century.

Comparing the confessional norms of the European churches reveals both similarities and differences. Protestants and Catholics were well aware of this at the time.[7] On theological topics such as predestination, every church wrestled with a range of theological opinions, each of which had been debated without resolution by their medieval forebears.

---

6 Eamon Duffy, *The Stripping of the Altars: Traditional Religion in England 1400–1580*, second ed. (Yale University Press, 2005), pp. 491–4, 586–93.

7 Richard A. Muller, *God, Creation, and Providence in the Thought of Jacob Arminius: Sources and Directions of Protestant Scholasticism in the Era of Early Orthodoxy* (Revell Books, 1991), p. 273.

These differences caused acute and prolonged conflict, and helped propel official resolutions such as the Lutheran Formula of Concord (1577), the Canons of the Synod of Dort (1618) among the Reformed, Charles I's Declaration on the Articles of Religion in the Church of England (1628), and the Roman Catholic Formulary of Alexander VII (1665).[8] Each church affirmed the priority of divine grace in the Christian life, and each also affirmed that some are predestined to salvation. Debate focused upon the extent of human freedom and whether God also predestines some for damnation. 'Double' or 'absolute' predestination claims that each person is predestined for either one or the other. Lutherans and Roman Catholics rejected this doctrine quite early, although Catholics in France debated it into the eighteenth century.[9] The Church of England never accepted the doctrine, and although much debate was had on it, Charles I's aforementioned Declaration became normative by stating that the Articles of Religion must be read in their plain sense, and therefore as not affirming double predestination. The Reformed, however, accepted it, first at the Synod of Dort and then in a more refined form in the third section of the Westminster Confession (1647).

Other matters show the same diversity. Like Roman Catholics and some Lutherans, the Church of England retained an episcopal hierarchy. Yet unlike Lutherans and Roman Catholics but more like the Reformed, Anglicans were rarely enthusiastic about artwork in churches. The liturgy of the Church of England was thus more truncated than that among Roman Catholics and Lutherans.[10] Yet the Church of England nonetheless retained ceremonies, a practice that the Belgic Confession rejected in its twenty-fifth article. The Anglican liturgical calendar was also reformed in such a way that it departed from developing Reformed orthodoxy. The Church of England commemorated saints, although it

---

8 Anglican debates will be discussed below. For Lutheranism, Robert Kolb, *Bound Choice, Election, and Wittenberg Theological Method: From Martin Luther to the Formula of Concord* (William B. Eerdmans, 2005); on the Synod of Dort, Carl Bangs, *Arminius: A Study in the Dutch Reformation* (F. Asbury Press, 1985), Chs 25–6, and Jonathan I. Israel, *The Dutch Republic: Its Rise, Greatness, and Fall 1477–1806* (Oxford University Press, 1995), Ch. 20; for Roman Catholicism, Birely, *Refashioning*, pp. 187–91, and William Doyle, *Jansenism* (St Martin's Press, 2000), esp. p. 91 for the Formulary.

9 Roman Catholics clarified their stance in Session VI of the Council of Trent; Lutherans rejected double predestination in Article XI of the Formula of Concord.

10 Nigel Yates, *Liturgical Space: Christian Worship and Church Buildings in Western Europe 1500–2000* (Ashgate, 2008), Chs 2, 4, 5.

rejected older ideas and practices concerning their role in intercession. In this, it stood apart from the Reformed, who wholly rejected a liturgical calendar, and from Lutherans and Roman Catholics, each of whom retained a liturgical calendar, although Lutherans rejected saintly intercession. Perhaps most importantly, unlike Lutherans and Reformed but like Catholics in France and Spain, the Church of England retained a medieval theology of the monarch as the anointed of the Lord. In France and England, this was bound up with a strong belief in the Royal Touch, the miraculous ability of kings to heal various diseases.[11] By 1600, no church had a theology uniquely its own. Each was defined by its own individual combination of continuities with, and reforms and rejections of, the medieval past.

Caroline England

Charles I ascended the throne amid considerable fanfare in 1625. None of the chaos that later overtook his reign was predictable at the time. By his own admission the new king planned to call parliaments frequently, but several political developments caused him to unexpectedly alter course. First, because Parliament refused to provide the necessary funds for continued war with Spain, the king recognized that he would soon have to sign a humiliating peace treaty. Second, the Duke of Buckingham, the king's best friend and political advisor, was assassinated by John Felton, a religious and political radical who was understandably resentful over his unpaid military service. Felton also claimed, however, that his actions were inspired by Parliamentary complaints against the Duke's failed military leadership and his purportedly 'Arminian' religious convictions. When some members of Parliament claimed that Felton was a hero for his actions, it appeared that they were willing to countenance terrorism.[12] Finally, when the king dissolved Parliament in early 1629, the House of Commons erupted in violence. The Speaker was physically coerced into remaining seated, which allowed additional resolutions to be read, many of which concerned religion. Not only

---

[11] Marc Bloch, *The Royal Touch: Monarchy and Miracles in England and France*, trans. J. E. Anderson (Routledge, 1989); J. H. Elliott, 'King and *Patria* in the Hispanic World', reprinted in *Spain, Europe & the Wider World 1500–1800* (Yale University Press, 2009), pp. 173–92; Luis R. Corteguera, 'King as Father in Early Modern Spain', in *Memoria y Civilización*, 12 (2009), pp. 49–69.

[12] Michael Braddick, *God's Fury, England's Fire: A New History of the English Civil Wars* (Penguin, 2008), pp. 40–5.

were members of the Commons prohibited from leaving, but one was assaulted for attempting to do so.[13] After order was restored, public opinion of Parliament, particularly the House of Commons, was understandably low.[14] A failed war, a successful assassination, and the Parliamentary melee left the king in no rush to call Parliament for the foreseeable future.

The religious background

Religious tensions permeated the events of 1628–9. England was like many other European countries: it had a national church of which every citizen was expected to be part. Political toleration of religious difference was quite rare; only in 1648, with the Peace of Westphalia, was limited toleration granted to select religious minorities in much of Europe. Every national church had to deal with the fact that an 'underground' of religious dissent existed within its walls, and because dissenters had no formal mechanism for confessional self-definition, a wide variety of ideas circulated among them. Since the reign of Elizabeth I, some reforming movements sought to transform the English church in foundational ways, usually by removing those elements that appeared similar to Roman Catholicism. Collectively, these groups are often labelled 'Puritan', although this term unhelpfully implies theological homogeneity vis-à-vis Reformed theology. Not all dissenters were attached to the doctrinal and disciplinary norms of the Reformed churches. In England as elsewhere, dissent encompassed a wide range or orthodox and heterodox convictions, and an equally wide range of opinions on how to deal with the state. In the late-sixteenth and seventeenth centuries, English religious history was not defined by a simple dichotomy between 'Puritan' and 'Anglican', but between dissenters of differing stripes and those who defended the Church of England.

Most people believed that unorthodox theological opinions nurtured, and were in turn nurtured by, political extremism. Few accusations carried more political weight than that of heresy. This exact scenario played out in the 1580s and 1590s, when John Whitgift, Archbishop of Canterbury, and an obscure priest named Richard Hooker took issue with the dissenter Thomas Cartwright. In response to Cartwright's

---

13 Kevin Sharpe, *The Personal Rule of Charles I* (Yale University Press, 1992), pp. 46–55.
14 Conrad Russell, *The Crisis of Parliaments: English History 1509–1660* (Oxford University Press, 1971), p. 310.

complaint against saying the Gloria Patri and the Athanasian Creed, Archbishop Whitgift wrote, 'I must suspect the matter, not well understanding whereunto these glances of yours at "Gloria Patri, and Athanasius' creed," do tend.' Whitgift continued, 'he that is offended with the oft repetition of saying of either of them, I cannot tell what I should judge of him. But undoubtedly there is a great cause why I should suspect him at the least of singularity and unquietness.'[15] In his *Lawes of Ecclesiasticall Politie*, Richard Hooker was no less critical, arguing that Cartwright and his supporters had intentionally 'renued' ancient heresy: 'The authors of this venime beinge dead and gon, theire wicked doctrine notwithstandinge continueth.'[16] The very title of Hooker's work indicated his concern with civil and ecclesiastical order. Other writers, such as James VI of Scotland, were also concerned with dissenting political doctrine. In his popular *Basilicon Doron*, a work of political theology written for his son Henry in 1597, the king described Puritans as 'phanaticke spirits' and the 'verie pestes in the Church and Common-weale, whom no deserts can oblige, neither oaths or promises binde, breathing nothing but sedition and calumnies, aspiring without measure, railing without reason, and making their owne imaginations (without any warrant of the word) the square of their conscience'.[17] Arguments such as these were not about being 'anti-Calvinist', as most English had a fairly rosy view of the reform movements on the European continent. Whitgift, Hooker and James VI were instead concerned with maintaining the societal bonds of theological, liturgical and political fellowship.

When James VI of Scotland became James I of England in 1603, he continued Elizabeth I's work in restraining the spread of dissenting ideologies. His first target was the Geneva Bible, a translation that was banned but widely available in England. The Geneva Bible was controversial because it contained a commentary which included the repeated claim that righteous subjects could execute kings who failed to defend true religion. The 'King James' or Authorized Version of the

---

15 John Whitgift, *The Defence of the Answer to the Admonition* (1574), Tract IX, John Ayre (ed.), *The Works of John Whitgift*, Vol. 2 (Oxford, 1852), p. 481.

16 Richard Hooker, *Of the Lawes of Ecclesiasticall Politie*, V.42.13 (1597), W. Speed Hill (ed.), *The Folger Library Edition of the Works of Richard Hooker* (Cambridge, MA, Harvard University Press, 1977), p. 177.

17 Cited from Johann Sommerville (ed.), *King James VI and I: Political Writings* (Cambridge University Press, 1994), pp. 26–7; *Basilicon Doron* translates as *The Royal Gift*.

Bible was produced so that the English would have a translation of Scripture without such subversive content.[18] It is generally recognized that the king was quite elastic in his ecclesiastical policy, which mirrors and perhaps even maps his international ecumenical efforts. James VI and I proactively sought peace with his European neighbours and also sought to pave the way towards an ecumenical council.[19] The king cultivated relations with groups as diverse as the Greek Orthodox and Dutch Reformed churches, and sought to use the French Protestant Synod of Tonneins as the basis for reconciliation between the Lutheran and Reformed churches.[20] He also sent a small delegation to the Reformed Synod of Dordrecht (Dort) in 1618–19. Royal involvement in each of these was due to the king's conciliarism.

The Synod of Dort was called to deal with controversy surrounding Arminius, a deceased pastor and professor of theology who advocated revising the Belgic Confession. Debate raged between Remonstrants, the followers of Arminius, and their opponents, the Counter-Remonstrants. These arguments reveal much about seventeenth-century intellectual history. First, they underscore the importance of scholasticism among seventeenth-century Protestants, who participated in and even helped spur the post-Tridentine renewal of scholastic thought. After Trent, Thomism was the first scholastic school to see a revival, within and then beyond Catholicism.[21] Second, we see how unresolved medieval disputes shaped the development of Protestant orthodoxies. A central theological divide within medieval scholasticism was between theological rationalism, most famously represented by Thomas Aquinas, and theological voluntarism, which became the dominant trend in Reformed theology. Arminius was a theological rationalist, which set him apart from most of his Reformed contemporaries.

Finally, the Arminian controversy highlights the relationship between the doctrines of creation and salvation. Aquinas held that divine reason

---

18 Alister McGrath, *In the Beginning: The Story of the King James Bible and How It Changed a Nation, a Language, and a Culture* (Doubleday, 2001), pp. 114–29.

19 W. B. Patterson, *King James VI and I and the Reunion of Christendom* (Cambridge University Press, 1997), p. 154.

20 Patterson, *Reunion*, pp. 158–80.

21 Ulrich G. Leinsle, *Introduction to Scholastic Theology*, trans. Michael J. Miller (Catholic University of America Press, 2010), p. 290; Frits G. M. Broeyer, 'Traces of the Rise of Reformed Scholasticism in the Polemical Theology of William Whitaker (1548–1595)', in Willem J. van Asselt and Eef Dekker (eds), *Reformation and Scholasticism: An Ecumenical Enterprise* (Baker Academic, 2001), p. 160.

determines all actions performed by the divine will. Creation, as a product of the divine will, reflects the order that is inherent in divine reason. The voluntarist tradition held that God created the world as a wholly free act. Thus the laws of nature reveal only the unconstrained operation of the divine will, rather than the determinations and constraints set by divine reason. These different understandings of creation worked themselves out in divergent understandings of the laws of nature. Theological rationalism could account for secondary causation within the natural order because it believed that natural laws reflected the order of divine reason. God is involved in creation, but does not actively will all that goes on within it. Creation is ordered by laws and these allow for a certain level of contingency. Voluntarists such as John Calvin, however, had a low estimate of secondary causation, and were far more inclined to ascribe historical and natural events to providential action.[22] These two, very different theologies of creation had implications for soteriology. Arminius held that God has willed the *means* of salvation, rather than the salvation of individuals.[23] Human beings may therefore either reject or accept the divine initiative. These views were condemned at Dort, which affirmed an exclusively voluntarist understanding of salvation as depending upon the freely willed act of God for an elect few.

The British found Dort a chaotic and disheartening experience.[24] John Hales, one of the English delegates, stated that he 'bid John Calvin goodnight' after Dort.[25] The delegation sought unsuccessfully to ameliorate the condemnation of the Remonstrants, which they refused to sign, and although they accepted the Synod's canons, they did so with the express intent of underscoring points of doctrinal agreement with the Lutherans. This pan-Protestant emphasis was the brainchild of the king, who had instructed his delegates to resist doctrinal development and instead advocate only those points of earlier doctrinal consensus.[26] Some English welcomed the condemnation of Arminius, but others were less sanguine about the outcome of the Synod.

---

22 Susan E. Schreiner, *The Theater of His Glory: Nature and the Natural Order in the Thought of John Calvin* (Baker Book House, 1995), pp. 30–2.

23 Muller, *God, Creation, and Providence*, pp. 123–4, 161–70.

24 Anthony Milton, *Catholic and Reformed: The Roman and Protestant Churches in English Protestant Thought, 1600–1640* (Cambridge University Press, 1995), pp. 418–26; Peter White, *Predestination, Policy, and Polemic: Conflict and Consensus in the English Church from the Reformation to the Civil War* (Cambridge University Press, 1992), Ch. 9.

25 Cited in White, *Predestination*, p. 183.

26 White, *Predestination*, pp. 180, 200–1.

Importantly, the Church of England never accepted Dort's canons. A watershed event for the Dutch Reformed therefore did not become such for the English church. Only among some dissenters did the term 'Arminian' become an insult tantamount to 'popery', and the two terms became polemically entwined under Charles I. The logic behind this equation is unclear; neither Arminius nor his followers had an interest in liturgy. The Remonstrants did, however, want the Dutch Republic to seek peace with Spain, the largest Catholic power in Europe. For more extreme dissenters, this betrayed the apocalyptic war against the papal Antichrist.[27] Other elements of the Remonstrant political programme, notably their advocacy of toleration for religious minorities, made no headway in England. The theological rationalism of English thinkers such as Richard Hooker was due to the sixteenth-century revival of Thomism. There was no Arminianism *avant la lettre*, only a shared scholastic background among all Europeans, Protestant and Catholic.

British problems

The years between 1629 and 1640 are known in English history as the 'personal rule' of Charles I. The term refers to a period when a king ruled without Parliament. There is no evidence that Charles I intentionally began a personal rule in England in 1629, and because the Irish and Scottish parliaments both met in the 1630s, we cannot claim that the king was hostile to parliaments. Charles I's personal rule was a period of stability. The 1630s opened with England at peace with both France and Spain. This allowed for the growth of English maritime trade, particularly with Europe, and raw materials were increasingly imported from both the New World and India.[28] The king decreased the national debt by almost half, streamlined and increased poor relief, and reformed and expanded the navy.[29] One recent historian has even referred to this period as the 'Pax Carolana'.[30]

Religious controversy undid the king's peace, but this was aided by Charles I's greatest political error: his seeming distance from his own

---

27 Israel, *Dutch Republic*, p. 423.
28 Keith Wrightson, *Earthly Necessities: Economic Lives in Early Modern Britain* (Yale University Press, 2000), pp. 180–1; Mark Kishlansky, *A Monarchy Transformed: Britain 1603–1714* (Penguin, 1996), pp. 117–18.
29 Kishlansky, *Monarchy Transformed*, p. 121; Sharpe, *Personal Rule*, p. 475; Richard Cust, *Charles I: A Political Life* (Pearson Longman, 2007), pp. 190–2.
30 Sharpe, *Personal Rule*, Ch. 2.

people.³¹ English monarchy, more so than Scottish and Irish monarchy, was predicated on public spectacles such as coronation, royal processions, and most especially the Royal Touch. The medieval origins of the practice should not be interpreted as making the Caroline regime more 'Catholic' than 'Protestant'. The early English reformers had no opposition to Edward VI using the Royal Touch; when the boy king was on his deathbed, he consecrated cramp rings for warding off bodily pain.³² Some rebels became sharply opposed to the Royal Touch during the civil wars, but the most consistent enemies of the Royal Touch from the mid-sixteenth century onward were the Jesuits, who opposed all notions of sacral kingship as an affront to papal power.³³ Charles I rarely dispensed the Royal Touch, and just as rarely embarked upon royal processions.³⁴ This weakened his popularity. Furthermore, he was not crowned in Scotland until 1633, and his refusal to participate in Presbyterian worship – like his father, he insisted on using the English Prayer Book in Scotland – angered many of the Presbyterians who lived there.

The kingdoms of England, Ireland and Scotland together comprised a composite monarchy: the union of two or more kingdoms, each with its own legal traditions and governmental structures, under one monarch.³⁵ The history of composite monarchy in the British Isles is often called the 'British problem'.³⁶ Composite monarchies were not uncommon in early-modern Europe, but they were often unstable. For example, Scotland and Ireland were jealous of England's economic superiority. The religions of the kingdoms were also different, and dissimilar religious loyalties were bound up with divergent political allegiances. Ireland was predominantly Roman Catholic, although a royalist element allied to the English Crown had existed in Ireland for a century. Under Elizabeth I, England had the 1559 Prayer Book in English, but

---

31 Cust, *Charles I*, pp. 170–1.

32 Bloch, *Royal Touch*, pp. 188–9.

33 Paul Kléber Monod, *The Power of Kings: Monarchy and Religion in Europe, 1589–1715* (Yale University Press, 1999), pp. 51–3.

34 Andrew Lacey, *The Cult of King Charles the Martyr* (Boydell Press, 2003), p. 34.

35 J. H. Elliott, 'A Europe of Composite Monarchies', reprinted in *Spain, Europe & the Wider World*, pp. 3–24.

36 J. G. A. Pocock, 'British history: A plea for a new subject' (1973/4), reprinted in *The Discovery of Islands: Essays in British History* (Cambridge University Press, 2005), pp. 24–43; John Morrill, 'The British Problem, c. 1534–1707', in Brendan Bradshaw and John Morrill (eds), *The British Problem, c. 1534–1707: State Formation in the Atlantic Archipelago* (Macmillan, 1996), pp. 1–38.

Introduction 13

in Ireland a Latin translation of the more traditional 1549 Prayer Book was used.[37] Confessional development also varied; the Church of Ireland adopted the Eleven Articles of Archbishop Parker in 1560 while the Church of England adopted the Thirty-Nine Articles of Religion in 1571. The more elaborate Irish Articles of Religion was composed in 1615, but does not appear to have been adopted.[38] Only in the 1630s was there a canonical and confessional convergence between the Irish and English churches.

The Scottish Reformation was yet another story. Scotland's church was an unhappy hybrid of loyalties. The most recent history of the Scottish Reformation describes it as 'unnervingly aggressive' to the point of 'sanctifying violence' because it proceeded by way of 'religious terrorism'.[39] This has implications for understanding English history and accentuates the reality of the British problem. Scottish Presbyterianism proactively cultivated a theology of armed, revolutionary resistance which some religiously and politically disaffected English were drawn to. However, the Scottish state church was not Presbyterian until the end of the seventeenth century. Murray G. H. Pittock has written against 'the legend of a solely Presbyterian Reformation', and he estimates that, even at the end of the seventeenth century, upwards of half the Scottish population was Episcopalian.[40] Yet in some places, traditional Christian holy days such as Christmas were banned by Presbyterian revolutionaries – a practice that was copied in England during and after the civil wars.[41]

The difficulties of ruling a composite monarchy could be ameliorated by increasing its uniformity in religion, law and government.[42] In the 1630s, Scotland, England and Ireland experienced a shared pattern of ecclesiastical reform. In 1636 a collection of canons was drawn up for the Scottish church and in 1637 Charles I introduced the Book of

---

37 John McCafferty, *The Reconstruction of the Church of Ireland: Bishop Bramhall and the Laudian Reforms, 1633–1641* (Cambridge University Press, 2007), pp. 10–12.

38 McCafferty, *Reconstruction*, pp. 59–68.

39 Alec Ryrie, *The Origins of the Scottish Reformation* (Manchester University Press, 2006), pp. 123, 124.

40 Murray G. H. Pittock, *A New History of Scotland* (Sutton, 2003), p. 160, and *Inventing and Resisting Britain: Cultural Identities in Britain and Ireland, 1685–1789* (St Martin's Press, 1997), p. 10.

41 Margo Todd, 'The problem of Scotland's Puritans', in John Coffey and C. H. Lim (eds), *The Cambridge Companion to Puritanism* (Cambridge University Press, 2008), p. 179.

42 Elliott, 'Composite Monarchies', pp. 15–16.

Common Prayer to Scotland; together these brought the Church of Scotland into doctrinal and liturgical conformity with the Irish and English churches. These reforms are often treated as an ideology and termed 'Laudianism' after William Laud, whom the king appointed to the See of Canterbury in 1633. It is unclear that Laud was the primary force behind these changes, although he was widely blamed for them at the time.[43] The Caroline reforms were distinguished by the restoration of the altar in the church, an increased appreciation for religious artwork, the rapid growth of devotional writing, and permission for the freer expression of liturgical devotion, such as bowing at the name of Jesus or towards the altar. These changes were controversial among more than just dissenters. The Caroline convergence defined the Anglican tradition from 1660 onward. In Scotland, the first Prayer Book liturgy was greeted with riots, with its opponents deriding it as 'popery'.[44] Scottish Presbyterians drafted a National Covenant in 1638 which emboldened and strengthened their place in the Scottish church. The Bishops' Wars followed in 1639 and 1640, with the result that the Prayer Book was withdrawn, Scottish episcopacy remained tenuously in existence, and Charles I was humiliated and in need of financial assistance. The personal rule was over. Parliament was summoned.

A world turned upside down

It is now known that the Scottish Covenanters were in contact with a small group in the English House of Commons who identified with their religious aims of abolishing the Prayer Book, and their political aims of circumscribing royal authority. These English even encouraged the Covenanters to invade England in 1640, which initiated the second Bishops' War.[45] By 1640, a junta had formed in the House of Commons which sought the destruction of the Church of England and a radical alteration of the government and civil law.[46] In the first parliament of 1640, known as the 'Short Parliament' because Charles I

---

43 Julian Davies, *The Caroline Captivity of the Church: Charles I and the Remoulding of Anglicanism* (Clarendon Press, 1992), Chs 1–2; Cust, *Charles I*, pp. 133–47.

44 J. S. A. Adamson, *The Noble Revolt: The Overthrow of Charles I* (Weidenfeld & Nicolson, 2007), p. 5.

45 Braddick, *God's Fury*, pp. 104–6; Adamson, *Revolt*, pp. 13, 44.

46 Adamson, *Revolt*, p. 96; Conrad Russell, *The Fall of the British Monarchies 1637–1642* (Oxford University Press, 1991), p. 462.

quickly dissolved it on account of its intransigence, the junta's aims were frustrated. In yet another illustration of the British problem, the junta's relief came neither from Scotland nor from England, but quite unexpectedly from Ireland, where a Catholic uprising was launched in 1641 against Protestants. The total number of Protestant deaths is difficult to ascertain; recent estimates range between 527 and 1,259.[47] Stories of the uprising were, however, manipulated by the junta, horrors were invented, and in some publications the number of Protestants killed was exaggerated by as much as 300,000.[48] With a propaganda campaign and a political crisis, much of the English population was on edge. In 1641, the Archbishop of Canterbury and the Earl of Strafford were impeached by Parliament and later executed. The junta then led the House of Commons in making the outrageously illegal claim that Parliament, rather than the king, was in control of the armed forces.[49] By 1642, relations between king and Parliament had broken down, with the fundamental divide between Crown and Commons.

Civil war raged in all three kingdoms from 1642 to 1646, and again in 1648 until the king was beheaded on 30 January 1649. The Irish and Welsh populations were strongly royalist.[50] The English junta and its supporters joined with the Scottish Covenanters against the royalists in Scotland and England. As Conrad Russell has noted, the two revolutionary movements were 'interdependent, and whatever threatened one carried an implied threat to the other'.[51] Between 1642 and 1645, the fortunes of each side waxed and waned. It appeared in 1645 that the royalists, after a series of victories, would emerge victorious; but at the battle of Naseby excessive zeal drove the king and his army to attack the New Model Army, which fought for the House of Commons, without waiting for reinforcements. All was lost.[52] Naseby was also the site of one of the most brutal acts by the rebels: the murder of one

---

47 S. J. Connolly, *Divided Kingdom: Ireland 1630–1800* (Oxford University Press, 2008), p. 46.

48 Braddick, *God's Fury*, pp. 167–8, 197; Connolly, *Divided Kingdom*, p. 108; Adamson, *Revolt*, pp. 420–30.

49 Braddick, *God's Fury*, p. 142; Adamson, *Revolt*, p. 336.

50 Connolly, *Divided Kingdom*, p. 67; Geraint H. Jenkins, *The Foundations of Modern Wales 1642–1780* (Clarendon Press/University of Wales Press, 1987), p. 35.

51 Russell, *Fall*, p. 491.

52 Ronald Hutton, *The Royalist War Effort 1642–1646* (Routledge, 2003), p. 178.

hundred women and the mutilation of those left alive.[53] The women were accused of being 'Irish whores', the implication being that they were Catholic. This episode was only a taste of things to come. The king surrendered in 1646 to the Covenanters, was ransomed to the English in 1647, and although he escaped was recaptured. In 1648, the New Model Army purged Parliament of those who objected to the radical course of events, leaving what is known to history as the 'Rump Parliament'.

The trial of Charles I was a farce. None of the justices initially nominated by the junta was willing to serve, leaving the Rump Parliament scrambling to find those willing to condemn the king.[54] Charles I repeatedly challenged the legality of the proceedings, and on the fourth day of the trial John Lilburne bluntly and bizarrely stated that the court was 'founded upon that *Authority of the Commons of England, in whom rests the Supreme Jurisdiction*'.[55] It is unclear that the king's enemies initially planned to execute him, but they did so on 30 January.[56] The event came as a shock to more than just royalists. Scottish Covenanters, who had hoped for a Presbyterian settlement in Scotland with Charles I still on the throne, declared Charles II their king. In England, however, there was no king, and the New Model Army proceeded to abolish the House of Lords in March 1649. Under the leadership of Oliver Cromwell, the New Model Army then went to war in Scotland and Ireland, destroying the Scottish and Irish parliaments. The horror at Naseby was then brought full circle. When Cromwell invaded Ireland in late 1649, thousands of Catholics were killed at Drogheda, including unarmed priests who were executed on the spot.[57] In the early 1650s, the Rump Parliament appeared to wield sovereignty, but tensions between it and Cromwell led to a military coup and Parliament's forced dissolution in 1653. Cromwell, who now reigned supreme, claimed that he had acted under divine inspiration.[58]

The Cromwellian regime was haunted by the memory of Charles I. The king's defiance of the Commons in his final days and his apparent

---

53 Jenkins, *Foundations of Modern Wales*, p. 17; Braddick, *God's Fury*, p. 377.
54 Diane Purkiss, *The English Civil War: Papists, Gentlewomen, Soldiers, and Witchfinders in the Birth of Modern Britain* (Basic Books, 2006), p. 554.
55 *Reliquae Sacrae Carolinae* (1650), Part II, p. 56.
56 Cust, *Charles I*, pp. 458–61.
57 Connolly, *Divided Kingdom*, p. 94.
58 Ian Gentles, *The New Model Army: In England, Ireland, and Scotland, 1645–1653* (Blackwell, 1993), pp. 433–4.

Introduction

fearlessness on the scaffold combined with popular sentiment to create a surge of pro-Caroline sentiment. The publication of the king's autobiographical *Eikon Basilike* the day of his death cemented his image as *the* royal saint and martyr. Although banned by the government, the work went through 39 English and almost two dozen foreign language editions in the first year of publication alone. It has every right to be called 'the most successful book of the [seventeenth] century'.[59] Attacks which claimed that the book was a forgery did nothing to undermine its popularity. Unofficial liturgies were written for 30 January, and, with the circulation of miracle stories about the Royal Touch being effected through the king's relics, we may conclude that Charles I garnered more support and loyalty dead than alive. But Cromwellian England was haunted in other ways as well. The absence of parliaments was a powerful sign of the absence of legal government. Taxes during the 1650s were also high – more than double what they had been during the personal rule of Charles I.[60] The rituals of state used by the Cromwellian regime echoed the rituals of royal splendour, although they lacked key traditional elements such as consecration and communion.[61]

The removal of these traditional elements was due to the anti-Anglican and especially anti-Catholic tenor of the government. As many as 3,600 Anglican clergy were removed from office over the course of the 1640s, the Prayer Book was banned, and its use became clandestine.[62] As the selection from John Evelyn in Chapter 5 illustrates, repression of Anglicans could be quite severe. The entire festive culture of the Anglican church, so deeply rooted in English folk culture and the agricultural year, was banned, including the celebration of Christmas, Easter and Whitsun/Pentecost, the three highest holy days when the Eucharist was traditionally celebrated. Christian weddings were also prohibited, and marriages became civil ceremonies.[63] The suffering of Irish Catholics was even greater. Approximately 12,000 Irish were enslaved and sent to work in the West Indies on sugar plantations, and some historians have discerned a push for 'ethnic cleansing' among some in the Cromwellian

---

59 Lacey, *King Charles the Martyr*, p. 81.

60 Barry Coward, *The Cromwellian Protectorate* (Manchester University Press, 2002), pp. 164–5.

61 Laura Lunger Knoppers, *Constructing Cromwell: Ceremony, Portrait, and Print, 1645–1661* (Cambridge University Press, 2000), pp. 107, 133.

62 Robert S. Bosher, *The Making of the Restoration Settlement: The Influence of the Laudians 1649–1662*, revised ed. (Dacre Press, 1957), p. 5.

63 Coward, *Protectorate*, p. 170.

regime.[64] In the event, the government agreed to exterminate 10 per cent of the population – approximately 130,000 people – although this too failed.[65] Cromwell did take much farmland from the Irish; owning 59 per cent of the land in 1641, their legal ownership was reduced to barely more than 6 per cent. Despite the restoration of much property back to the Irish under Charles II, by 1688 Irish ownership had increased to only 22 per cent.[66] Cromwell's frequent appeals to 'religious toleration' and 'the people' were not precursors of modern, liberal democracy, but applied only to the small number of religious groups legalized during his reign. Cromwell himself recognized his unpopularity.[67] After he died in 1658, his military republic rapidly collapsed.

Restoration

In 1660, Charles II was restored to his throne and the Church of England was restored with him. It is difficult to overstate the immense joy that greeted the king. According to his Declaration of Breda, Charles II intended to grant an undefined degree of religious toleration to those who could not accept the Church of England, the precise extent of which was left in the hands of the newly restored Parliament. Among the first things that Charles II did upon his return to England was practise the Royal Touch. Surviving records indicate that the king laid his hands on almost 100,000 of his subjects.[68] This was a key difference between the court of Charles I and that of his son: the latter cultivated his popularity. The great failure of Charles II was his sexual appetite. In this he was wholly opposite to his father, who was chaste and monogamous, and was known for lecturing young men on the importance of living virtuously.[69] Charles II was rebuked for his promiscuity by figures such as Gilbert Sheldon, Archbishop of Canterbury, and Richard Allestree, arguably the most popular Anglican writer of the seventeenth

---

64 S. J. Connolly, *Contested Island: Ireland 1460–1630* (Oxford University Press, 2007), p. 105; references to 'ethnic cleansing' in Coward, *Protectorate*, p. 147, and Crawford Gribben, 'Puritanism in Ireland and Wales', in Coffey and Lim, *Puritanism*, p. 165.

65 Coward, *Protectorate*, p. 145; computed from Connolly, *Contested Island*, p. 405.

66 Connolly, *Divided Kingdom*, p. 137.

67 Coward, *Protectorate*, p. 169.

68 Anna Keay, *The Magnificent Monarch: Charles II and the Ceremonies of Power* (Hambledon Continuum, 2008), p. 211.

69 Cust, *Charles I*, p. 188.

and eighteenth centuries.[70] The newly restored king, despite his embrace of earlier Caroline ceremonial, lacked the piety of his father. The looseness of Charles II's court sharply contrasted with the disciplined national church, such that by the end of the decade the euphoria of 1660 had waned considerably.

The religious settlement that developed in 1662 was a victory for the Church of England. The Declaration of Breda implied a royal willingness to create a broad church that would encompass moderate Presbyterians. This is not what transpired. Many features of the earlier Caroline church returned with the Restoration, in large part because they had become heavily theologized in debate with dissenters during the 1640s and 1650s. Altars were restored, artwork returned, and in cathedrals incense was burned on high holy days.[71] Charles I was made the first Anglican saint and included in the 1662 calendar of saints as King Charles the Martyr. Like 30 January, 29 May, the date when Charles II entered London and completed the Restoration, was given its own liturgy. The new Prayer Book further revived a liturgical role for the king from the medieval period. On Christmas, Easter and Whitsun the monarch received the alms of the chapel royal and placed them upon the altar before receiving the Eucharist. As Anna Keay has observed, this liturgical participation emphasized the king's 'priestly role'.[72] Finally, as this integration of monarchical intercession with the liturgical year indicates, the whole of Anglican festive culture was revived in 1660. Christmas was again celebrated and Christian marriage again solemnized with priestly blessings and the celebration of the Eucharist.

The re-focusing of confessional commitment against dissenters was a response to several failed rebellions in the early 1660s. Revolutionary fervour did not die out among dissenters. In 1661 and 1662, uprisings animated by religious extremism occurred in England. The Act of Uniformity was passed in 1662 and required clergy to vow that they would not overthrow either the Church of England or the Crown. Most clergy acceded to it. A total of 1,760 clergy were removed from ministry between the Restoration and the passing of the Act of Uniformity.[73] However, it must be recognized that many of the clergy and laity who

---

70 For Sheldon, W. M. Spellman, *The Latitudinarians and the Church of England, 1660–1700* (University of Georgia Press, 1993), p. 41; for Allestree, N. H. Keeble, *The Restoration: England in the 1660s* (Blackwell, 2002), p. 172.

71 Nigel Yates, *Buildings, Faith and Worship: The Liturgical Arrangement of Anglican Churches 1600–1900* (Oxford University Press, 1991), p. 63.

72 Keay, *Magnificent Monarch*, pp. 154–8.

73 Bosher, *Restoration Settlement*, p. 266.

were hostile to the Church of England left the national church in 1660.[74] The number of dissenters was quite small. In England and Wales, the dissenting population was merely 4–5 per cent of the population.[75] Pockets of dissent existed in Ireland, but the bulk of the population remained Roman Catholic; in Scotland, the national church comprised Episcopalian and Presbyterian commitments which were not finally separated until the 1690s. Throughout the reign of Charles II, the legal fortunes of dissent depended primarily upon the actions of its radical fringe. In 1663, uprisings were staged in England and Ireland, which finally turned Charles II against dissent.[76] Then came the Rathbone Plot, a failed regicide attempt in 1665 that was scheduled for 3 September, the anniversary of two Cromwellian military victories.[77] The entirety of Charles II's reign was plagued by plots, conspiracies, failed revolutions and attempted regicide. His most recent biographer describes the king as 'the luckiest monarch in English history'.[78] The 1660 settlement of church and state was not unprovoked, but was instead a series of responses to the zero-sum approach taken by a militant minority. Without the Restoration and its struggle for survival, Anglicanism would not exist today.

Contours of Caroline divinity

It remains now to outline some of the defining features of Caroline divinity. I do not intend to be exhaustive. I wish only to illuminate some current historical debates while drawing attention to themes that may be missed by readers unfamiliar with seventeenth-century intellectual history.

Humanism and scholasticism

Humanism and scholasticism were foundational for Caroline divinity. Humanist scholarship focused on the study of ancient texts, whether Christian, Greek or Roman, and laid an especial emphasis upon the knowledge of ancient languages. The humanist element within

---

74 Jenkins, *Foundations of Modern Wales*, pp. 183–4.
75 Keeble, *Restoration*, pp. 141–2; Jenkins, *Foundations of Modern Wales*, p. 195.
76 Ronald Hutton, *Charles II: King of England, Scotland, and Ireland* (Oxford University Press, 1989), pp. 210–11, 457.
77 Keeble, *Restoration*, pp. 154–7.
78 Hutton, *Charles II*, p. 447.

Anglicanism dates to its very foundation. Henry VIII invited Erasmus of Rotterdam, the greatest humanist of the sixteenth century, to teach in England; under Edward VI and Elizabeth I, Erasmus's New Testament paraphrases became required reading for all priests and had to be owned by all parishes along with the Book of Common Prayer, the Great Bible and the Book of Homilies. Erasmus remained quite popular in England until the 1650s, but many of his writings were put back into the print during the Restoration.[79] By the time of Charles I, university education had long been steeped in the study of ancient authors, the most important of whom were arguably Cicero and Aristotle. Their influence is all but impossible to overestimate. This is seen most clearly in the many references in the chapters that follow to moderation, virtue and, above all, duty. John Cosin writes of our duty to pray in Chapter 7; Jeremy Taylor describes the duties of marriage in Chapter 13; most importantly, Chapter 10 includes an excerpt from Roger L'Estrange's translation of Cicero's *De Officiis* (*On Duties*). Knowledge of ancient sources is of paramount importance for understanding Caroline divinity.

The other great tradition of seventeenth-century scholarship was scholasticism. Like humanism, scholasticism was defined by a particular method of study, namely the construction of logical argument in response to a stated question.[80] The scholastic method may be found especially in Chapter 10, with the writings of Robert Sanderson and Jeremy Taylor on conscience. And while only the introduction from Archbishop Laud's *Conference with Fisher the Jesuite* has been excerpted in Chapter 12, the *Conference* has been described as 'one of the last great scholastic works of divinity'.[81] Yet there is a considerable difference between the way that scholasticism developed among Anglicans and other European churches. Most important here is the development of theological prolegomena – critical, methodological reflections upon the nature of theology. Johann Gerhard (1582–1637), a Thomist scholastic and Lutheran pastor, was the first Protestant to author 'a well-organized prolegomenon to dogmatics'.[82] This stimulated the production

---

79 Gregory D. Dodds, *Exploiting Erasmus: The Erasmian Legacy and Religious Change in Early Modern England* (University of Toronto Press, 2009), pp. 233–64.
80 Paul Oskar Kristeller, *Renaissance Thought and its Sources* (Columbia University Press, 1979), p. 99.
81 Davies, *Caroline Captivity*, p. 58.
82 Robert D. Preus, *The Theology of Post-Reformation Lutheranism*, Vol. 1 (Concordia, 1970), p. 142. Gerhard's *Theological Commonplaces* is being translated under the direction of Benjamin T. G. Mayes.

of systems of doctrine among Lutheran and Reformed theologians in the seventeenth century, although among Roman Catholics the construction of theological systems dated to the post-Tridentine Thomist revival. The British episcopal churches reveal no concern with systematic theology. Anglicans produced no theological prolegomena, and only Roger Boyle, an Irish bishop, produced a doctrinal system – the *Summa Theologiae Christianae*, which was printed but once in 1681. Perhaps it is telling that in the seventeenth century Johann Gerhard was the most popular Lutheran theologian printed in England, with nearly two dozen combined English and Latin editions of his devotional writings appearing in print. Yet nothing of his *Theological Commonplaces* was translated into English. The truncated and idiosyncratic legacy of scholasticism within Anglicanism is an area that needs further research.

Arminianism?

Some readers will be familiar with the 'revisionist' thesis of the 1980s, which claimed that, under Charles I, the Church of England changed its confessional allegiance from Calvinism to Arminianism. We have already surveyed the shared scholastic background among all European Christians, and have also discussed the shared influence of Thomism upon both Remonstrants and Anglicans. There are good reasons for rejecting the revisionist thesis. First, the regime of Charles I, which was hostile to public debate on predestination, never printed the writings of Arminius. Only two short works by Arminius were translated in the seventeenth century, both in 1657 by Tobias Conyers, a dissenter. Arminius was not translated into English again until James Nichols and his son William Nichols, both Anglicans, translated and edited a large number of Arminius's writings in three volumes between 1825 and 1875. Known as the 'London Edition', this remains the standard English-language edition of his work. Second, the Remonstrant Confession of 1621 was not printed in England until 1676. A second English edition appeared in 1684 and a Latin edition in 1702. The text was not published in the London Edition and did not appear in English again until Mark A. Ellis published a bilingual edition in 2005.[83] The Remonstrant Confession is quite possibly the least-published confession in Anglo-American religious history. Third, when we turn to other

---

83 Mark A. Ellis (trans. and ed.), *The Arminian Confession of 1621* (Pickwick, 2005).

Remonstrant theologians, notably Simon Episcopius and Philip van Limborch, we find that their writings were just as rarely printed. The case is different when we turn to Grotius, whose political and theological writings were quite popular in England. Yet here we see the Erasmian humanism which Remonstrants and Anglicans deeply valued, rather than scholasticism.[84] Finally, scholarship on Arminius has grown since the 1980s, and in 2010 Keith D. Stanglin edited three dozen previously unpublished theological disputations by Arminius, while also drawing attention to the existence of an additional 31 unpublished letters.[85] These reveal Arminius as a theologian interested in far more than predestination, but not at all in matters of liturgy or monarchy, both of which were deeply important to Anglicans. Reducing Arminius to the status of a mere anti-Calvinist is reductive.[86] Reducing Anglican theology to either Arminianism or anti-Calvinism is equally reductive.

Typology

Typology, a method of biblical interpretation which held that Scripture contains 'types' or patterns that are repeated through salvation history, was a consistent feature of Caroline divinity. Through typology, the biblical past was connected to the English present, and heavenly worship made the model for earthly liturgy. As can be seen in Chapter 4, typological comparisons were drawn between the royal saint's martyrdom and the crucifixion of Christ; William Laud opens Chapter 11 by drawing a typological association between the kingdoms of Israel and England. The liturgical reforms that reached their apex under Charles I were also explained typologically. John Buckeridge and William Page understood the Church's liturgical worship as a literal participation in the heavenly liturgical worship described in Scripture. George Herbert and his imitators drew upon typology when they described the parish church either as a synagogue or as the Temple itself. And in Chapter 8, William Beveridge asks, 'Was the Temple an House of Prayer to them? So is the Church to us.' Through typology, the Old Testament provided every justification for the richness of Anglican ceremonial. Sacred space and sacred time are present in Scripture, not as historical

---

84 Israel, *Dutch Republic*, p. 514.
85 Keith D. Stanglin, *The Missing Public Disputations of Jacobus Arminius* (Brill, 2010), p. 40; before Stanglin, the most important work was Muller, *God, Creation, and Providence*.
86 Stanglin, *Missing*, pp. 35–6.

facts consigned to the past but as a living reality, typologically accessed and typologically understood.

Intelligibility

The 'typological imagination' may seem muddled and undisciplined to some readers. Typology should be understood as an argument about the *intelligibility* of human experience made through an appeal to Scripture, one of the two books authored by God for human wellbeing. The other book is creation, and it too reveals order. In Chapter 9, we read Thomas Browne's profession that 'there are two Books from whence I collect my Divinity; besides that written one of God, another of his servant Nature'. The first is written in 'mystical Letters' while the latter is composed of 'common Hieroglyphicks'. We have already noted key differences between theological voluntarism and theological rationalism. Anglicans tended quite strongly towards the latter. The Royal Society, which propelled the growth of natural philosophy and the rise of modern science, assumed that the universe is ordered and therefore intelligible.[87] Theological voluntarism could not and did not yield such an approach to the study of nature. If typology allows one to harmonize the Church's practices with the biblical past, then the study of nature allows the natural philosopher to discern the presence of humanity within a harmonious network of divinely authored natural laws.

Influence

It is often assumed that the late-seventeenth century saw the overthrow of Caroline divinity in favour of 'Latitudinarianism', a tepid brand of churchmanship defined in large part by a complacent comfort with heterodoxy and an emphasis upon moralism at the expense of heartfelt devotion and intellectual rigour. This thesis, which received its classical form in the words of John Henry Newman cited much earlier, has been rejected by a growing body of scholarship in the last 30 years.[88]

---

87 Peter Dear, *The Intelligibility of Nature: How Science Makes Sense of the World* (University of Chicago Press, 2006), p. 14.

88 Gerard Reedy, S.J., *The Bible and Reason: Anglicans and Scripture in Late Seventeenth-Century England* (University of Pennsylvania Press, 1985) was among the first to question the 'Latitudinarian' thesis; John Spurr, '"Latitudinarianism" and the Restoration Church', *The Historical Journal*, 31 (1) (1988), pp. 61–82, and '"Rational Religion" in Restoration England', *Journal of the History of Ideas*, 49 (4) (1988), pp. 563–85, followed with devastating effect;

It is no longer possible to claim that Anglicanism was dominated by Latitudinarianism in the century and a half preceding the development of Anglo-Catholicism. To the contrary, the Restoration saw the organic theological, devotional and liturgical growth of the British episcopal churches into the nineteenth century.[89] This was upset by, but did not fundamentally change with, the Dutch invasion of England in 1688.[90] Save for Anglicanism in America, the 'cult' of King Charles the Martyr was a defining feature of Anglican identity well into the nineteenth century.[91] The most popular work of theology among nineteenth-century American Episcopalians was John Pearson's *Exposition of the Creed*.[92] Typology was used in sermons, in teaching on the sacraments, and in liturgical commentaries on both sides of the Atlantic.[93] Anglican architecture remained Caroline in style, with a raised altar fenced by altar rails, despite later liturgical experimentation.[94] Far from being overthrown by an untimely Latitudinarian revolt, the Caroline convergence remained foundational to the Anglican way of life until the mid-nineteenth century, when it became more diffuse and overshadowed by new questions and arguments. Its influence nonetheless remains.

Conclusion

Three determinants have shaped the texts selected for the present volume. The first is popularity and influence. King Charles the Martyr

---

Spellman, *Latitudinarians*, argues that Latitudinarians were thoroughgoing Augustinians; Jan W. Wojcik, *Robert Boyle and the Limits of Reason* (Cambridge University Press, 1997), pp. 215–17 discusses the inadequacy of Latitudinarianism as a descriptive category.

89 The most important survey of the 'long eighteenth century' is J. C. D. Clark, *English Society 1660–1832: Religion, Ideology and Politics during the Ancient Regime*, second ed. (Cambridge University Press, 2000).

90 On the 'Glorious Revolution' as a Williamite offensive, see Jonathan I. Israel, 'The Dutch role in the Glorious Revolution', in Jonathan I. Israel (ed.), *The Anglo-Dutch Moment: Essays on the Glorious Revolution and its World Impact* (Cambridge University Press, 1991), pp. 105–62.

91 The Society of King Charles the Martyr, one of the Anglican Communion's largest devotional societies, is the long-lasting successor of the old 'cult'.

92 Robert W. Prichard, *The Nature of Salvation: Theological Consensus in the Episcopal Church, 1801–73* (University of Illinois Press, 1997), p. 82.

93 Prichard, *Salvation*, pp. 89–91; Peter B. Nockles, *The Oxford Movement in Context: Anglican High Churchmanship 1760–1857* (Cambridge University Press, 1994), pp. 206–9.

94 Yates, *Buildings, Faith and Worship*, pp. 185–7.

shaped the Anglican devotional and political ethos for two centuries and, as already noted, *Eikon Basilike* was the runaway international bestseller of its time; Richard Allestree's *The Whole Duty of Man* was reprinted on an almost-annual basis until the end of the eighteenth century and did much to disseminate a Ciceronian conception of duty; George Herbert's poetry inspired many imitators and did more than all of them combined to make theological and devotional poetry one of the most distinctive elements of the Anglican tradition. Second, I have included not just English sources, but those by Welsh, Scottish and Irish authors as well. Today it is something of a commonplace to identify Anglican history with England, but I would argue that amid the Caroline convergence of the early–mid-seventeenth century, the Anglican tradition became fundamentally British and has remained larger than England ever since. The present volume is, in many ways, an argument that the development of the Anglican tradition can only be understood with reference to the 'British problem'. Third, I have sought to include popular writings such as petitions and pamphlets, as well as lay religious writings by figures who are not well known today. Some, such as Anne Halkett, wrote with an unparalleled vibrancy and spiritual depth. The influence of other figures, notably Izaak Walton and Robert Boyle, has strangely bypassed the Anglican tradition while profoundly shaping the world at large. Walton's *Compleat Angler*, the third most reprinted book in the English language, helped inspire the conservation movement in North America in the late-nineteenth century.[95] Robert Boyle, quite possibly the greatest philosopher of science in the Anglican tradition, is one of the fathers of modern science and has been the subject of numerous historical studies. I hope that *The Beauty of Holiness* will help erode some of the older, less tenable assumptions about the historical development of Anglicanism. I hope, too, that it will communicate the very real blood, sweat and tears of many faithful Anglicans during a half-century that truly saw the best and worst of times. Restoration is ever possible.

---

95 The Izaak Walton League, which still exists today, was founded in the United States in 1922.

I

Roots

John Buckeridge, bishop of Rochester under James VI and I and mentor of William Laud, defended traditional liturgical piety. Although he drew upon historic precedent, he also drew upon Scripture, as the following selection exemplifies. Liturgy imitates the biblical pattern of worship revealed in texts such as the Lord's Prayer and the Apocalypse.

The sixt Reason is, *Praxis Ecclesiae Triumphantis*: the practise of the Triumphant Church in heaven; and this admitteth no refusal: for heavenly things are the exemplars and patternes, to which earthly things must bee conformed. Is there a Tabernacle to bee made on earth? must not the modell thereof bee taken from heaven? *Secundùm formam in monte*; thou shalt make it according to the forme shewed thee in the Mount.[1] Is there a forme of life to be prescribed to men on earth? Is it not to bee guided by the rule of heaven? Thy will be done, *Sicut in caelo, sic in terra*, In earth as it is in heaven;[2] the obedience of earth, must be squared by the line of heaven: and then, though our bodies be on earth, yet our conversation is in heaven.[3] The earth is the prison, or place of mans banishment; the out-house, and suburbs, in comparison of heaven, the Citie, and pallace of the great King. The earth is the place of Pilgrimage, and the valley of misery; and heaven is the Countrey of rest, and eternall felicitie. In earth all things are unperfect, and only inchoate: in heaven all things are consummate and in absolute perfection. Mans ambition by the subtiltie of the Serpent, was *Eritis sicut Di*: you shall be as gods:[4] but mans greatest exaltation after his fall is, *Eritis sicut Angeli*, you shall be as the Angels.[5] And if it be true, that the Church-government, the neerer it commeth to the Hierarchie of heaven, the more perfect, and absolute

---

1 [Exod. 25.40, 26.30.]
2 [Matt. 6.10.]
3 [Phil. 3.20.]
4 [Gen. 3.5.]
5 Matthew 22.23–33; Mark 12.18–27; Luke 20.27–40.

it is; it will also be true, that the neerer the worship, and Adoration of the Church militant resembleth the exact, and absolute patterne of the Triumphant Churches worship in heaven; the more pleasing and acceptable to God it must needs be. For surely this *Sicut in caelo*, reacheth principally to the worship of God: So that this is an undeniable proposition which must necessarily be granted:

Such, as is the Adoration and gesture of the Saints, in the worship of God, and of the Lambe, at the supper of the Lambe in Heaven: such must be the Adoration & gesture of the Saints in earth, in the worship of God, at the Supper of the Lambe on earth.

But the Saints in the worship of God, and of the Lambe, doe use the Adoration of falling downe and kneeling, at the Supper of the Lambe in Heaven.

Therefore the Saints must use the Adoration of falling downe, or kneeling, in the worship of God, at the Supper of the Lambe on earth.

For that there is a Supper *in via*, in the way, there can bee no doubt to him, that readeth Christes words, *A certaine man made a great Supper, and bade many*.[6] And that there is a Supper *in patria*, in the Countrey and kingdome of Heaven; there can be no doubt, to him that beleeveth *S. John*, that pronounceth them blessed, that are called to the Supper of the Lambe.[7] The first Supper is *sub Sacramentis*, under Sacraments: for so long as we live here in this vale of misery, and our soule is clad about with sinfull flesh, we have need of Elements, which God hath ordeined to convey his graces to us; and because we cannot see, *but as in a glasse, or darke speaking*, all vailes are not taken from us. But when *we shall see, as we are seene, face to face*,[8] wee shall bee admitted to that Supper, which is *sine Sacramentis*, without all Sacraments: and as we shall be *sicut Angeli*, as the Angels of God, so we shall be fedde, *sicut Angeli*, as the Angels of God, without the meanes of any creature, or Element at all.

Now, if they at the marriage Supper of the Lambe consummate in Heaven, doe bow downe and kneele, much more must wee, that are onely admitted to the marriage Supper, that is the contract and espous-

---

6 [Luke 14.16.]
7 [Apocalypse 19.9.]
8 1 Corinthians 13.9–12.

als, that is made by the holy Spirit, in the Church militant in earth, bow and kneele. And so much the rather, because the blessed Saints that bow and kneele in Heaven, doe onely make *Confessionem Laudis*, confession of praise, and give glory and honour to God, in signe of their Joy, which is so absolute, that all teares are wiped from their eyes. And therefore the Saints on earth that make *Confessionem peccatorum & miseriae*, confession of their sinnes and miseries, in token of their sorrow and contrition, ought much more to bow downe, and kneele, to pacifie the anger of God.

Now that the Saints in heaven doe bow downe, or fall on the ground and kneele, when they worship (in bodie if their bodies bee there, or else in soule and spirit) and adore God, and sing praise to him that sitteth on the Throne; it is apparent in many places in the *Revelation* of S. *Joh. Cap.*4.10. The foure and twenty Elders fall downe before him that sate upon the Throne, and worship him that liveth for ever and ever, and cast their Crownes before the Throne. And *cap.* 5, 8. the foure and twentie Elders fell downe before the Lambe: and *ver.*14. the foure and twenty Elders fell downe and worshipped him that liveth for ever and ever. And c.7.*ver.*9. having put a certaine number for an uncertaine, twelve thousand of every one of the twelve Tribes: *A great number clothed in white robes, and Palmes in their hands, cryed, Salvation to our God, which sitteth upon the Throne, and unto the Lambe. And all the Angels stood round about the Throne, and about the Elders, and the foure beasts; and fell before the Throne on their faces, and worshipped God, saying, Amen: Blessing, and glory, and wisdome, and thanksgiving, and honour, and power, and might, bee unto our God for ever and ever, Amen.* And that these are Saints in glory, appeareth after, *ver.*14. *These are they that come out of great tribulations, and have washed their Robes, and made them white in the blood of the Lambe: therefore are they before the Throne of God, and serve him day and night in his Temple: and he that sitteth on the Throne shall dwell among them: They shall hunger no more, neither thirst any more, neither shall the Sunne light on them, nor any heate; For the Lambe which is in the middest of them shall feede them, and shall leade them unto living fountaines of waters, and God shall wipe away all teares from their eyes.*

Now these are the Endowments of another life; wee are in great tribulation, as long as wee are in this life; these came out of great tribulation: wee doe now wash our selves in the blood of the Lambe, and while wee live we cannot get out all the spots of sinne and lust; these have washed their Robes, and made them white in the blood of the Lambe. This life is, *Esuries & sitis Iustitiae*: the hunger and thirst of righteousnesse; the life to come, hath no hunger nor thirst, because they live at the well head, and sea of all goodnesse; and their cup doth alwaies overflow. I omit other circumstances: for these proove sufficiently, that the Saints which the Apostle describeth, are Possessors in the Kingdom of glory, not Travellers in the way of grace. And the Text saith,[9] The Lambe which is in the middest of the Throne, shall feede them: that must necessarily be, *Coena gloriae*, the Supper of glory; the vision and contemplation of God and Christ, face to face without all Sacrament.

And in all this worship; that the consummated Saints give to God, it is said, that the Angels, and the Elders, and the beasts fall downe before the Throne on their faces, and worship God:[10] So in heaven there is no worship without prostration and kneeling.

. . .

If all this worship bee given to God, that sitteth on the Throne, and to the Lambe, by the Angels, and Elders, and Beasts, and Saints, when they worship God, and are feasted at the Supper of the Lambe, in glory in heaven; why should not their practise bee a warrant to the Saints in earth, to use like falling downe, or kneeling, in the worship of God, at the feast of the Lambe in grace, on earth? since the practise of the Church Triumphant may well be received as a patterne, and guide by the Church militant, whose example so long as shee followeth, shee can never erre; whose imitation is her readiest way to perfection?

John Buckeridge, *A Discourse concerning Kneeling at the Communion* (1617), pp. 206–11

Lancelot Andrewes's Form of Consecration *was published posthumously. This excerpt is followed by prayers consecrating the baptistery, the pulpit, the lectern, the holy table, the place of matrimony, and the church floor, under which people were sometimes buried.*

Let us dedicate and offer up unto God this Place with the same prayer that King *David* did dedicate and offer up his, 1 *Chron*. 29.10.

Blessed be thou O Lord our God, and the God of our Fathers for ever and ever, &c. *usque ad finem vers. 18. paucis mutatis. Deinde*[11]

---

9 [Verse 17.]
10 [Cap.7.7, 11.]
11 *All the way to the end . . . With a few changes having been made. Then*; the changes are unspecified.

Most glorious God, the Heaven is thy Throne, and the Earth thy Footstool; what house then can be built for thee, or what place is there that thou canst rest in? Howbeit we are taught by thy Holy Word, that thy will is not to dwell in the dark Cloud,[12] but that thy delight hath been ever with the Sons of Men; so that in any place whatsoever, where two or three are gathered together in thy name, thou art in the midst of them;[13] But specially in such places as are set apart and sanctified to thy name, and to the memory of it, there thou hast said, thou wilt vouchsafe thy gracious Presence after a more special manner, & come to bless us.

Wherefore in all Ages of the world, thy Servants have separated certain places from all profane and common uses, and hallow'd unto thy Divine Worship and service, either by inspiration of thy blessed Spirit, or by express Commandment from thine own mouth.

By inspiration of thy holy Spirit. So didst thou put into the heart of thy Holy Patriarch *Jacob* to erect a stone in *Bethel* to be an house to thee, which act of his thou didst call for, and highly allow of.[14]

By express Commandment from thine own mouth. So did *Moses* make thee the Tabernacle of the Congregation in the Desert, which thou didst honour by covering it with a Cloud, and filling it with thy Glory.

And after, when it came into the heart of thy servant *David* to think it was in no wise fitting that himself should dwell in an house of Cedar, and the Ark of God remain but in a Tabernacle, thou didst testifie with thine own mouth, that in that *David* was so minded to build a House to thy Name, it was well done of him, to be so minded, though he built it not.[15]

The material Furniture for which house though his Father plentifully prepared, yet *Solomon* his Son built it and brought it to perfection. To which House thou wer't pleased visibly to send fire from Heaven to consume the Sacrifice, and to fill it with the Glory of thy presence before all the people.[16]

And after, when for the sins of thy people that Temple was destroyed, thou didst by thy Prophets, *Aggai* and *Zachary* (by shewing how inconvenient it was that they should dwell in seeled houses, and let thy

---

12 Exodus 20.18–21; cf. Psalm 18.11ff.
13 Matthew 18.20.
14 Genesis 28.10–22.
15 1 Chronicles 29.
16 1 Kings 6–8.

house lie waste) stir up the spirit of *Zorobabel*, to build thee the second Temple anew: which second House likewise by the fullness of the Glory of thy presence, thou didst shew thy self to like and allow of.[17]

Neither only wer't thou well pleased with such as did build thee these Temples, but even with such of the people afterwards, as being moved with Zeal added unto their Temple, their *Mother Church*, lesser places of prayer, by the names of Synagogues, in every Town throughout the Land; for the Tribes to ascend up to worship thee, to learn thy holy will and to do it. Which very Act of the Centurion, to build thy people a Synagogue, thou didst well approve and commend in the Gospel.[18]

And by the bodily presence of thy Son our Saviour at the feast of the Dedication, testified by S. *John*, didst really well allow of, and do honour to such devout Religious services, as we are now about to perform.[19]

Which also by thy holy Word hast taught us, that thine Apostles themselves, and the Christians in their time, as they had houses to eat and drink in; so had they also where the whole Congregation of the Faithful came together in one place, which they expresly called Gods Church, and would not have it despised, nor abused, nor eaten, nor drunken in, but had in great Reverence, being the very place of their holy Assemblies.[20]

By whose godly examples the Christians in all Ages successively have erected and consecrated sundry godly houses, for the Celebration of Divine Service and Worship (Monuments of their Piety and Devotion) as our eyes see this day.

We then as Fellow-Citizens with the Saints and of the Household of God, being built upon the Foundation of the Apostles and Prophets, Jesus Christ himself being the head cornerstone, walking in the Steps of their most holy Faith, and ensuing the examples of these thy Patriarchs, Prophets, and Apostles have together with them done the same work (I say) in building and dedicating this house, as an habitation for thee, and a place for us to assemble and meet together for the observation of thy Divine Worship, invocation of thy Name, reading, preaching and hearing thy most holy Word, administring thy most holy Sacraments; and above all in thy most holy place, the very gate of Heaven upon

---

17 Haggai 2.20–23; Zechariah 4; Ezra 5–6.
18 Luke 7.3–11.
19 John 10.22–23; also known as Hanukkah.
20 1 Corinthians 11.17–33.

earth, as *Jacob* nam'd it, to do the work of Heaven;[21] to set forth thy most worthy praise, to laud and magnify thy most glorious Majesty, for all thy goodness to all men; especially to us of the Household of Faith. Accept therefore we beseech thee, most gracious Father, of this our bounden duty and service; accept this for thine house; and because Holiness becomes thine house for ever, sanctifie this house with thy gracious presence, which is erected to the honour of thy most glorious Name.

Now therefore, arise O Lord, and come into this place of thy rest, thou and the ark of thy strength; Let thine eye be open towards this House day and night; Let thine ears be ready towards the prayers of thy children, which they shall make unto thee in this place, and let thine heart delight to dwell here perpetually: And whensoever thy servants shall make to thee their petitions in this House, either to bestow thy good graces, & blessings upon them, or to remove thy punishments and judgements from them, hear them from Heaven thy dwelling place, the Throne of the glory of thy Kingdom, and when thou hearest have mercy; and grant, O Lord, we beseech thee, that here and elsewhere thy Priests may be cloathed with Righteousnesse, and thy Saints rejoyce in thy Salvation.[22]

And whereas both in the Old and New Testament thou hast consecrated the measuring out and building of a material Church, to such an excellent Mysterie, that in it is signified and represented the fruition of the joy of thy Heavenly kingdome, we beseech thee that, in this material Temple made with hands, we may so serve and please thee in all holy Exercises of Godliness and Christian Religion, that in the end we may come to that thy Temple on high, even to the holy places made without hands, whose Builder and Maker is God; so as when we shall cease to pray to thee on Earth, we may with all those that have in the like manner erected such places to thy Name, and with all thy Saints eternally praise thee in the highest Heavens, for all thy goodness vouchsafed us for a time here on earth, and laid up for us there in thy Kingdom for ever and ever; and that for thy dear Sons sake, our blessed Saviour Jesus Christ, to whom, &c.

Blessed Father, who hast promised in thy holy Law, that in every place where the remembrance of thy Name shall be put, thou wilt come unto us and bless us; according to that thy promise come unto us and

---

21 Genesis 28.17.
22 Psalms 13.5, 20.5, 132.9; 2 Corinthians 5.1–6.

bless us, who put now upon this place the memorial of thy Name, by dedicating it wholly and only to thy Service and Worship.

Blessed Saviour, who in the Gospel, with thy bodily presence, didst honour and adorn the Feast of the dedication of the Temple; at this dedication of this Temple unto thee be present also, and accept, Good Lord, and prosper the work of our hands.

Blessed Spirit, without whom nothing is holy, no person or place is sanctified aright, send down upon this place thy sanctifying power and grace, hallow it, and make it to thee an holy habitation for ever.

Blessed and glorious Trinity, by whose Power, Wisdom and Love all things are purged, lightened, and made perfect; enable us with thy Power, enlighten us with thy Truth, perfect us with thy Grace, that both here and elsewhere acknowledging the glory of thy eternal Trinity, and in the Power of thy Divine Majesty worshipping the Unity, we may obtain to the fruition of the glorious Godhead, Trinity in Unity, and Unity in Trinity to be adored for ever.

God the Father, God the Son, and God the Holy Ghost accept, sanctifie, and bless this place to the end whereunto, according to his own Ordinance, we have ordain'd it, to be a Sanctuary to the most High, and a Church for the living God: The Lord with his favour ever mercifully behold it, and so send upon it his spiritual Benediction and Grace, that it may be the House of God to him and Gate of Heaven to us. *Amen.*

Lancelot Andrewes, *The Form of Consecration of a Church or Chappel* (1659), pp. 15–34

This declaration, also known as the Book of Sports, *protected traditional recreational activities. It did not reflect an 'Anglican' consensus against 'Puritan' scruples; many orthodox churchmen maintained an austere Sabbath observance. The declaration did, however, reveal a royal unwillingness to accept the Puritan critique of less stringent practice.*

By the King.

O UR *Deare Father of blessed Memory, in his returne from Scotland, comming through* Lancashire, *found that his Subjects were debarred from Lawful Recreations upon Sundayes after Evening Prayers ended, and upon Holy dayes: And Hee prudently considered, that if these times were taken from them, the meaner sort who labour hard all the weeke, should have no Recreations at all to refresh their spirits. And after His returne, Hee farther saw that His loyall Subjects in all other parts of His Kingdome did suffer in the same kinde, though perhaps not in the same degree: And did therefore in His Princely wisedome, publish a Declaration to all his loving Subjects concerning lawfull Sports to be used at such times, which was printed and published by His royall Commandement in the yeere 1618. In the Tenor which hereafter followeth.*[23]

By the King.

WHEREAS *upon Our returne the last yere out of Scotland, We did publish Our Pleasure touching the recreations of Our people in those parts under Our hand: For some causes Us thereunto mooving, Wee have thought good to command these Our Directions then given in* Lancashire *with a few words thereunto added, and most appliable to these parts of Our Realmes, to bee published to all Our Subjects.*

Whereas Wee did justly in Our *Progresse thorough* Lancashire, rebuke some Puritanes and precise people, and tooke order that the like unlawfull carriage should not be used by any of them hereafter, in the prohibiting and unlawfull punishing of Our good people for using their lawfull Recreations, and honest exercises upon Sundayes and other Holy dayes, after the afternoone Sermon or Service: Wee now finde that two sorts of people wherewith that Countrey is much infected, (Wee meane Papists and Puritanes) have maliciously traduced and calumniated those Our just and honourable proceedings. And therefore lest Our reputation might upon the one side (though innocently) have some aspersion layd upon it, and that upon the other part Our good people in that Countrey be misled by the mistaking and misinterpretation of Our meaning: We have therefore thought good hereby to cleare and make Our pleasure to be manifested to all Our good People in those parts.

It is true that at Our first entry to this Crowne, and Kingdome, Wee were informed, and that too truely, that Our County of Lancashire abounded more in Popish Recusants[24] then any County of England, and thus hath still continued since to Our great regreet, with little amendment, save that now of late, in Our last riding through Our said County, Wee find both by the report of the Judges, and of the Bishop of that diocesse, that there is some amendment now daily beginning, which is no small contentment to Us.

---

23 The original declaration follows.
24 Roman Catholics.

The report of this growing amendment amongst them, made Us the more sorry, when with Our owne Eares We heard the generall complaint of Our people, that they were barred from all lawfull Recreation, & exercise upon the Sundayes afternoone, after the ending of all Divine Service, which cannot but produce two evils: The one, the hindering of the conversion of many, whom their Priests will take occasione hereby to vexe, perswading them that no honest mirth or recreation is lawfull or tolerable in Our Religion, which cannot but breed a great discontentment in Our peoples hearts, especially of such as are peradventure upon the point of turning; The other inconvenience is, that this prohibition barreth the common and meaner sort of people from using such exercises as may make their bodies more able for Warre, when Wee or Our Successours shall have occasion to use them. And in place thereof sets up filthy tiplings and drunkennesse, & breeds a number of idle and discontented speeches in their Alehouses. For when shall the common people have leave to exercise, if not upon the Sundayes & holydaies, seeing they must apply their labour, & win their living in all working daies?

Our expresse pleasure therefore is, that the Lawes of Our Kingdome, & Canons of Our Church be aswell observed in that Countie, as in all other places of this Our Kingdome. And on the other part, that no lawfull Recreation shall bee barred to Our good People, which shall not tend to the breach of Our aforesayd Lawes, and Canons of Our Church: which to expresse more particularly, Our pleasure is, That the Bishop, and all other inferiour Churchmen, and Churchwardens, shall for their parts bee carefull and diligent, both to instruct the ignorant, and convince and reforme them that are mis-led in Religion, presenting them that will not conforme themselves, but obstinately stand out to Our Judges and Justices: Whom We likewise command to put the Law in due execution against them.

Our pleasure likewise is, That the Bishop of that Diocesse take the like straight order with all the Puritanes and Precisians within the same, either constraining them to conforme themselves, or to leave the County according to the Lawes of Our Kingdome, and Canons of Our Church, and so to strike equally on both hands, against the contemners of Our Authority, and adversaries of Our Church. And as for Our good peoples lawfull Recreation, Our pleasure likewise is, That after the end of Divine Service, Our good people be not disturbed, letted,[25] or discouraged from any lawful recreation, Such as dancing, either men or women, Archery for men, leaping, vaulting, or any other

---

25 Hindered.

such harmelesse Recreation, nor from having of May-Games, Whitson Ales, and Morris-dances,[26] and the setting up of May-poles[27] & other sports therewith used, so as the same be had in due & convenient time, without impediment or neglect of Divine Service: And that women shall have leave to carry rushes to the Church for the decoring of it, according to their old custome. But withall We doe here account still as prohibited all unlawfull games to bee used upon Sundayes onely, as Beare and Bullbaitings,[28] Interludes,[29] and at all times in the meaner sort of people by Law prohibited, Bowling.[30]

And likewise We barre from this benefite and liberty, all such knowne recusants, either men or women, as will abstaine from comming to Church or divine Service, being therefore unworthy of any lawfull recreation after the said Service that will not first come to the Church, and serve God: Prohibiting in like sort the said Recreations to any that, though conforme in Religion, are not present in the Church in the Service of GOD, before their going to the said Recreations. Our pleasure likewise is, That they to whom it belongeth in Office, shall present and sharpely punish all such as in the abuse of this Our liberty, will use these exercises before the ends of all Divine Services for that day. And We likewise straightly command, that every person shall resort to his owne Parish Church to heare Divine Service, and each Parish by it selfe to use the said Recreation after Divine Service. Prohibiting likewise any Offensive weapons to bee carried or used in the said times of Recreations. And Our pleasure is, That this Our Declaration shall bee published by order from the Bishop of the Diocesse, through all the Parish Churches, and that both Our Judges of Our Circuit, and Our Justices of Our Peace be informed thereof.

Given at Our Mannour of Greenwich the foure and twentieth day of May, in the sixteenth yeere of Our Raigne of England, France and Ireland, and of Scotland the one and fiftieth.[31]

---

26 A form of English folk dancing.

27 As part of springtime festivities, poles were set up around which music was played, and games and dancing took place. Puritans alleged that maypoles were pagan in origin. There is no evidence to support their contention.

28 Regardless of religious persuasion, many in the seventeenth century considered these cruel forms of animal treatment.

29 Theatre.

30 Bowling often involved gambling.

31 The closing which follows is by Charles I.

Now out of a like pious Care for the service of God, and for suppressing of any humors that oppose trueth and for the Ease, Comfort, & Recreation of Our well deserving People, Wee doe ratifie and publish this Our blessed Fathers Declaration: The rather because of late in some Counties of Our Kingdome, Wee finde that under pretence of taking away abuses, there hath been a generall forbidding, not onely of ordinary meetings, but of the Feasts of the Dedication of the Churches, commonly called Wakes. Now Our expresse will and pleasure is, that these Feasts with others shall bee observed, and that Our Justices of the peace in their severall Divisions shall looke to it, both that all disorders there may be prevented or punished, and that all neighbourhood and freedome, with manlike and lawfull Exercises bee used. And Wee farther Command Our Justices of the Assize in their severall Circuits, to see that no man doe trouble or molest any of Our loyall and duetifull people, in or for their lawfull Recreations, having first done their duetie to God, and continuing in obedience to Us and Our Lawes. And of this Wee command all Our Judges, Justices of the Peace, as well within Liberties as without, Mayors, Bayliffes, Constables, and other Officers, to take notice of, and to see observed, as they tender Our displeasure. And Wee farther will, that publication of this Our Command bee made by order from the Bishops through all the Parish Churches of their severall Diocesse respectively.

Given at Our Palace of Westminster the eighteenth day of October, in the ninth yeere of Our Reigne.

God save the King.

James VI and I & Charles I, The Kings Majesties Declaration to His Subjects, Concerning lawfull Sports to bee used (1617/1633)

2

Developments and Convergence

Developments

Arguments about predestination were widespread during the reign of Charles I. With this declaration, the king rebuffed all who speculated on the matter, whether 'Calvinist' or 'Arminian'. In the short run, this was a failure. In the long run, however, the declaration had tremendous influence. It was prefixed to the Articles of Religion in the 1662 Book of Common Prayer and for centuries offered the single most important gloss upon the Articles, which the king declared should be interpreted in a non-speculative manner.

HIS MAJESTIES
DECLARATION.

B<small>EING</small> *by Gods ordinance, according to Our just Title,* Defender of the Faith, *and supreame Governour of the Church, within these Our Dominions, Wee hold it most agreeable to this Our Kingly Office, and Our owne Religious zeale, to conserve and maintaine the Church committed to Our charge in the unitie of true Religion, and in the bond of peace: and not to suffer unnecessary Disputations, altercations, or questions to bee raysed, which may nourish faction both in the Church and Common-wealth. Wee have therefore upon mature deliberation, and with the advice of so many of Our Bishops as might conveniently bee called together, thought fitte to make this Declaration following. That the Articles of the Church of England (which have been allowed and authorized heretofore, and which Our Clergie generally, have subscribed unto) doe containe the true doctrine of the Church of England, agreeable to Gods word: which Wee doe therefore ratifie and confirme, requiring all Our loving Subjects to continue in the uniforme profession thereof; and prohibiting the least difference from the sayd Articles, which to that end Wee command to be new printed, and this Our declaration to be published therewith.*

That We are supreame Governour of the Church of England: and that if any difference arise about the externall policie, concerning Injunctions, Canons, or other Constitutions whatsoever thereto belonging: the Clergie in their Convocation is to order and settle them, having first obtained leave under Our broad Seale so to doe: and Wee approving their sayd Ordinances and Constitutions, providing that none be made contrary to the Lawes and Customes of the Land.

That out of Our Princely care, that the Churchmen may doe the worke which is proper unto them: the Bishops and Clergie, from time to time in Convocation, upon their humble desire shall have licence under Our broad Seale, to deliberate of, and to doe all such things, as being made plaine by them & assented unto by Us, shall concerne the settled continuance of the doctrine & discipline of the Church of England now established: from which We will not endure any varying, or departing in the least degree.

That for the present, though some differences have been ill raised, yet We take comfort in this, that all Clergie-men within Our Realme, have always most willingly subscribed to the Articles established, which is an argument to Us, that they all agree in the true usuall literall meaning of the sayd Articles, and that even in those curious points in which the present differences lie, men of all sorts take the Articles of the Church of England to bee for them, which is an argument againe, that none of them intend any desertion of the Articles established.

That thereof in these both curious and unhappy differences, which have for so many hundred yeeres, in different times and places, exercised the Church of Christ. Wee will that all further curious search be layd aside, and these disputes shut up in Gods promises as they be generally set foorth to Us, in the holy Scriptures; and the generall meaning of the Articles of the Church of England according to them. And that no man hereafter shall either print or preach, to draw the Article aside any way, but shall submit to it in the plaine and full meaning thereof: And shall not put his owne sense or Comment to bee the meaning of the Article, but shal take it in the literall and Grammaticall sense.

That if any publique Reader in either Our Universities, or any Head or Master of a Colledge, or any other person respectively in either of them, shall affixe any new sense to any Article, or shall publiquely reade, determine, or hold any publique disputation, or suffer any such to bee held either way, in either the Universities or Colledges respectively; or if any Divine in the Universities shall preach or print any thing either way, other then is already established in Convocation with Our Royall assent: he, or they the offenders, shall bee liable to Our displeasure; and the Churches censure in Our Commission Ecclesiasticall, as well as any other: and Wee will see there shall bee due execution upon them.[1]

Charles I, Declaration on the Articles of Religion (1628)

Bowing at the name of Jesus in the liturgy was a point of sharp controversy. Giles Widdowes and William Prynne, who wrote against the practice, were answered by William Page in 1631. The selection below labelled Append. *contains Widdowes's complaint; it is followed by Page's response, labelled* Answere. *These arguments reference a sermon on Philippians 2.8–11 by Lancelot Andrewes, who defended liturgical bowing by appealing to the eschatological vision of humanity bowing, by divine command, at the name of Jesus.*

Append.

For first, it is no duty of the Text, *viz.* of *Phil.* 2.9, 10. as the first Patriots of it affirme: First, because this opinion doth utterly disprove it to be an indifferent, arbitrary, humane Ceremony, as these latter make it: since no duty of the Text that hath immediate reference to the very person of Christ, *as this bowing hath*,[2] can be a ceremony, which is really distinguished from a religious duty.

Answere.

True sir, if it were a morall and substantiall duty belonging unto God, then could it not agree with a ceremony:[3] but so long as it is but rituall and circumstantiall, a ceremony and it may agree well enough together; insomuch that I may well call it a cerimoniall duty; which although it be indifferent in respect of Gods essentiall and substantiall service, yet is it in it selfe not only an innocent and harmelesse, but also a very usefull, reverent, and significant ceremony, but an humane ceremony, none of our authors call it; if they should so call it, their saying were true, for so farre the ceremony is a duty humane as it results from the 18 canon, which being ecclesiaticall is humane. For one and the same ceremony may be a duty both divine and humane: for men

---

1 The Articles of Religion follow.
2 Lancelot Andrewes, *Ninety-Six Sermons* (1629), p. 476.
3 Page earlier defines a ceremony as 'an outward signe of some inward worship or service, or some other religious signification' (6).

prophecying, to be uncovered, is a ceremony, and because it is commanded, the same is also a duty: and because commanded in Scripture it is a ceremoniall duty divine or of the text; and because commanded by the Church it is also a ceremoniall duty humane or of the Canon. And the matter is very ordinary for one and the same duty to be commanded both by the law of God and men, as likewise for one and the same sinne to be forbidden by both those severall lawes.

Againe the learned *Bishop* doth not say this bowing hath immediate refrence to the person of Christ but it is *mediante nomine*, this name coming betweene, we doe it to the name and from thence to the person; we divide them not, but conjoyne them, for these are the Bishops words, (*the text saith doe it to the name, the name is not the sound but the sense, the caution is easy then, doe it to the sense have mind on him that is named and doe his name the honour and spare not.*)[4] But suppose it had such immediate reference to Christ himselfe, might it not be a ceremony for all this, for what shall we thinke of kneeling, lifting up the hands and eyes unto God in prayer, they have immediate reference unto God, yet I hope they be but Ceremonies.

But a *Ceremony is really distinguished from a religious duty.*

It is not; a ceremony indeede not commanded, is no duty but any ceremony whatsoever it be, if it be commanded by lawfull authority, that ceremony is a duty; if by authority of the Scripture, it is a duty of the text; if of the Church, it is a duty of the Canon; Yea, and if it be a ceremony commanded in the service of God, we may well call it a religious duty, as religious is opposed to civill. But if by religious, you meane that which is inward, of the heart and syncere, and so opposite to outward, which may be fained & hypocriticall, then bowing of the knee is not the religious duty it selfe, but only a signe of it, as M. *Calvin* hath very well observed upon this place. *Adoration is here signified*, saith he, *which is proper unto God, a signe or token whereof, is bowing of the knee.*[5] So that this bowing of the knee is but an outward signe of that religious service and obedience we owe unto Christ. For it is the subjection and bowing of the heart which makes the religious duty; otherwise if the bowing of the knee were the duty, then the *Jewes* were dutifull worshippers of Christ, when they bowed *their knees before him*; but because their hearts did not stoope to him; therefore the text saith they did but *mock him.*[6]

---

4 Andrewes, *Sermons*, p. 477.
5 John Calvin, *Commentary on Philippians*, on 2.10.
6 [Matt. 27.29.]

Likewise, wee use to bow to the King, and to our superiours: which bowing is not distinguished from our bowing to God by the outward act; it is the heart therefore that must distinguish and sever them: for from my respect to my superiours, for Gods sake, I call this civill honour and reverence; but from my relation and bowing to God for his owne sake, I call that religious and divine worship: For sometime the text enjoyneth us the inward worship of God, as where it is said *God is a spirit and they that worship him, must worship him in spirit and in truth*, but doth not hereby exclude the outward.[7]

And sometimes againe it commandeth the outward, but alwaies includes the inward, as where it is said *give up your bodies a living sacrifice, holy and acceptable unto God*, and so here, the bowing of the knee is commanded.[8]

And sometimes it commandeth both, as *come let us worship*, there is the inward, *and fall downe and kneele before the Lord our maker*, there is the outward service;[9] so then, this bowing, being but a signe of a religious Duty, may well enough be a ceremony; nay, I doe not see how it can be otherwise.

William Page, A Treatise or Justification of Bowing at the Name of Jesus
(1631), pp. 7–10

Little Gidding

Little Gidding was a religious community in Caroline England, supported by Charles I and affiliated with figures such as Richard Crashaw and, most famously, George Herbert. It was not a monastic community but might be described as an 'intentional community'. Little Gidding had all the support necessary for an equally influential and long life, but it was branded the 'Arminian Nunnery' by its opponents and finally destroyed by the rebels in 1647.

The Story Books of Little Gidding are a collection of dialogues that were had in the community. They were recorded by Nicholas Ferrar, although the leader of the community was first Mary Ferrar and then her granddaughter, Mary Collet.

---

7 [John 4.34.]
8 [Rom. 12.1.]
9 [Psal. 95.6.]

THE FEAST OF THE PURIFICATION
1630 (1631)
Formation and design of the Little Academy.

It was the same Day wherein the Church celebrates that great Festivall of the Purification, that the Mayden Sisters, longing to bee Imitatours of those glorious Saints by whose Names they were called (for all bare Saints Names, and shee that was elected CHEIFE, that of the Blessed Virgin Mary) having entered into a joynt Covenant betweene themselves and some others of nearest Blood (which according to their severall relations they stiled FOUNDER, GUARDIAN, and VISITOUR) for the performance of divers religious exercizes, least, as sweet Liquors are oftentimes corrupted by the sowrenesse of the Vessells wherein they are infused, there should arise in their hearts a Distaste or Abuse of those excellent things for which they purposed; they therefore resolved, together with the Practize of Devotion, to intermingle the study of wisedome, searching and enquiring diligently into the knowledge of those things which appertaine to their Condition and Sex.

Finding in themselves, and observing in others that doe sincerely pursue vertue, that the greatest barre of Perfection was Ignorance of the truth, whereby through misapprehension many prejudiciall things were embraced, and many most behovefull to their ends and most delightfull in performance were not onely neglected but abhorred: which, having by many particulars experimented in themselves, doubting that they were alike abused in most of those things which wee have received by Tradition from our Fathers, they determined with firme promises each to other to make a particular survey of those opinions and practizes which the world recommends or disallows, weighing them not in the scales of common Judgement, but of true and right Reason, according to the weights and by the standard of Scripture; wherein being excellently versed, so as they were most able to repeat by heart both the Booke of Psalms and most part of the New Testament, they found that there was neither Action nor Opinion that could bee propounded but might receive a clear solution and direction from that Booke.

Wherefore, not upon presumption of their own Abilities, but on Confidence of GODS gracious assistance to their humble and diligent Indeavours, they agreed every day at a sett houre to conferre together of some such subject as should tend either to the information of the understanding or to the exciting of the Affections, to the more ready and fervent prosecution[10]

---

10 Pursuit.

Developments and Convergence

of vertues and better performance of all such duties as in their present or other Course of Life hereafter should be required of them.

The first proceedings, as it alwaies happens in great attempts that have no presidents to direct, were both in forme and substance farre short of that whereunto they were in the end reduced.

Wherefore, as Artists upon the full accomplishment of their workes cast aside the first draughts, so silencing what was lesse exactly done, I shall goe on with the recording of things from that time which themselves accompt the beginning, being about the end of May. Onely, by way of introduction, as Porches were anciently sett in the Fronts of greater Buildings, I will sett downe the passages of two or three severall daies, which may well serve for a preface to the Reader for this following booke, as in truth they were maine arguments to the Confirmation of their minds who were the Actours of this and other noble undertakings.

Dialogues at Little Gidding sometimes began with hymns, such as the two following.

> Teach us by his example, Lord,
> For whom we honour Thee to-day;
> And grant his witness of Thy word
> Thy church enlighten ever may.
>
> And as beloved, O Christ, he was,
> And therefore leaned upon Thy breast,
> So let us also in Thy grace
> And on Thy sacred bosom rest.
>
> Into us breathe that life divine
> Whose testimony he commands;
> About us cause Thy light to shine,
> Light which no darkness comprehends.
>
> And let Thy ever blessed Word
> Which all things did create of nought,
> Anew create us now, O Lord!
> Whose ruin sin hath almost wrought.
>
> Thy holy faith we do profess;
> Us to Thy fellowship receive.
> Our sins we heartily confess:
> Thy pardon therefore let us have.

And as to us Thy servant gives
Occasion thus to honour Thee:
So also let our words and lives
As lights and guides to others be.

That rage, whereof the psalm doth say,
   Why are the Gentiles grown so vaine?
Appeared in part upon this day,
   When Herod had the infants slaine.
Yet, as it saith, they raged in vaine,
   Though many innocents they slew,
For Christ they purposed to have slaine,
   Who all their counsels overthrew.

Thus still vouchsafe thou to restraine
   All Tyrants, Lord, pursuing thee;
Thus let our vast desires be slaine,
   That thou mayst living in us bee.
So whilst wee shall enjoy our breath,
   Wee of thy Love our songs will frame,
And with those Innocents our death
   Shall also glorify thy Name.

In Type those many died for one,
   That One for many more was slaine;
And what they felt in Act alone,
   Hee did in will and Act sustaine.
Lord, grant that what thou hast decreed
   In will and Act wee may fulfill,
And though wee reach not to the deed,
   For us, oh Lord, accept the will.

E. Cruwys Sharland (ed.), *The Story Books of Little Gidding* (London, 1899), pp. 1-2, 40, 59-60

This is the prayer that Nicholas Ferrar composed upon learning that George Herbert was on his deathbed.

O most mighty God, and mercifull Father, we most humbly beseech thee, if it be thy good pleasure, to continue to us that singular benefit which thou hast given us in the friendship of thy servant, our dear brother, who now lieth on the bed of sickness. Let him abide with us yet awhile, for the furtherance of our faith. We have indeed deserved by our ingratitude, not only the loss of him, but whatever other opportunities thou hast given us for the attainment of our salvation. We do not deserve to be heard in our supplications; but thy mercies are above all thy works. In consideration whereof we prostrate ourselves in all humble earnestness, beseeching thee, if so it may seem good to thy Divine Majesty, that thou wilt hear us in this, who hast heard us in all the rest, and that thou wilt bring him back again from the gates of death: that thou wilt yet a while spare him, that he may live to thy honour, and our comfort. Lord, thou hast willed that our delights should be in the Saints on earth, and in such as excel in virtue: how then should we not be afflicted, and mourn when thou takest them from us! Thou hast made him a great help, and furtherance of the best things amongst us, how then can we but esteem the loss of him, a chastisement from thy displeasure! O Lord, we beseech thee that it may not be so: we beseech thee, if it be thy good pleasure, restore unto us our dear brother, by restoring him to his health: so will we praise and magnify thy name, and mercy with a song of thanksgiving. Hear us, O Lord, for thy dear Son's sake, Jesus Christ our Saviour. Amen.

P. Peckard, *Memoirs of the Life of Nicholas Ferrar* (Cambridge, 1790), pp. 314-16[11]

Convergence

A canonical convergence is found in the Constitutions and Canons Ecclesiastical of the churches of England (1604), Ireland (1634) and Scotland (1636). The Church of England passed a revised set of canons in 1640, but these were rejected by Parliament and are not included below.

English Canons

I.

The Kings Supremacie over the Church of England, *in causes Ecclesiasticall, to be maintained.*

As our duty to the Kings most Excellent Majesty requireth, we first decree and ordain, that the Archbishop of *Canterbury*, (from time to

---

11 Original Source British Library (W67/0799 DSC).

time,) all Bishops of this Province, or Deans, Archdeacons, Parsons, Vicars, and all other Ecclesiastical persons, shall faithfully keep and observe, and (as much as in them lieth) shall cause to be observed and kept of others, all and singular Laws and Statutes made for the restoring to the Crown of this Kingdome, the ancient jurisdiction over the State Ecclesiastical, and abolishing of all forein power repugnant to the same. Furthermore, all Ecclesiastical persons having cure of Souls, and all other Preachers, and Readers of Divinity Lectures, shall to the uttermost of their wit, knowledge and learning, purely and sincerely (without any colour or dissimulation) teach, manifest, open, and declare four times every year (at the least) in their Sermons and other Collations and Lectures, That all usurped and forein power, (forasmuch as the same hath no establishment nor ground by the Law of God) is for most just causes taken away and abolished: and that therefore no manner of obedience, or subjection within his Majesties Realms and Dominions, is due unto any such forein power: but that the Kings power within his Realms of *England*, *Scotland*, and *Ireland*, and all other his Dominions and Countreys, is the highest power under God, to whom all men, as well inhabitants as born within the same, do by Gods Laws owe most loyalty and obedience, afore and above all other Power and Potentates in the earth.

II.

Impugners of the Kings Supremacy censured.

Whosoever shall hereafter affirm, that the Kings Majesty hath not the same authority in causes Ecclesiastical that the godly Kings had amongst the Jews, and Christian Emperors in the Primitive Church, or impeach in any part his regal Supremacy in the said causes restored to the Crown, and by the Laws of this Realm therein established, let him be excommunicated *ipso facto*,[12] and not restored but only by the Archbishop, after his repentance and publick revocation of those his wicked errours.

III.

The Church of England *a true and Apostolical Church.*

Whosoever shall hereafter affirm, that the Church of *England* by Law established under the Kings Majesty, is not a true and an Apostolical

---

12 By the deed itself.

Church, teaching and maintaining the doctrine of the Apostles, let him be excommunicated *ipso facto*, and not restored but onely by the Archbishop, after his repentance and publick revocation of this his wicked errour.

IV.

Impugners of the publick worship of God established in the Church of England *censured.*

Whosoever shall hereafter affirm, that the form of Gods worship in the Church of *England*, established by the Law, and contained in the Book of Common Prayer, and administration of Sacraments, is a corrupt, superstitious, or unlawful worship of God, or containeth any thing in it that is repugnant to the Scriptures, let him be excommunicated *ipso facto*, and not restored but by the Bishop of the place, or Archbishop, after his repentance and publick revocation of such his wicked errours.

V.

Impugners of the Articles of Religion established in the Church of England *censured.*

Whosoever shall hereafter affirm, that any of the nine and thirty Articles agreed upon by the Archbishops, and Bishops of both Provinces, and the whole Clergie in the Convocation holden at *London*, in the year of our Lord God, one thousand five hundred sixtie two, for the avoiding of diversities of opinions, and for the establishing of consent touching true Religion, are in any part superstitious or erroneous, or such as he may not with a good conscience subscribe unto, let him be excommunicated *ipso facto*, and not restored but only by the Archbishop, after his repentance and publick revocation of such his wicked errors.

Irish Canons

I.

Of the agreement of the church of England and Ireland, in the profession of the same Christian Religion.

For the manifestation of our agreement with the Church of England in the confession of the same Christian Faith, and the doctrine of the Sacraments: Wee doe receive and approve the Booke of Articles of Religion agreed upon by the Archbishops, and Bishops, and the whole Clergie in the Convocation holden at London in the yeare of our Lord God, 1562 for the avoyding of diversities of opinions, and for the establishing of consent touching true Religion. And therefore if any hereafter shall affirme that any of those Articles are in any part superstitious or erroneous, or such as he may not with a good conscience subscribe unto, let him be excommunicated, and not absolved before he make a publique revocation of his errour.

Scottish Canons

CHAPTER I.
Of the CHURCH of SCOTLAND

1. The Religion of CHRIST teacheth us, to honour Secular Princes, as the Viceregents of GOD upon earth; And therefore, as our duetie to the King's most excellent Majestie obliedgeth, It is decreed, and ordayned, That all Arch-Bishops, Bishops, and all other Ecclesiasticall persons; all Readers of Divinitie Lectures, all Masters, Principalls, Primars, Regents, Fellowes, and all who-so-ever have Charge of Schools, Colledges, and Universities, shall faythfullie keepe and observe, and (as much as in them lyeth) cause to be observed, and kept of others, all singular Lawes and Statutes made for the restoring to the CROWNE of this Kingdome, the aunctient Jurisdiction over the Estate Ecclesiasticall, and abolishing all Forraygne Power, repugnant to the same. And farther-more, shall purelie, and sincerelie, to the uttermost of their wit and Learning, teach, make open, and declare in their Doctrine, Exhortations, Lectures, Instructions, & Conferences at all fit times & occasions, That all usurped and forraygne power (for-as-much as the same hath no establishment, nor ground by the Law of GOD) is, for most just causes, taken away, and abolished; and that therefore no manner of obedience or subjection within His Majesties Realms and Dominions, is due unto any such forraygne power. But that the King's power within His Realms of SCOTLAND, ENGLAND, IRELAND, and all other His Dominions & Countreys, is the highest power under GOD; to whom all men, as well inhabitants, as borne within the same, doe by GOD'S Law owe most loyaltie and obedience; afore & above all powers, and Potentates on earth.

A liturgical convergence is found in the production and promulgation of the Scottish Prayer Book. The theology of the Preface reflects that of Thomas Cranmer's Preface to the Prayer Books of 1549 and 1552: just as there is one Lord, one faith, and one Baptism, so too where there is one monarch there should be one doctrine and one liturgical use.

THE PREFACE.

THE Church of Christ hath in all ages had a prescript forme of Common prayer, or Divine service, as appeareth by the ancient Liturgies of the Greeke and Latine Churches. This was done, as for other great causes, so likewise for retaining an uniformitie in Gods worship: a thing most beseeming them that are of one and the same profession. For by the forme that is kept in the outward worship of God, men commonly judge of Religion. If in that there be a diversitie, straight they are apt to conceive the Religion to bee diverse. Wherefore it were to be wished, that the whole Church of Christ were one as well in forme of publike worship, as in doctrine: And that as it hath but one Lord, and one Faith, so it had but one heart, and one mouth. This would prevent many schismes and divisions, and serve much to the preserving of unitie. But since that cannot be hoped for in the whole Catholike Christian Church, yet at least in the Churches that are under the protection of one Soveraigne Prince the same ought to be endeavoured.

It was not the least part of our late Soveraigne King JAMES of blessed memorie his care, to work this uniformitie in all his Dominions: but while he was about to do it, it pleased God to translate him to a better kingdome. His MAJESTIE that now raigneth, (and long may He raigne over us in all happinesse) not suffering his Fathers good purpose to fall to the ground, but treading the same path, with the like zeale and pious affection, gave order soon after his coming to the Crown, for the framing of a book of Common prayer, like unto that which is received in the Churches of England and Ireland, for the use of this Church. After many lets and hinderances, the same cometh now to be published, to the good, we trust, of all Gods people, and the increase of true pietie, and sincere devotion amongst them.

But as there is nothing, how good and warrantable soever in it selfe, against which some will not except: so it may be that exceptions will be taken against this good and most pious work, and perhaps none more pressed, then that we have followed the Service book of England. But we should desire them that shall take this exception, to consider, that being as we are by Gods mercie of one true profession, and otherwise united by many bonds, it had not been fitting to vary much from theirs, our especially coming forth after theirs, seeing the disturbers of the Church both here and there, should by our differences, if they had been great, taken occasion to worke more trouble. Therefore did wee think meet to adhere to their forme, even in the festivals, and some other rites, not as yet received, nor observed in our Church, rather then by omitting them, to give the Adversarie to think, that we disliked any part of their Service.

Out first Reformers were of the same minde with us, as appeareth by the ordinance they made, that in all the Parishes of the Realme, the Common prayer should be read weekly on Sundaies, and other Festivall dayes, with the Lessons of the old and new Testament, conforme to the order of the book of Common prayer (meaning that of England; for it is known that divers years after we had no other order for common prayer). This is recorded to have been the first head concluded in a frequent Councell of the Lords and Barons professing Christ Jesus. We keep the words of the historie; *Religion was not then placed in rites and gestures, nor men taken with the fancie of extemporarie prayers.*[13] Sure, the publike worship of God in his Church, being the most solemne action of us his poor creatures here below, ought to be performed by a Liturgie advisedly set and framed, and not according to the sudden and various fancies of men. This shall suffice for the present to have said. The God of mercie confirme our hearts in his truth, and preserve us alike from prophaneness and superstition. Amen.

The Scottish liturgy influenced all later Anglican liturgy with its epiclesis, the Eucharistic prayer which asks God the Father 'to blesse and sanctifie with thy word and holy Spirit these thy gifts and creatures of bread and wine'. An epiclesis was included in the 1549 Prayer Book but removed in subsequent revisions. Through continued Scottish use, the epiclesis has become a standard feature of Anglican liturgy.

ALMIGHTY God our heavenly Father, which of thy tender mercy didst give thy onely Sonne Jesus Christ to suffer death upon the Crosse for our redemption, who made there (by his one oblation of himself once offered) a full, perfect, and sufficient sacrifice, oblation, and satisfaction for the sinnes of the whole world, and did institute, and in his holy gospel command us to continue a perpetuall memory of that his precious death and sacrifice, untill his coming again: Heare us,

---

13 [The historie of the Church of Scotland, *pag.* 218.] by John Knox.

O mercifull Father, we most humbly beseech thee, and of thy almighty goodnesse vouchsafe so to blesse and sanctifie with thy word and holy Spirit these thy gifts and creatures of bread and wine, that they may bee unto us the body and blood of thy most dearly beloved Son: so that wee receiving them according to thy Sonne our Saviour Jesus Christs holy institution, in remembrance of his death and passion, may be partakers of the same his most precious body and bloud: who in the night that he was betrayed, *took bread*,[14] and when he had given thanks, he brake it, and gave it to his disciples, saying, Take, eat, this is my body, which is given for you; do this in remembrance of me. Likewise, after supper he *took the cup*,[15] and when he had given thanks, he gave it to them, saying, Drinke yee all of this, for this is my bloud of the new testament, which is shed for you, and for many, for the remission of sins: do this as oft as ye shall drink it in remembrance of me.

The Church of Scotland, The Book of Common Prayer (1637), no pag.

---

14 [At these words (*took bread*) the Presbyter that officiates is to take the Paten in his hand.]

15 [At these words (*took the cup*) he is to take the chalice in his hand, and lay his hand upon so much, be it in chalice or flagons, as he intends to consecrate.]

3

Civil War

Popular pamphlets

The 1640s saw the publication of thousands of pamphlets and petitions. The three excerpted here represent three genres. Locke's pamphlet represents popular providentialism, the reading of recent events (and rumours) as signs of God's will. All religious groups published such writings during and after the civil wars. The petition from Thomas Aston is one of many that he collected in defence of the Church of England. Finally is a petition for the Royal Touch, a theme whose importance will be seen more clearly in Chapter 4.

> Of one *Mary Wilmore*, wife to *John Wilmore* rough Mason, who was delivered of a Childe without a head, and credibly reported to have a firme Crosse on the brest, as this ensuing Story shall relate.

This Kingdome once glorying in the flourishing title of Albion: which is as much as happinesse and tranquility, (*tam Eccles. quam Respub.*)[1] but now being clouded and maskt with various distractions, as are apparently knowne and made manifest to the whole world, in so much that she is made a laughing stocke, and a scorne to all Nations, may now with the Publican cry, *Lord have mercy on me a sinner:*[2] or with *Eccebolius*, chiefe Captain of the Apostates, who in *Constantines* time tooke upon him the note of a zealous Christian: in the reigne of *Julian* he became a Pagan; *Julian* being dead then he would become a Christian: but being sensible of his mutability and inconstancy, prostrated himselfe flat upon the ground at the Porch of the Temple, crying with a loud voyce, Tread on me, tread on me, for I am unsavoury salt.

---

1 As in the Church, so in the Republic.
2 Luke 18.13.

I feare me we have too too many of these unsavoury and wheeling Rotundities frequent amongst us, but I pray God it happeneth not to them as it did to *Julian* Uncle to *Julian* the Apostate, for their contemning and slighting Gods holy ordinances, who comming into a Church at Antioch, profaned the Lords Table by pissing upon it, saying in scorne, that the Divine Providence tooke no care of outward ceremonies. But not long after divine Justice found him out, for being taken with a disease that rotted his bowels, his excrements leaving their wonted passage, ran through his throat and blasphemous mouth in as stinking a manner, as the poysoned trash and beggarly rudiments are fomented now adayes from the impudent mouthes of unlearned and ignorant Teachers, the event of whose pernicious and illiterate doctrine will lead me to this ensuing story of Gods wrath and judgements to over curious and nice zelots of our times.

In Mears-Ashby in Nottinghamshire one *Mary Wilmore* wife of *John Wilmore*, rough Mason, being great with childe, and much perplext in minde, to thinke that her childe when it pleased God she should be delivered, should be baptized with the signe of the Crosse: The Minister of the Parish being a very honest and conformable man, not suiting with the vaine babling and erroneous Sycophants, as there are too too many thereabouts inhabiting, desires her husband to goe to Hardwicke, a Village neare adjoyning to one Master *Bannard* a reverend Divine, to know his opinion concerning the Crosse in Baptisme: whose answer was, That it was no wayes necessary to salvation, but an ancient, laudable, and decent ceremony of the Church of England, Which answer being related to her from her husband, it is reported she should say, I had rather my childe should bee borne without a head, then to have a head to be signed with the signe of the Crosse.

Haply this woman through her weaknesse, or too much confiding in the conventicling Sectaries, *Qui quicquid in buccam venerit blatterant*:[3] might thinke she did well, supposing as shee was taught by them, the Crosse in Baptisme to bee a pernicious, popish and idolatrous ceremony: yet see *Uzzah*, 2 *Sam.* 6.6, 7. 1 *Chron.* 13.9, 10. *vid. Judg.* 8.27. though thy intent in doing a seeming good action be never so good, yet if thou have not warrant for not so doing, thou and thine actions may happly perish together, as the sequell of this story will declare. It pleased God about a month after, shee was accordingly delivered of a Monster, *Rudes indegestaque moles*, a child without a head, to the shame of the

---

3 *Everything which they babble came into her mouth.*

parents, in not having that part whereon it might have been markt with that token whereof it should never after have beene ashamed.

What strange judgements of God have wee seene, saith *Pollychronus*, in the times of revolters? as we may see in the third yeare of Queene *Elizabeth* of ever blessed memory, when as in *Moore* and *Geofferey*, two of the divells agents, publisht their prodigious and hereticall tenents, to the allurement of many faithfull and constant beleevers: the yeare after was many monstrous births. A man childe was born at Chichester in Suffex, the head, armes, and legs whereof were like Anatomy, the brest and belly monstrous big from the navell, about the necke a great coller of flesh and skin growing, like to the double ruffes and neckerchiefes then in use, and many more like accidents, *qua nunc norandi non est locus*.[4] Good Lord therefore which hast made and fashioned us, and as there is one Lord, one faith, and one baptisme, one God and Father of all, even so Lord grant that wee may joyntly agree in love, and that there remaine amongst us a godly consent and loving concord, and that nothing bee done in contention and vainglory: and suffer us not to exercise our selves in the workes of the flesh, as hatred, emulations, contentions, heresies, seditions, needless and unprofitable questions, which tend to rebellion and discord, breeding ungodlinesse, and make dissention: breake thou the bonds of Sathan, and the malice of those who extinguish the bond of peace.

By *John Locke, Cleric.*

FINIS.

John Locke, *A Strange and Lamentable accident that happened lately at Mears-Ashby in Northamptonshire* (1642)

To the *Kings* Most Excellent *Majesty*,
And to the Right Honourable the Lords,
and the Honourable the House of Commons
assembled in Parliament.

The most humble Petition of divers *Baronets, Knights, Justices, Gentry, Ministers, and Freeholders, Inhabitants of the County of* Kent, *within the Diocesse of* Canterbury.

---

4 *Now is not the place where they must be observed* (substituting *notandi* for *norandi*).

Most humbly shewing,

That notwithstanding this Kingdome, hath by the singular providence of Almighty God, for many yeares last past, happily flourished, above all other Nations in the Christian World, under the Religion and Government by Law established: Yet hath it beene of late most miserably distracted through the sinister practises of some private persons ill affected to them both.

By whose meanes the present Government is disgraced and traduced, The Houses of God are prophaned, and in part defaced, The Ministers of Christ are contemned and despised, The Ornaments, and many Utensils of the Church are abused, The Liturgy and Booke of Common Prayer depraved, and neglected, That absolute modell of Prayer, *The Lords Prayer*, vilified, The Sacraments of the Gospell in some places unduly administred, in other places omitted, Solemne dayes of fasting observed, and appointed by private persons, Marriages illegally Solemnized, Burials uncharitably performed, And the very Fundamentall of our Religion subverted, by the publication of a new Creed, and teaching the abrogation of the Morall Law. For which purpose, many offensive Sermons are dayly Preached, and many impious Pamplets printed, and in contempt of authority, Many doe what seemeth good in their owne eyes, onely as if there were no King, nor Government, in this our Israel.[5]

Whereby Almighty God is highly provoked, his sacred Majesty dishonoured, The peace of the Kingdome endangered, The Consciences of the people disquieted, The Ministers of Gods Word disheartened, and the Enemies of the Church emboldned in their enterprises.

For redresse whereof, May it please this Great and Honourable Councell, speedily to command a due observation of the Religion and Government, by Law established; in such manner, as it may seeme best to the Piety and Wisdome of his Royall Majesty, and this Honourable Court.

Your Petitioners as they shall Confidently expect a blessing from Heaven upon this Church and Kingdome, So shall they have this further cause to implore the Divine Assistance upon this Most Honourable Assembly.

---

5 Cf. Judges 21.25.

Subscribed by

Knight Barronets, and Knights	24.
Esquires and Gentlemen of note, above	300.
Divines	108.
Freeholders, and Subsidie men	800.

All within the Diocesse of *Canterbury*.

Thomas Aston, *A Collection of Sundry Petitions* (1642), pp. 26–7

THE
Humble *Petition* of divers hundreds
of the Kings poore Subjects, afflicted
with that grievous Infirmitie,
CALLED
The Kings Evill.

Whereas divers of your Majesties loving and faithfull Subjects in great and considerable numbers, not onely in and about the City of *London*, and the suburbs thereof, but also in all parts of your Majesties Dominions, are oppressed with that grievous and afflicting Maladie, called *The Kings Evill*, which, as it is proper onely to our *English* Nation, is curable by the Kings of *England*, no Soveraigne of any Kingdome else having that miraculous medicinall vertue infused upon them,[6] but onely the Monarchs of this Nation, to whose sacred hands, as it appeares, both by example and History, this healing propertie is circumscribed and confined ever since that holy King of famous memory, *Edward* the Confessor, by the vertuall contact and imposition of his hands upon a party afflicted with that tumorous and insufferable disease asswaged the present paine, and afterward remitting the said afflicted person to the hands of his Physitians and Chirurgions, who finishing that worke which the good King had begun, gave a perfect cure to the said contagious and hideous Maladie; ever since which time, as the Crowne hath descended upon his successors from *William* the Conqueror, to your sacred Majestie, so hath that said healing vertue likewise hereditarily descended upon all his successors even to your most excellent Majesty, who have also as well as the most religious and holy of all your

---

6 Although unknown to the author of the petition, the Royal Touch was also practised in France.

predecessors, given sufficient and luculent[7] testimonies of your royall abilities that way, in the cure of that noysome and contagious disease. Your majesty, like the good *Samaritan*, pouring in oyle and balme into the wounds of those wretched persons that have long time desperately laine and languished even to death of that miraculous and supernaturall evill, the cure of which is one of the greatest of your royall Majesties prerogatives, which no force can deprive your Highnesse of, nor no humane mean hath power to annihilate; the rest of the Princely attributes hereditary to this Crowne of *England*, and its regall possessors, being subject to humane casualties, and dying with the possessors, this blessed cure being progressive, and like fame increasing by succession; so that there is no one happinesse which the subject of *England* possesseth in their Soveraigne of so much value to them as this is, which is freely and charitably imparted to them to the great comfort & saving of the healths, lives and limbs of many thousands of your Majesties poore subjects, impossibilited of being cured by any other means then the contaction and imposition of your Majesties sacred hands.

. . .

To conclude, all of us are a sort of miserable undone wretches, who are nothing without the sudden expression of your gracious favour towards us, which wee can no way enjoy, unlesse your sacred Majestie be pleased to consigne some way whereby wee may be enabled to approach your royall presence, which we can no way doe, so long as your Majestie resides at *Oxford*, invironed with so many legions of souldiers, who will be apt to hinder our accesse to your Court and Princely Person, which others that have formerly laboured with our Malady have so freely enjoyed at *London* when you were resident at your palace at *White-hall*, where we all wish your Majestie, as well for the cure of our infirmitie, as for the recovery of the State, which hath languished of a tedious sicknesse since your Highnesse departure from thence, and can no more be cured of its infirmitie then wee, till your gracious returne thither, which, that it may the sooner be effected, wee your Majesties loyall Subjects and humble Petitioners, shall ever pray, *&c.*

Anonymous, Petition for the Royal Touch (1643), pp. 3–4, 8

---

7 Lucid.

The execution of Charles I

There are two versions of the king's final speech. The first version, King Charls his Speech Made upon the Scaffold, *was printed in 1649 with the statement 'Published by Spetiall Authority' on the cover. The author is unknown. The second version was printed in the* Reliquae *in 1650. The latter is transcribed here, with substantive 1649 variants footnoted.*

Tuesday, Jan. 30. 1648.

About ten in the Morning the King was brought from S. *James*'s walking on foot through the Park with a Regiment of Foot, part before and part behind him, with Colours flying, Drummes beating, his private Guard of Partizans, with some of his Gentlemen before, and some behind bare-headed, Dr. *Juxton* next behind him, and Col. *Thomlinson* (who had the charge of him) talking with the King bare-headed from the Park, up the stairs into the Gallery, and so into the[8] *Cabinet Chamber*, where he used to lie, where he continued at his Devotion, refusing to dine (having before taken the *Sacrament*) onely about an hour before he came forth he drank a glass of Claret Wine, and ate a piece of bread about twelve at noon.

From thence he was accompanied by Doctor *Juxton*, Col. *Thomlinson*, and other Officers, formerly appointed to attend him, and the private Guard of Partizans, with Musketeers on each side, through the Banquetting-house, adjoyning to which the Scaffold was erected, between White-Hall Gate, and the Gate leading into the Gallery from S. *James*'s:[9] The Scaffold was hung round with black, and the floor covered with black, and the Ax and Block laid in the middle of the Scaffold. There were divers Companies of Foot, and Troops of Horse placed on the one side of the Scaffold toward *Kings street*, and on the other side toward *Charing Cross*, and the multitudes of people that came to be spectators very great.

Because we have no other Relation of what His Majesty then spake, save what his Enemies have set forth; nor had his Majesty any copy (being surprized and hastned by those that thirsted after His Blood) save onely a few Heads in a little Scrip of Paper, which the Souldiers took from the Bishop of *London*, to whom He gave it: therefore the Reader

---

8 1649 marginalia: [It is observ'd, The King desired to have the use of the Cabinet, and the little room next to it, where there was a Trap-door.]

9 1649 marginalia: [It was neare [if not in] the very place where the first blood in the beginning of the late troubles was shed, when the Kings Cavaliers fell upon the Citizens, killed one, and wounded about 50 others.]

must be content with this Copy which they have published (some few words being altered to make the sense perfect, which either wilfully, or by mistake of the Writer or Printer were perverted.)[10]

The King being come upon the Scaffold, and looking about him upon the people, who were kept off by Troops of Horse, so that they could not come near to hear him, omitted what he had purposed to have spoken to them (as 'tis thought) and turning himself to the Souldiers and Officers (the Instruments of the Regicide) spake to them this effect:[11]

His MAJESTIES Speech.

King. *I Shall very little be heard of any body here, I shall therefore speak a word unto you here: indeed I could hold my peace very well, if I did not think that holding my peace would make some men think that I did submit to the Guilt as well as to the Punishment; but I think it is my duty to God first, and to my Countrey, for to clear my self both as an honest Man, a good King, and a good Christian. I shall begin first with my* Innocency: *In truth I think it not very needfull for me to insist long upon this, for all the world knows that I never did begin a War with the two Houses of Parliament; and I will call God to witness, to whom I must shortly make an account, that I never did intend for to incroach upon their Priviledges: they began upon me; it is the Militia they began upon; they confest that the Militia was mine, but they thought it fit for to have it from me: And to be short, if any body will look upon the dates of Commissions, of their Commissions and mine, and likewise to the Declarations, will see clearly that they began these unhappy Troubles, not I: so that as the guilt of these enormous Crimes that are laid against me, I hope in God that God will clear me of; I will not, I am in charity: God forbid that I should lay it upon the two Houses of Parliament, there is no necessity of either, I hope they are free of this guilt: for I do believe that ill Instruments between them and me, has been the chief cause of all this blood-shed, so that by way of speaking, as I find my self clear of this, I hope (and pray God) that they may too: yet for all this, God forbid that I should be so ill a Christian as not to say that Gods judgements are just upon me: Many times he does pay Justice by an unjust Sentence, that is ordinary: I will onely say this,*

---

10 This paragraph is not contained in 1649.

11 1649: 'The King being come upon the Scaffold look'd very earnestly on the block, and asked Colonel Hacker if there were no higher; and then spake thus (directing his speech chiefly to Col. Thomlinson).'

That an unjust Sentence[12] *that I suffered for to take effect, is punished now by an unjust Sentence upon me, that is so: for I have said, to shew you that I am an innocent man.*

Now for to shew you that I am a good Christian, I hope there is[13] *a good man that will bear me witness, That I have forgiven all the world, and even those in particular that have been the causers of my death; who they are, God knowes, I do not desire to know, I pray God forgive them. But this is not all, my Charity must go farther, I wish that they may repent, for indeed they have committed a great sin in that particular: I pray God with St. Stephen, this be not laid to their Charge; nay not onely so, but that they may take the right way to the Peace of the Kingdom; for my Charity commands me, note onely to forgive particular men, but my Charity commands me to endeavour to the last gasp the Peace of the Kingdom; So (Sir) I do wish with all my soul, (and I do hope there is some*[14] *will carry it further) that they may endeavour the Peace of the Kingdome.*

Now (Sirs) I must shew you both how you are out of the way, and will put you in the way: first you are out of the way, for certainly all the way you ever have had yet as I could finde by any thing, is in the way of conquest; certainly this is an ill way: for Conquest (Sir) in my opinion is never just, except there be a good just cause, either for matter of wrong or just Title, and then if you go beyond it, the first quarrell that you have to it is that it makes it unjust at the end that was just at first: But if it be onely matter of Conquest, then it is a great Robbery, as a Pirat said to Alexander, *that He was the great Robber, he was but a petty Robber: and so, Sir, I do think the way that you are in, is much out of the way. Now Sir, for to put you in the way, believe it you will never do right, nor God will never prosper you, untill you give God his due, the King his due (that is, my Successors) and the people their due: I am as much for them as any of you: You must give God his due, by regulating rightly his Church (according to his Scriptures) which is now out of order: For to set you in a way particularly now I cannot, but onely this, A Nationall Synod freely called, freely debating among themselves, must settle this, when that every Opinion is freely and clearly heard.*

For the King, indeed I will not (then turning to a Gentleman that touched the Ax, said, hurt not the Ax, that may hurt me.[15] *For the King) the Lawes of the Land will clearly instruct you for that; there-*

---

12 [Straffords.]
13 [Pointing to Dr. *Juxton*.]
14 [Turning to some Gentlemen that wrote.]
15 [Meaning if he did blunt the edge.]

fore because it concerns my own particular, I onely give you a touch of it.

For the people: And truly I desire their Liberty and freedome as much as any body whosoever; but I must tell you, That their Liberty and freedome consists in having of Government; those Lawes, by which their Life and their Goods may be most their own. It is not for having share in Government (Sir) that is nothing pertaining to them; A Subject and a Soveraign are clean different things, and therefore untill they do that, I mean, That you do put the people in that Liberty as I say, certainly they will never enjoy themselves.

Sir, It was for this that now I am come here: If I would have given way to an Arbitrary way, for to have all Lawes changed according to the power of the sword, I needed not to have come here, and therefore I tell you (and I pray God it be not laid to your charge) That I am the Martyr of the people.

In truth Sirs, I shall not hold you much longer, for I will onely say this to you, That in truth I could have desired some little time longer, because I would have put this that I have said in a little more order, and little better digested then I have done; and therefore I hope you will excuse Me.

I have delivered my Conscience, I pray God that you do take those courses that are best for the good of the kingdom and your own salvations.

Dr. *Juxton.* Will your Majesty (though it may be very well known Your Majesties affections to Religion, yet it may be expected that you should) say somewhat for the worlds satisfaction?

King. *I thank you very heartily (my Lord) for that, I had almost forgotten it: In truth Sirs, My Conscience in Religion I think is very well known to all the World; and therefore I declare before you all, That I die a Christian, according to the profession of the Church of England, as I found it left me by my Father; and this honest man*[16] *I think will witnesse it.* Then turning to the Officers, said: *Sirs, excuse me for this same, I have a good cause, and I have a gracious God, I will say no more.* Then turning to Colonel *Hacker,* he said: *Take care they do not put me to pain, and sir, this, and it please you:* But then a Gentleman coming near the Ax, the King said, *Take heed of the Ax, pray take heed of the Ax;* then the King to the Executioner said, *I shall say but very short Prayers, and when I thrust out my hands*—Then the King called to Doctor *Juxton* for his *Night cap,* and

---

16 [Pointing to Dr. *Juxton.*]

having put it on, he said to the Executioner, *Does my hair trouble you?*[17] who desired him to put it all under his Cap, which the King did accordingly by the help of the Executioner and the Bishop: Then the king turning to Dr. *Juxton*, said, *I have a good Cause and a gracious God on my side.*

Doctor *Juxton*. There is but one Stage more, This Stage is turbulent and troublesome; it is a short one: But you may consider, it will soon carry you a very great way: it will carry you from earth to heaven; and there you shall find a great deal of cordial joy and comfort.

King. *I go from a corruptible to an incorruptible Crown; where no disturbance can be, no disturbance in the world.*

Dr. *Juxton*. You are exchanged from a Temporal to an Eternall Crown; a good exchange.

The King then said to the Executioner, is my hair well? Then the King took of His Cloak and his George,[18] giving his George to Doctor *Juxton*, saying, Remember[19] — Then the King put off his Doublet, and being in his Wastcoat, put his Cloak on again, then looked upon the block, said to the Executioner, *You must set it fast.*

Executioner. It is fast Sir.[20]

King. *When I put my hands out this way, stretching them out, then*—

After that having said two or three words (as he stood) to himself, with hands and eyes lift up; Immediately stooping down, laid his neck upon the Block: And then the Executioner again putting his hair under his Cap, the King said (thinking he had been going to strike) stay for the sign.

Executioner. Yes I will & it please your Majesty.

And after a very little pause, the King stretching forth his hands, The Executioner at one blow severed his head from his body; the head being off, the Executioner held it up, and shewed it to the people; which done, it was with the Body put in a coffin covered with black Velvet for that purpose,[21] and conveyed into his Lodgings there: And from

---

17 The hair was placed under the night cap so that the executioner could see the king's neck and thus behead him with one blow.

18 The ornate and decorated badge of the Order of the Garter, the oldest chivalric order in England, which featured St George slaying the dragon. The king was the head of the order.

19 [It is thought for to give it to the Prince.]

20 1649 inserts two lines:
  King. It might have been a little higher.
  Executioner. It can be no higher Sir.

21 1649 concludes here with: 'The Kings Body now lies in his Lodgings in White-Hall. Sic transit Gloria Mundi.' (*Thus passes the glory of the world.*)

thence it was carried to his house at S. *James*'s, where his body was put in a Coffin of Lead, laid there to be seen by the people; and about a fortnight after it was carried to *Windsor*, accompanied with the Duke of *Lenox*, the Marquesse of *Hartford*, and the Earle of *Southampton*, and Doctor *Juxton*, Bishop of *London*, and others, and interred in the Chappel Royall in the Vault with *King Henry* the eight, having onely this Inscription upon his Coffin.

CHARLES KING OF ENGLAND.

His Majesties last Speech, *Reliquae Sacrae Carolinae*[22] (1650), pp. 90–8

---

22 Sacred Caroline Relics.

4

The Cult of King Charles the Martyr

Eikon Basilike[1]

The king's collection of prayers and meditations, first printed on the day of his death, was the runaway bestseller of the seventeenth century. The volume consisted of prayers, which were printed in italics, and prose meditations, which were not. More than anything else, this cemented the king's image as an imitator of Christ.

II. Upon the Earle of Straffords death.[2]

But thou, O God of infinite Mercies, forgive Me that act of sinful complyance, which hath greater aggravations upon me then any man. Since I had not the least temptation of envy, or malice against him, and by my place should, at least so far, have been a preserver of him, as to have denied my consent to his destruction.

O Lord, I acknowledge my transgression, and my sin is ever before me.

Deliver me from bloud guiltinesse O God, thou God of my salvation, and my tongue shall sing of thy righteousnesse.

Against thee have I sinned, and done this evil in thy sight, for thou sawest the contradiction between my heart and my hand.

Yet cast me not away from thy presence, purge me with the blood of my Redeemer, and I shall be cleane; wash me with that precious effusion, and I shall be whiter then snow.

Teach me to learn Righteousnesse by thy Judgments, and to see my frailty in thy Justice: while I was perswaded by shedding one mans blood to prevent after troubles, thou hast for that, among other sins, brought upon me, and upon my Kingdoms, great, long, and heavy troubles.

Make me to prefer Justice, which is thy will, before all contrary clamours, which are but the discoveries of mans injurious will.

---

1 The Royal Image.
2 This prayer works quite heavily off Psalm 51.

It is too much that they have once overcome me, to please them by displeasing thee: O never suffer Me for any reason of State, to go against my reason of Conscience, which is highly to sin against thee, the God of Reason, and Judge of our Consciences.

What ever, O Lord, thou seest fit to deprive me of, yet restore unto me the joy of thy Salvation, and ever uphold me with thy free Spirit; which subjects my will to none, but thy light of Reason, Justice, and Religion, which shines in my Soul, for thou desirest Truth in the inward parts, and integrity in the outward expressions.

Lord hear the voice of thy Sonnes, and my Saviours blood, which speaks better things; and make me, and my people, to hear the voice of Joy and Gladnesse, that the bones which thou hast broken, may rejoyce in thy Salvation.

XVI. Upon the Ordinance against the Common-Prayer-Book.

It is no news to have all Innovations ushered in with the name of Reformations in Church and State, by those, who seeking to gain reputation with the Vulgar for their extraordinary parts and piety, must needs undo whatever was formerly setled never so well and wisely.

So hardly can the pride of those that study Novelties, allow former times any share or degree of wisdom and godlinesse.

And because matter of prayer and devotion to God justly bears a great part in Religion, (being the Souls more immediate converse with the Divine Majesty) nothing could be more plausible to the people, then to tell them, they served God amisse in that point.

Hence our publick Liturgy, or Forms of constant Prayers, must be (not amended, in what upon free and publick advice might seem to sober men inconvenient for matter or manner, to which I should easily consent, but) wholly cashiered and abolished; and after many popular contempts offered to the Book, and those that used it according to their Consciences, and the Laws in force, it must be crucified by an Ordinance, the better to please either those men, who gloried in their extemporary vein & fluency: or others, who conscious to their own formality in the use of it, thought they fully expiated their sin of not using it aright, by laying all the blame upon it, and a total rejecting of it as a dead letter, thereby to excuse the deadnesse of their hearts.

As for the matter contained in the Book, sober & learned men have sufficiently vindicated it against the cavils and exceptions of those, who thought it a part of piety, to make what profane objections they could against it; especially for Popery and Superstition; whereas no doubt the

Liturgy was exactly conformed to the Doctrine of the Church of *England*: and this by all Reformed Churches is confessed to be most sound and Orthodox.

For the manner of using set and prescribed Forms, there is no doubt, but that wholsome words being known and fitted to mens understandings, are soonest received into their own hearts, and aptest to excite & carry along with them judicious and fervent affections.

Nor do I see any reason why Christians should be weary of a well-composed Liturgy (as I hold this to be) more then of other things, wherein the constancy abates nothing of the excellency and usefulnesse.

I could never see any reason, why any Christian should abhor, or be forbidden to use the same Forms of prayer, since he prayes to the same God, believes in the same Saviour, professes the same Truths, reads the same Scriptures, hath the same duties upon him, and feels the same daily wants for the most part, both inward and outward, which are common to the whole Church.

XXVIII. Meditations upon Death, after the Votes of Non-Address,[3] and His Majesties closer Imprisonment in *Carisbrook-Castle*.

As I have leisure enough, so I have cause more then enough to meditate upon, and prepare for My Death; for I know there are but few steps between the prisons and graves of Princes.

It is Gods indulgence, which gives Me the space, but Mans cruelty, that gives Me the sad occasions for these thoughts.

For, besides the common burthen of morality, wch lies upon Me, as a Man; I now bear the heavy load of other mens ambitions, fears, jealousies, and cruel passions, whose envy or enmity against Me, makes their own lives seem deadly to them, while I enjoy any part of Mine.

I thank God, My prosperity made Me not wholly a stranger to the contemplations of mortality.

Those are never unseasonable, since this is always uncertain: Death being an eclypse, which oft happeneth as well in clear, as cloudy dayes.

But My now long and sharp adversity, hath so reconciled in Me those natural Antipathies between Life and Death, which are in all men, that I thank God, the common terrors of it are dispelled; and the special horror of it, as to My particular much allayed: For, although My death at present may justly be represented to Me, with all those terrible ag-

---

3 The decision of the English Parliament in January 1648 to terminate negotiations with the king.

gravations, which the policy of cruel and implacable enemies can put upon it (affairs being drawn to the very dregs of malice) yet I blesse God, I can look upon all those stings, as unpoysonous, though sharp; since My Redeemer hath either pulled them out, or given Me the Antidote of his death against them; which as to the immaturity, unjustice, shame, scorn, and cruelty of it, exceeded whatever I can fear.

Indeed, I did never finde so much the life of Religion, the feast of a good Conscience, and the brazen wall of a judicious integrity and constancy, as since I came to these closer conflicts wth the thoughts of Death.

I am not so old, as to be weary of life; nor (I hope) so bad, as to be either afraid to dye, or ashamed to live: true, *I am so afflicted, as might make me sometime even desire to dye*; if I did not consider, That it is the greatest glory of a Christian life, to *dye daily*, in conquering by a lively faith, and patient hopes of a better life; those partial and quotidian deaths, which kill us (as it were) by piece-meals, and make us overlive our own fates; while we are deprived of health, honour, liberty, power, credit, safety, or estate, and those other comforts of dearest relations, which are as the life of our lives.

Another relation from the Lady Elizabeths *own Hand.*

Eikon Basilike *expanded to include additional material by the king, including his final correspondence with his daughter, the princess Elizabeth. This is one of his most important and influential letters; it propelled the theological convergence of his own reign into that of his son. Under Charles II, Andrewes's* Sermons *went through three editions in 1661; Hooker's* Works *were printed in 1662, 1666, 1676 and 1682; and Laud's* Conference *was printed in 1673 and 1686. Each edition of Hooker's* Works *carried the endorsement of Charles I on the title page, and other writings by Andrewes and Laud were also widely printed.*

What the King said to me the 29 of Jan. 1648. being the last time I had the happinesse to see Him, He told Me, He was glad *I* was come, and although He had not time to say much, yet somewhat He had to say to Me, which He had not to another, or leave in writing; because He feared their cruelty was such, as that they would not have permitted Him to write me. He wished me not to grieve and torment My self for Him, for that would be a glorious death that He should dye; it being for the Laws and Liberties of this Land, and for maintaining the true Protestant Religion. He bid me reade Bishop *Andrew*'s Sermons, *Hooker's Ecclesiastical Polity,* and Bishop *Laud*'s Book against *Fisher*, which would ground me against Popery. He told me, He had forgiven all His Enemies, and hoped God would forgive them also; and commanded us, and all the rest of my Brothers and Sisters, to forgive them. He bid me tell My Mother, That His thoughts had never strayed from Her, and that His love should be the same to the last. Withal He commanded me and my Brother, to be obedient to her: And bid me send His blessing to the rest of my Brothers and Sisters, with commendation to all His friends. So after He had given me his blessing, I took my leave.

Further, He commanded us all to forgive those people, but never to trust them; for they had been most false to Him, and to those that gave them power, and He feared also, to their own Souls; and desired Me not to grief for Him, for He should dye a Martyr, and that He doubted not but the Lord would settle His Throne upon His Son, and that we should be all happier, then we could have expected to have been, if He had lived: with many other things, which at present I cannot remember.

Elizabeth.

Charles I, *Eikon Basilike* (1649), in *Reliquae Sacrae Carolinae* (1650), Part II, pp. 7–8, 93–4, 171–2, 339

Popular responses

Popular outrage at the king's beheading took numerous forms. Especially important were stories that circulated about the Royal Touch being effected through the king's relics, and typological comparisons of the king with Christ.

Loving Countreymen, this is a briefe and faithfull Relation of a mayd dwelling and living now in *Detford*, foure miles distant from *London*, daughter to M^ris *Baylie*; which mayd being about the age of fourteen or fifteen years, hath long time been grievously tormented with the disease which is called the *Kings Evill*, which evill continued its force so long upon her, that it putrified and corrupted, not onely the unseen parts of her body, but her face and her eyes, in so much that she became blinde therewith. Her mother being a carefull and loving woman, having more regard to the welfare of her childe, then she had to the wealth of the world, endeavoured (as farre as her Purse or pains would extend) to do her good. But alas, all that ever she could do was but lost labour, only through Gods great mercy she kept the Girle alive, though her pains every day encreased more and more. Yet notwithstanding this, M^ris *Baylie* sought to many skilfull folks, hoping in time to have some remedy for her daughter; amongst others, she employed one M^r. *Stipkins*, a man of very good knowledge and understanding in the practice of Surgery, being very well approved of for his skill both in the City of *London* and many parts of the Countreys adjacent: This M^r. *Stypkins* often frequented Mistris *Baylies* house in hope to cure her daughter of the Evill; but all he could doe would little prevaile, though for a time, while he was present, she found some ease, yet when he was gone from her she became as bad or worse then she was before; so that all the help that man could do could not cure her disease: wherefore those that were neighbours dwelling neere unto her perswaded her mother even to give over, and let God work his will with her; & some others that ministred to the Damsell, bid her, serve God and be content, and prepare for Heaven, for there was no likelihood of long remaining in this World. And thus was the poore silly[4] soule past all hopes of recovery, being discomforted with words, blind of her sight, forsaken by the Physicians, and left off by acquaintance. But yet for all these doings the Lord provided for this poore creature such a miraculous blessing, whereby to preserve her life, and cure her blindnesse, the like was never known since our Saviour Christ and his blessed Apostles lived on the Earth,[5] as will appear by this following Discourse.

Here followeth a true and faithfull Discourse concerning the daughter of Mistris Baylie, *who had been long time possessed of the disease called the* Kings Evill: *and how at last she was cured by a Handkircher that was dipt in the Kings Blood that day he was beheaded.*

It is an old saying and a true, that when men and women are at weakest, then is God full as strong, and the same God he was before; as may appear by these examples which are here set down. Though the three Children (we read in the Scripture) were cast into a fiery Furnice, the Lord sent an Angel to deliver them out. Though *Daniel* was cast into the Denne amongst Lyons, yet God provided so for him, they had no power to hurt him. Though *Jonas* was cast into the depth of the Sea, the Lord sent a Whale to bring him to Land. Though *Job* was tormented and buffeted by the divell, the Lord restored him to his former estate. Though *Paul* suffered shipwrack, yet the Lord suffered him not to be utterly lost. Though the man spoken of in the Gospell was borne blinde, which no man could

---

4 Simple.
5 Acts 19.12.

cure, yet the Lord Jesus Christ could cure him by working a Miracle upon him, by annoynting his eyes with Clay, whereby he received sight. Even so hath the Almighty Lord of Heaven restored this poor forlorn Mayd of *Detford* to her sight again, by way of Miracle, and thus it was:

It hapned, by Gods appointment, that one Master, *John Lane*, now living in *London* in the *Old-Change*, a Woollen Draper by profession, hearing of the misery that M^ris *Baylies* daughter was in, he having a Handkircher about him which had been dipped in the Kings blood on the day that he was beheaded. This Mr *Lane* gave her a piece of the same Handkircher, which the mayd tooke, and applied to her sores, and wiping her eyes with the bloody side of the Handkircher, hath through Heavens providence recovered her eyesight, and is become lusty and strong, and able to doe any thing both abroad and at home, as is fitting for one of her age and growth to doe, and many hundreds of people come daily to see her both from *London* and other places; and all that ever saw her in her sicknesse, and sees her now in health, do confesse that it is a work the Lord hath done, whereby his Name might be glorified, and the Kings death thought upon. And those that desire to know further of the matter, may both see and talke with the Mayd at her mothers house at *Detford*.

And now beloved Christians, let us consider what a precious Jewell we lost, when we parted from our Kings life; whose Blood after his death was of such a valuable vertue, that it made the blinde to see, by no other meanes but by stroaking and applying the Handkircher to the soarnesse of the places where her griefe lay, which she did morning and evening. And though, by Gods good pleasure this one poore creature hath recovered her life by his death, yet there are many thousands that stand in great need of helpe for the same Disease, which never can be cured, for want of a King that can safely say, *I touch, God heals*.[6] Now there are some that will say, why doe not all them that are troubled with the *Kings Evill*, make suit & get some of the Kings Blood to cure them? the answer is, that it is not to be had for love nor money; for where any is, they either keepe it secretly, or if it be known, they will not part from it. But it fared better with such poor distressed souls while the King lived, for he was so gracious, that when there were a numberlesse company of poore distressed people, he would appoint them a time to give them a visit, and be as good as His word; and when His patients came into His presence, He scorned not to touch the poorest creatures sores, and handle their wounds to doe them good, while the corruption of their Diseases ranne upon his Princely fingers, and by the vertue

---

6 In the liturgy for the Royal Touch, the king spoke these words when he laid his hands upon the sick.

The Cult of King Charles the Martyr

of the same they had their perfect cure. Where is the man to be found that now can doe so? surely not alive in *England*. Here are them left that can kill the Kings friends; but here are none that can cure the Kings Evill.

And now I hold it not amisse to speake something of the happy estate that we lived in while the King lived, and how our fortunes are crost by His death; and this shall be done by way of comparison. First, suppose there were a rich man living, as *Job* was at the first, having many children, plenty of servants, store of Corne on the ground, and Cattell in the field, and flocks of sheep feeding on the pleasant mountaines: would it not greatly grieve this rich man to part with his children, to forgoe his riches, to be turned out of his habitation, to be cast in prison, and to have his servants banished out of his sight? Even so fared our Soveraigne Lord King *Charles*, His Wife was banished, His Children dispersed, His Servants disinherited, His goods taken from Him, and at last His Princely Head brought to the Block, which well may make the heart of every Christian tremble to think on.

In the holy Book of God is written thus, *Touch not the Lords Anoynted, nor doe my Prophets no harme.* And in 1 Pet. 2.17. we are forewarned, *to feare God, and honour the King.* Exod. 22.28. *Thou shalt not speake evill of the King.* Eccles. 10.20. *Curse not the King in thy thought.* But alas, how far is the feare of God hidden from our eyes! How many times hath *Charles* the first, the Lords Anoynted been, not onely toucht, but buffeted, kickt and spurned at? How many seditious persons have been suffered to speak evill against His Majesty, and with spitefull tongues and slanders scandalize and abuse him to his face? yea, how many thousand envious Matchevils[7] have not onely cursed him in their thoughts, but openly said, they hoped to wash their hands of His hearts blood? And last of all, instead of *Feare God, honour the King*, they have forgotten their duty to both.

To conclude, he was a *Salomon*, for wisdome; a *David*, for courage, and a *Job*, for patience. He was a forgiver of injuries, a lover of Religion, a hater of lewdnesse, a friend to his enemies, a maintainer of the Truth, Defender of the Faith, a protector of his Subjects, and a help of the poor. The Lord in mercy send that no worse come in His place now he is gone from us.

FINIS.

Anonymous, *A Miracle of Miracles* (1649)

---

7 Machiavellis. Niccolo Machiavelli (1469–1527) was an Italian political theorist who advocated the ruthless use of political power.

Our Saviour was watched the night before he suffered; in the morning sent to *Pilat*, from him to *Herod*, then back again to the *Common Judgment Hall*, where he was condemned, and at the third hour led forth to be crucified: But our Sovereign was watched many nights before he suffered; for all the time of his triall his Chamber was fil'd with barbarous Souldiers, who deprived him of his rest, and of all manner of privacy, which was more bitter to him then death. At last, our Saviour suffered death: so did our Sovereign, at the very same hour of the day; for our Saviour gave up the Ghost at the ninth hour, which is our three of the clock in the afternoon: the same hour put a period to our Soveraigns life, and to the happinesse of three Kingdoms.

<small>Guarded night and day with Souldiers.</small>

<small>The King suffered the 30 of Jan: at three in the afternoon, 1648.</small>

Let us now see how he did bear this; even as his Saviour had done, *who for the joy that was set before him, endured the crosse, despising the shame.*[8]

He contemned an Earthly Crown, for the assured hope he had of an Immortall Crown, *that fadeth not away:*[9] And so, like his Saviour, *When he was reviled, he reviled not again, but was led like a sheep unto the slaughter, and opened not his mouth.*[10] As Christ prayed for them that crucified him: so did our Sovereign pour out many devout prayers for his Enemies, which might serve to melt their hearts, if they were not harder than *Adamant*. As Christ wept over *Jerusalem* so did our Sovereign weep over his three Kingdoms; being more sorry for the miseries that are to come upon them, then for all that had hapned unto himself. As women, beholding Christs passion, *wept*: so many women, beholding their *Soveraign* on a Scaffold, *wept bitterly*; unto whom he might have said (as our *Saviour* said unto the other, *Weep not for me, ye Daughters of Jerusalem, but weep for your selves*).[11]

<small>He despised an earthly Crown for an immortall Crown.</small>

<small>He prayed for his Enemies.</small>

<small>His Spectators wept to see him on the Scaffold.</small>

---

[8] Hebrews 12.2.
[9] 1 Peter 5.4.
[10] Isaiah 53.7.
[11] Luke 23.28.

He died for the Church and his peoples liberties.	Christ gave himself for the Church, he died for the people: so our Soveraign in another sense, gave himself for the Church, and died for his people; for he might have saved his life, if he would have consented to destroy the Church, and inslave his people: so that (as he said on the Scaffold) he was the
The Martyr of the people.	Martyr of the people, Martyred by them, and for them. When our Saviour suffered, there were terrible signs and wonders, and darknesse over all the
Signs and Wonders.	Land: so during the time of our Soveraigns Martyrdom, there were strange signs seen in the sky, in divers places of the Kingdom; and it was thought very prodigious, that when he suffered, the Ducks forsook their Pond at Saint *Jameses*; and came as far as *Whitehall*, fluttering about the Scaffold: so that he might have said unto his bloudy Murder-
Job 12.7.	ers, *Ask the Beasts, and they will tell thee; and the Fowls of Heaven, and they will instruct thee*, what an unnaturall murther ye are now committing.
Collonel Tomlinson.	When our Saviour suffered, the Centurion, beholding his passion, was convinced that he was the Son of God, and feared greatly: so one of the centurions who guarded our Soveraign, beholding his most Christian, Pious and Magnanimous carriage, was convinced, and is to this day stricken with great fear, horror and astonishment.

Thus from the Throne to the Block, have his cruel, traiterous and bloud-thirsty Enemies brought the most Virtuous, Religious and Pious Prince in the Christian World.

Anonymous, *The Life and Death of King Charles the Martyr, Parallel'd with our Saviour in all his Sufferings* (1649), p. 6

Poetry

The Welsh royalists Katherine Philips and Henry Vaughan were among the earliest to compose poems on King Charles the Martyr. Beginning in the eighteenth century, poetry about the royal saint was a standard feature of poetic cycles on the liturgical year. The king remained a popular subject of poetic reflection into the nineteenth century.

In Answer to a Libellous Copy of Rimes made by Vavasor Powell.

I Think not on the State, nor am concern'd
Which way soever the great helm is turn'd:
But as that son whose father's dangers nigh
Did force his native dumbness, and untie
The fettered organs; so here's a faire cause
That will excuse the breach of Nature's laws.
Silence were now a sin, nay Passion now
Wise men themselves for Merit would allow.
What noble eye could see (and careless pass)
The dying Lion kick'd by every Ass?
Has *Charles* so broke God's Laws, he must not have
A quiet Crown nor yet a quiet Grave?
Tombs have been Sanctuaries; Thieves lie there
Secure from all their penalty and fear.
Great *Charles* his double misery was this,
Unfaithful Friends, ignoble Enemies.
Had any Heathen been this Prince's foe,
He would have wept to see him injur'd so.
His Title was his Crime, they'd reason good
To quarrel at the Right they had withstood.
He broke God's Laws, and therefore he must die;
And what shall then become of thee and I?
Slander must follow Treason; but yet stay,
Take not our Reason with our King away.
Though you have seiz'd upon all our defence,
Yet do not sequester our common Sense.
But I admire not at this new supply:
No bounds will hold those who at Sceptres fly.
Christ will be King, but I ne're understood
His Subjects built his Kingdom up with bloud,
Except their own; or that he would dispence,
With his commands, though for his own defence.
Oh! to what height of horrour are they come,
Who dare pull down a Crown, tear up a Tomb!

Katherine Philips, 'Upon the Double Murther of K. CHARLES I', *Poems* (1664), pp. 1–3

A King and no King! Is he gone from us,
And stoln alive into his Coffin thus?

This was to ravish Death, and so prevent
The Rebells treason and their punishment.
He would not have them damn'd, and therefore he
Himself deposed his own Majesty.
Wolves did pursue him, and to fly the Ill
He wanders (Royal Saint!) in sheep-skin still.
Poor, obscure shelter! if that shelter be
Obscure, which harbours so much Majesty.
Hence prophane eyes! The mysterie's so deep,
Like *Esdras* books, the vulgar must not see't.[12]

   Thou flying Roll, written with tears and woe,
Not for thy Royal self, but for thy Foe:
Thy grief is prophecy, and doth portend.
Like sad *Ezekiel*'s sighs, the Rebells end.
Thy robes forc'd off, like *Samuel*'s when rent,
Do figure out anothers Punishment.
Nor grieve thou hast put off thy self a while,
To serve as Prophet to this sinful Isle;
These are our days of *Purim*, which oppress
The Church, and force thee to the Wilderness.
But all these Clouds cannot thy light confine,
The Sun in storms and after them, will shine.
Thy day of life cannot be yet compleat,
'Tis early sure; thy shadow is so great.

   But I am vex'd, that we at all can guess
This change, and trust great *Charles* to such a dress.
When he was first obscur'd with this coarse thing,
He grac'd *Plebeians*, but prophan'd the King.
Like some fair Church, which Zeal to Charcoals burn'd,
Or his own Court now to an Ale-house turn'd.

   But full as well may we blame Night, and chide
His wisdom, who doth light with darkness hide:
Or deny Curtains to thy Royal Bed,
As take this sacred cov'ring from thy Head.
Secrets of State are points we must not know;
This vizard is thy privy Councel now.

   Thou Royal Riddle, and in every thing
The true white Prince, our Hieroglyphic King!
Ride safely in his shade, who gives thee Light:

---

12 2 Esdras 14.37–48.

And can with blindness thy pursuers smite.
O may they wonder all from thee as farr
As they from peace are, and thy self from Warr!
And wheresoe're thou dost design to be
With thy (now spotted) spottles Majestie,
Be sure to look no Sanctuary there,
Nor hope for safety in a temple, where
Buyers and Sellers trade: O strengthen not
With too much trust the Treason of a Scot!

    Henry Vaughan, 'The King Disguis'd', *Thalia Rediviva* (1678), pp. 1–3

5

Interregnum

The British Church

In 1633, George Herbert published his classic poem 'The British Church'. In 1650, Henry Vaughan published a response which bore the same title. The stark contrast reveals the radically different outlooks among Anglicans pre- and post-Civil War.

I Joy, deare Mother, when I view
Thy perfect lineaments, and hue
   Both sweet and bright.

Beautie in thee takes up her place,
And dates her letters from thy face,
   When she doth write.

A fine aspect in fit aray,
Neither too mean, nor yet too gay,
   Shows who is best.

Outlandish looks may not compare:
For all they either painted are,
   Or else undrest.

She on the hills, which wantonly
Allureth all in hope to be
   By her preferr'd,

Hath kiss'd so long her painted shrines,
That ev'n her face by kissing shines,
   For her reward.

She in the valley is so shie
Of dressing, that her hair doth lie
   About her eares:

While she avoids her neighbour's pride,
She wholly goes on th' other side,
   And nothing wears.

But dearest Mother, (what those misse)
The mean thy praise and glorie is,
   And long may be.

Blessed be God, whose love it was
To double-moat thee with his grace,
   And none but thee.

        George Herbert, 'The British Church', *The Temple* (1633), p. 102

A<small>H</small>! he is fled!
And while these here their *mists*, and *shadowes* hatch,
  My glorious head
Doth on those hills of Myrrh, and Incense watch.
    Hast, hast[1] my deare,
    The Souldiers here
    Cast in their lotts againe,
    That seamless coat
    The Iewes[2] touch'd not,
    These dare divide, and staine.

        2.

   O get thee wings!
Or if as yet (until these clouds depart,
   And the day springs,)
Thou think'st it good to tarry where thou art,
    Write in thy books
    My ravish'd looks,

---

1 Haste.
2 Jews.

Slain flock, and pillag'd fleeces,
And haste thee so
As a young Roe
Upon the mounts of spices.

O rosa campi! O lilium convallium! quomodo nunc facta es pabulum aprorum![3]

Henry Vaughan, 'The British Church', Silex Scintillans (1650), p. 22

Christmas controversies

A major point of controversy between Anglicans and Dissenters before and after the Civil War concerned the celebration of Christmas. Anglicans regarded its celebration as a mark of Christian orthodoxy. Refusing Christmas amounted to refusing Christ, because it refused recognizing the event of Incarnation.

ALL after pleasures as I rid one day,
My horse and I, both tir'd, bodie and minde,
With full crie of affections, quite astray;
I took up in the next inne I could finde.

There when I came, whom found I but my deare,
My dearest Lord, expecting till the grief
Of pleasures brought me to him, readie there
To be all passengers most sweet relief?

O Thou, whose glorious, yet contracted light,
Wrapt in nights mantle, stole into a manger;
Since my dark soul and brutish is thy right,
To Man of all beasts be not thou a stranger.

Furnish and deck my soul, that thou mayst have
A better lodging then a rack or grave.

---

3 O rose of the plain! O lily of the valleys! You have now been made as the food of wild boars!

THE shepherds sing; and shall I silent be?
  My God, no hymne for thee?
My soul's a shepherd too; a flock it feeds
  Of thoughts, and words, and deeds.
The pasture is thy word; the streams, thy grace
  Enriching all the place.
Shepherd and flock shall sing, and all my powers
  Out-sing the day-light houres.
Then we will chide the sunne for letting night
  Take up his place and right:
We sing one common Lord; wherefore he should
  Himself the candle hold.
I will go searching, till I find a sunne
  Shall stay till we have done;
A willing shiner, that shall shine as gladly,
  As frost-nipt sunnes look sadly.
Then we will sing, and shine all our own day,
  And one another pay:
His beams shall cheer my breast, and both so twine,
Till ev'n his beams sing, and my musick shine.

  George Herbert, 'Christmas', *The Temple* (1633), pp. 72–3

UNFOLD thy face, unmaske thy ray,
  Shine forth, bright Sunne, double the day:
Let no malignant misty fume,
Nor foggy vapour once presume
To interpose thy perfect sight
This day, which makes us love thy light
For ever better that we could
That blessed object once behold,
Which is both the circumference
And center of all excellence:
Or rather neither, but a treasure
Unconfined without measure:
Whose center and circumference
Including all preheminence,
Excluding nothing but defect,

And infinite in each respect;
Is equally both here and there,
And now and then, and every where;
And alwaies one himselfe the same,
A beeing farre above a name.
Draw neer then, and freely poure
Forth all thy light into that houre
Which was crowned with his birth,
And made heaven envy earth.
Let not his birth-day clouded be,
By whom thou shinest, and we see.

    Christopher Harvey, 'The Nativitie', *The Synagogue* (1640), pp. 10–11

AWAKE, glad heart! get up, and Sing,
It is the Birth-day of thy King,
  Awake! awake!
  The Sun doth shake
Light from his locks, and all the way
Breathing Perfumes, doth spice the day.

2.

Awak, awak![4] heark, how th' *wood* rings,
Winds whisper, and the busie *springs*
  A Consort make;
  Awake, awake!
Man is their high-priest, and should rise
To offer up the sacrifice.

3.

I would I were some *Bird*, or Star,
Flutt'ring in woods, or lifted far
  Above this *Inne*
  And Rode of sin!
Then either Star, or *Bird*, should be
Shining, or singing still to thee.

---

4 Awake.

4.

I would I had in my best part
Fit Roomes for thee! or that my heart
   Were so clean as
   Thy manger was!
But I am all filth, and obscene,
Yet, if thou wilt, thou canst make me clean.

5.

Sweet *Jesu*! will then; Let no more
This Leper haunt, and soyl thy door,
   Cure him, Ease him
   O release him!
And let once more by mystick birth
The Lord of life be borne in Earth.

II

How kind is heav'n to man! If here
One sinner doth amend
Strait there is Joy, and ev'ry sphere
   In musick doth Contend;
And shall we then no voices lift?
   Are mercy, and salvation
Not worth our thanks? Is life a gift
   Of no more acceptation?
Shal he that did come down from thence,
   And here for us was slain,
Shal he be now cast off? no sense
   Of all his woes remain?
Can neither Love, nor suff'rings bind?
   Are we all stone, and Earth?
Neither his bloudy passions mind,
   Nor one day blesse his birth?
   Alas, my God! Thy birth now here
   Must not be numbred in the year.

Henry Vaughan, 'CHRISTS Nativity',
Silex Scintillans (1650), pp. 61–2

Reader, the Title of this Solemn Day,
And what it doth import, doth bid thee stay,
And read, and wonder. 'Tis that Mystery
That Angels gaze upon; Divinity
Assuming Humane Flesh; Th' Eternal Son
Of the Eternal God, is Man become.
But why this strange Assumption? or what end
Equivalent, could make him so descend
So far beneath himself, and equalize
the Miracle of such an enterprise?
Yet stay and wonder: Undeserved Love
To Man, to sinful man, did only move
This stoop from Heaven to Earth, and all to win
And rescue lost and fallen Man from Sin
And Guilt, and Death, and Hell, and re-install
Him in that Happiness lost by his Fall,
And greater, Everlastingly to dwell
In Blessedness: So that thou canst not tell
Which of the two the greater Wonder proves,
Thy Saviour's Incarnation, or his Love.
But both conclude thou dost not give, but pay
A Debt, in the Observance of this Day.

Matthew Hale, Ninth Poem upon Christmas-Day,
Contemplations Moral and Divine (1677), pp. 517–18[5]

Liturgy and episcopacy

Anthony Sparrow first published his Rationale *in 1655. It quickly became the most popular commentary on the Prayer Book in the seventeenth century. Like many works dating from the Interregnum, it was published anonymously; only with the second, expanded edition of 1657 did Sparrow identify himself as the author. The Preface was unchanged in later editions.*

The Preface.

The present Age pretends so great Love to *Reason*, that, this RATIONALE may even for its *Name*, hope for acceptance, which it will the sooner

---

5 [Without date.]

have, if the Reader know, that the Author vents it not for a full and just, much less a publick and authentick Piece, but as his own private Essay (wholy submitted to the censure of our Holy Mother *The Church*, and the Reverend Fathers of the same, and) composed on purpose to keep some from moving that way, which, it is feared, some will say, it leads to. The Authors designe was not, by *Rhetorick* first to Court the *Affections*, and then by their help, to carry the *understanding*. But quite contrary, by *Reason* to work upon the *Judgement*, and leave *that* to deal with the *affections*.

The Poor *Liturgie* sufrers from two extremes, one sort sayes, *it is old superstitious Roman Dotage*. The other, *it is Schismatically New*. This Book endeavours to shew particularly, what Bishop JEWEL (Apol. p. 177)[6] says in general. 1 *That it is agreeable to Primitive usage*, and so, not *Novel*. 2 THAT IT IS A REASONABLE SERVICE, and so, not *superstitious*. As for those that love it, and suffer for the love of it, this will shew them *Reasons*, why they should suffer on, and love it still more and more. To end, if the Reader will cast his Eye upon the sad Confusions in point of prayer, (wherein are such contradictions made, as God Almighty cannot grant) and lay them as *Rubbish* under these *Fundamental Considerations*; First, How many *Set Forms* (of Petition, Blessing, and Praise) be recorded in the Old and New Testament, used both in *the Church Militant and Triumphant*; 2 How much of the Leiturgie is *very Scripture*; 3 How Admirable a Thing *Unity Unity* in Time, Form, &c. is; 4 How many millions of poor souls are in the world; ignorant, infirm by nature, age, accidents, (as blindness, deafness, loss of speech, &c.) which respectively may receive help by *Set Forms*, but cannot so well (or not at all) by extemporary voluntary effusions, and then upon all these will build what he reads in this Book; he will, if not be convinced to joyn in Communion with, yet perhaps be so sweetned, as more readily to pardon those, who still abiding in their former Judgements, and being more confirmed hereby, do use THE ANTIENT FORM.

Anthony Sparrow, *A Rationale upon the Book of Common-Prayer of the Church of England* (1655), no pag.

In the third edition of the Synagogue *(1657), Harvey added several poems defending Holy Orders and a fairly polemical commendatory verse by Izaak Walton.*

---

6 John Jewel, *An Apology of the Church of England* (1564), Book VI.

THE Bishop? Yes: why not? What doth that name
        Import that is unlawful, or unfit?
To say the Overseer is the same
In substance, and no hurt, I hope, in it:
    But sure if men did not despise the thing,
    Such scorn upon the name they would not fling.

Some Priests, some Presbyters, I mean, would be
Each Overseer in his sev'rall cure,
But one superiour, to oversee
Them all together, they will not endure:
    This the maine diff'rence is, that I can see,
    Bishops they would not have, but they would be.

But who can shew of old that ever any
Prebyteries without their Bishops were;
Though Bishops without Presbyteries many,
At first must needs be, almost every where?
    That Presbyters from Bishops first arose,
    T' assist them, 's probable, not these from those:

However, a true Bishop I esteem
The highest officer the Church on earth
Can have, as proper to it self, and deem
A Church without one an imperfect birth,
    If constituted so at first, and maimed,
    If whom it had, it afterward disclaimed.

All order first from unitie ariseth,
And th' essence of it is subordination.
Who ever this contemnes, and that despiseth,
May talk of, but intends not, reformation.
    'Tis not of God, of nature, or of art,
    T' ascribe to all what's proper to one part,

To rule and to be ruled are distinct
And sev'rall duties, sev'rally belong
To sev'ral persons can no more be link't
In all together, than amidst the throng
    Of rude unruly passions, in the heart,
    Reason can see to act her soveraigne part.

But a good Bishop, as a tender father,
Doth teach and rule the Church, and is obey'd.
And rev'renc'd by it, so much the rather,
By how much he delighteth more to lead
   All by his own example in the way,
   Then punish any, when they go astray.

Lord, thou the Bishop, and chief Shepherd, art
Of all that flock, which thou hast purchased
With thine own blood: to them thou do'st impart
The benefits, which thou hast merited,
   Teaching, and ruling, by thy blessed spirit,
   Their souls in grace, til glory they inherit.

The stars which thou dost hold in thy right hand,
The Angels of the Churches, Lord, direct
Clearly thy holy will to understand,
And do accordingly: Let no defect,
   Nor fault, no not in our New Prelaticks,
   Provoke thee to remove our candle-sticks.

But let thy Urim and thy Thummim be
Garments of praise t' adorne thine holy ones:
Light and perfection let all men see
Brightly shine forth in those rich precious stones,
   Of whom thou wilt make a foundation,
   To raise thy new Hierusalem[7] upon.

And, at the brightnesse of its rising, let
All nations with thy people shout for joy:
Salvation for wals and bulwarks set
About it, that nothing may it annoy.
   Then the whole world thy diocesse shall be,
   And Bishops all but Suffragans to Thee.

Christopher Harvey, 'The Bishop',
The Synagogue (1657), pp. 31–3

---

7 Jerusalem.

SIR.

I Lov'd you for your *Synagogue*, before
I knew your person; but now love you more,
  Because I finde
It is so true a picture of your minde:
    Which tunes your sacred lyre
    To that eternal quire;
    Where holy *Herbert* sits
    (O shame to prophane wits)
And sings his and your Anthems, to the praise
Of him that is the first and last of dayes.

These holy Hymns had an Etherial birth:
For they can raise sad souls above the earth
  And fix them there
Free from the worlds anxieties and feare.
    Herbert and you have pow'r
    To do this: ev'ry hour
    I read you kills a sin,
    Or lets a virtue in
To fight against it: and the Holy Ghost
Supports my frailties, lest the day be lost.

This holy war, taught by your happy pen,
The Prince of Peace approves. When we poor men
  Neglect our armes;
W'are circumvested with a world of harms.
    But I will watch, and ward,
    And stand upon my guard,
    And still consult with you,
    And *Herbert*, and renew
My vows, and say, Well fare his, and your heart,
The Fountains of such Sacred Wit and Art.
                      Iz. Wa.

Izaak Walton, 'To My Reverend friend the Author of the *Synagogue*', Commendatory Verse in Christopher Harvey, *The Synagogue* (1657), p. 67

Oppression

Evelyn's Diary, *which was not published until the nineteenth century, contains historical information about topics ranging from the exiled Caroline court to the founding of the Royal Society. The excerpts below are a small selection of entries dating from the Interregnum.*

[*January*, n.d., 1648/9]. The villainy of the rebels proceeding now so far as to try, condemn, and murder our excellent King on the 30th of this month, struck me with such horror, that I kept the day of his martyrdom a fast, and would not be present at that execrable wickedness; receiving the sad account of it from my brother George, and Mr. Owen, who came to visit me this afternoon, and recounted all the circumstances.

3rd December [1654]. Advent Sunday. There being no Office at the church but extemporary prayers after the Presbyterian way, for now all forms were prohibited, and most of the preachers were usurpers, I seldom went to church upon solemn feasts; but, either went to London, where some of the orthodox sequestered Divines did privately use the Common Prayer, administered sacraments, &c., or else I procured one to officiate in my house; wherefore, on the 10th, Dr. Richard Owen, the sequestered minister of Eltham, preached to my family in my library, and gave us the holy Communion.

25th December. Christmas-day. No public offices in churches, but penalties on observers, so as I was constrained to celebrate it at home.

9th [*March*, 1655]. I went to see the great ship newly built by the Usurper, Oliver, carrying ninety-six brass-guns, and 1000 tons burthen. In the prow was Oliver on horseback, trampling six nations under foot, a Scot, Irishman, Dutchman, Frenchman, Spaniard, and English, as was easily made out by their several habits. A Fame held a laurel over his insulting head; the word, *God with us.*

25th [*December*, 1657]. I went to London with my wife, to celebrate Christmas-day, Mr. Gunning preaching in Exeter chapel, on Micah vii. 2. Sermon ended, as he was giving us the Holy Sacrament, the chapel was surrounded with soldiers, and all the communicants and assembly surprised and kept prisoners by them, some in the house, others carried away. It fell to my share to be confined to a room in the house, where yet I was permitted to dine with the master of it, the Countess of Dorset, Lady Hatton, and some others of quality who invited me. In the afternoon, came Colonel Whalley, Goffe, and others, from Whitehall, to examine us one by one; some they committed to the Marshal, some to prison. When I came before them, they took my name and abode, examined me why, contrary to the ordinance made, that none should any longer observe the superstitious time of the Nativity (so esteemed by them), I durst offend, and particularly be at Common Prayers, which they told me was but the mass in English, and particularly pray for Charles Stuart; for which we had no Scripture. I told them we did not pray for Charles Stuart, but for all Christian Kings, Princes, and Governors. They replied, in so doing we prayed for the King of Spain, too, who was their enemy and a Papist, with other frivolous and ensnaring questions, and much threatening; and, finding no colour to detain me, they dismissed me with much pity of my ignorance. These were men of high flight and above ordinances, and spake spiteful things of our Lord's Nativity. As we went up to receive the Sacrament, the miscreants held their muskets against us, as if they would have shot us at the altar; but yet suffering us to finish the office of Communion, as perhaps not having instructions what to do, in case they found us in that action. So I got home late the next day; blessed by God!

22nd [*October*, 1658]. Saw the superb funeral of the Protector. He was carried from Somerset-House in a velvet bed of state, drawn by six horses, housed with the same; the pall held by his new Lords; Oliver lying in effigy, in royal robes, and crowned with a crown, sceptre, and globe, like a king. The pendants and guidons were carried by the officers of the army; the Imperial banners, achievements, &c. by the heralds in their coats; a rich caparisoned horse, embroidered all over with gold; a knight of honour, armed cap-a-pié,[8] and, after all, his guards, soldiers, and innumerable mourners. In this equipage, they proceeded to Westminster: but it was the joyfullest funeral I ever saw; for there were none that cried but dogs, which the soldiers hooted away with a barbarous noise, drinking and taking tobacco in the streets as they went.

25th [*April*, 1659]. A wonderful and sudden change in the face of the public; the new Protector, Richard, slighted; several pretenders and parties strive for the government: all anarchy and confusion; Lord have mercy on us!

---

8 Head to foot.

29th [May]. The nation was now in extreme confusion and unsettled, between the Armies and the Sectaries, the poor Church of England breathing as it were her last; so sad a face of things had overspread us.

11th [October]. The Army now turned out the Parliament. We had now no government in the nation; all in confusion; no magistrate either owned or pretended, but the soldiers, and they not agreed. God Almighty have mercy on, and settle us!

21st. A private fast was kept by the Church of England Protestants in town, to beg of God the removal of His judgments, with devout prayers for His mercy to our calamitous Church.

William Bray (ed.), *Diary and Correspondence of John Evelyn, F.R.S.* (1859), vol. 1, pp. 256, 321–2, 323, 347, 348, 349, 350, 351

6

Restoration

The Return of the King

The Restoration began with Charles II promising forgiveness to almost all who were involved in the rebellion and part of the Cromwellian regime. The excitement and joy expressed in Evelyn's diary entries reflect the general tenor of the British kingdoms after the king's arrival in May 1660.

KING CHARLES II. HIS DECLARATION
TO ALL HIS LOVING SUBJECTS OF THE
KINGDOM OF ENGLAND.

DATED FROM HIS COURT AT BREDA IN HOLLAND,
THE 4/14 OF APRIL 1660.

CHARLES by the grace of GOD King of *England*, *Scotland*, *France* and *Ireland*, Defender of the Faith, To all our loving Subjects of what degree or quality soever, greeting. If the general distraction and confusion which is spread over the whole Kingdom, doth not awaken all men to a desire and longing that these wounds which have so many years together been kept bleeding, may be bound up, all we can say will be to no purpose; However, after this long silence, we have thought it our duty, to declare how much we desire to contribute thereunto: And that as we can never give over hope in good time to obtain the Possession of that Right which GOD and Nature hath made our due, So we do make it our daily suit to the Divine Providence, that He will in Compassion to Us and our Subjects (after so long misery and sufferings) remit us and put us into a quiet and peaceable Possession of that Our Right, with as little blood and damage to Our people, as is possible; Nor do we desire more to enjoy what is Ours, than that all our Subjects may enjoy what by Law is theirs, by a full and entire Administration of Justice throughout the Land, and by extending our mercy where it is wanting and deserved.

And to the end That the fear of punishment may not engage any conscious to themselves of what is past, to a perseverance in Guilt for the future, by opposing the quiet and happinesse of their Country, in the restoration both of King, Peers and People, to their just ancient and fundamental Rights: We do by these presents Declare, That we do grant a full and generall Pardon, which we are ready to pass under our great Seal of *England*, to all our Subjects of what degree or quality soever, who within fourty dayes after the publication hereof shall lay hold upon this our grace and favour, and shall by any publick Act declare their doing so; And that they return to the Loyalty and Obedience of good Subjects, excepting only such Persons as shall hereafter be excepted by *Parliament*, Those only excepted. Let our Subjects how faulty soever, relye upon the word of a King, solemnly given by this present *Declaration*, That no Crime whatsoever committed against us or our Royal Father before the publication of this, shall ever rise in judgment, or be brought in question against any of them, to the least indamagment, either in their Lives, Liberties or Estates, or (as far forth lies in our power) so much as to the prejudice of their Reputation, by any reproach or term of distinction from the rest of our best Subjects. We desiring and ordaining, that hence forward all Notes of discord, separation and difference of Parties, be utterly abolished among all our Subjects, whom we invite and conjure to a perfect Union among themselves under our Protection, for the resettlement of our just Rights and theirs in a *free Parliament*; By which upon the word of a King we will be advised.

And because the passion and un-charitablnesse of the times have produced several opinions in Religion, by which men are engaged in parties and animosities against each other, which when they shall hereafter unite in a freedom of conversation will be composed or better understood: We do declare a Liberty to Tender Consciences, and that no man shall be disquieted or called in question for differences of opinion in matters of Religion, which do not disturb the Peace of the Kingdom; And that we shall be ready to consent to such an Act of Parliament, as upon mature Deliberation shall be offered to us for the full granting that indulgence: And because in the continued distractions of so many years, and so many great Revolutions, many Grants and Purchases of Estates have been made to and by many Officers and Soldiers, and others, who are now possessed of the same, and who may be liable to Actions at Law upon several Titles, We are likewise willing that all such differences, & all things relating to such Grants, Sales and Purchases, shall be determined in Parliament, which can best provide for the just satisfaction of all men who are concerned.

And we do further declare, That we will be ready to consent to any Act or Acts of Parliament to the purposes aforesaid, and for the full satisfaction of all Arrears due to the Officers and Souldiers of the Army, under the Command of General MONCK: And that they shall be received into our Service upon as good pay and conditions as they now enjoy. Given under our sign *Manuel* and privy signet at our Court at *Breda* this fourteenth day of *April*, 1660. In the twelveth year of our Reign.

Charles II, The Declaration of Breda (1660)

29th [May, 1660]. This day, his Majesty, Charles the Second came to London, after a sad and long exile and calamitous suffering both of the King and Church, being seventeen years. This was also his birth-day, and with a triumph of above 20,000 horse and foot, brandishing their swords, and shouting with inexpressible joy; the ways strewed with flowers, the bells ringing, the streets hung with tapestry, fountains running with wine; the Mayor, Aldermen, and all the Companies, in their liveries, chains of gold, and banners; Lords and Nobles, clad in cloth of silver, gold, and velvet; the windows and balconies, all set with ladies; trumpets, music, and myriads of people flocking, even so far as from Rochester, so as they were seven hours in passing the city, even from two in the afternoon till nine at night.

6th [*July*]. His Majesty began first to *touch for the evil!* according to custom, thus: his Majesty sitting under his state in the Banqueting-house, the chirurgeons cause the sick to be brought, or led, up to the throne, where they kneeling, the king strokes their faces, or cheeks with both his hands at once, at which instant a chaplain in his formalities says, "He put his hands upon them, and he healed them." This is said to every one in particular. When they have been all touched, they come up again in the same order, and the other chaplain kneeling, and having angel gold strung on white ribbon on his arm, delivers them one by one to his Majesty, who puts them about the necks of the touched as they pass, whilst the first chaplain repeats, "That is the true light who came into the world." Then follows, an epistle (as at first a Gospel) with the Liturgy, prayers for the sick, with some alteration; lastly the blessing; and then the Lord Chamberlain and the Comptroller of the Household bring a basin, ewer and towel, for his Majesty to wash.

William Bray (ed.), *Diary and Correspondence of John Evelyn, F.R.S.* (1859), Vol. 1, pp. 355, 357

Mitre and crown

Sudbury's sermon was occasioned by the first consecration of bishops in England in almost 20 years; the royal coronation took place two years later. The Act of Uniformity envisioned a truly restored and peaceful England, and is well complemented by the ideal of the Royal Touch: the king healing the sick.

1 TIM. 3.1.

This is a true saying, If a man desire the Office of a Bishop, he desireth a good work.

There needs no other *Preface* or Introduction to commend *this* saying to our attention, then this which the Apostle hath set before it, *This is a true saying*. For seeing there is not *any* saying in *this* book which is not as true as *this*, we may be *sure* there is some difference between the truth of *this* and *other* sayings, which made the Apostle *so particularly* commend it to us. And though it be not easie to determine positively *what it is*, it is not hard to say *what it might be*.

For first, it is easie to perceive what great need there was to arm and fence it well against the contradiction of such as would oppose and *gainsay* it. For there is not *any* saying in *this* book which hath met with *more* and *greater* opposition and contradiction. The Office of a Bishop hath been the *mark* at which not onely the *profess'd Enemies* of the Church have bent *their* bows and shot *their* arrows; but likewise *they* who have the greatest contention with each other, which of them should be the better, if not the only Christian Church; they on the one side contending for one Bishop over the whole Church, and making all the rest but his Ministers; the other would have as many Bishops as there are Ministers, which is in effect to have none.

But secondly, the truth of this saying is likewise a matter of *great* importance, worthy of more then ordinary *regard*, which might move the Apostle to commend it to a *more then ordinary* attention. For there is not a word in it which will not require and deserve a distinct and particular consideration. First, here is the Office of a Bishop; secondly, the Work belonging to that Office; thirdly, the Goodness of that Work; fourthly, the Desire of that Office, and of the good Work: the one set down by way of supposition, *If a man desire the Office of a Bishop*; the other by way of inference or conclusion thereupon, *he desireth a good work.*

...

There is therefore a *necessity* of *this* Office, with *this* Power and Authority, to preserve *Truth* and *Peace* and *Unity*, and to prevent the *manifold* and *great* mischiefs which Parity, the Mother of *Anarchy* and *Confusion*, would soon produce: which must needs be greater in the *Church*, then in the *State*. For there is *nothing* that so *effectually* rules the Multitude as *Religion*, the *name* whereof is *so* venerable, that they are more apt to follow their *Preachers* then their *Princes*; because they look upon them as the Ministers of God, whose *Office* it is to teach them *his word* and will; and are afraid to think amisse of any thing which they hear from *them*, lest in so doing they should set themselves against *God*: whereby it comes to passe that there is scarce any *Errour* so *grosse* which some of them will not *believe*, or any *Wickedness* so *great* which some of them will not *practice*, and think thereby to do God service, if it be preach'd to them as a matter and duty of *Religion*. And how much this may tend to the disturbance of the publick Peace and Government, is easie to be seen. For remedy whereof, if the sovereign *Prince* interpose his power only, he runs the hazard of being reputed an *enemy* of *God* and of *Religion*, then which nothing can be more prejudicial to him not only in point of *reputation*, but of *safety* likewise.

There is no better Remedy against all *this* mischief, then that *wise* and *good*, *grave* and *learned* men, such as are *able by sound Doctrine both to exhort and to convince the gain-sayers*,[1] should be set up over the rest, with *Power* and *Authority* to *charge them that they teach no other Doctrine*, as St. *Paul* writes to *Timothy*, whom he left at *Ephesus* to this end, 1 Tim. 1.3. *and to stop the mouths of such unruly and vain talkers, who subvert whole houses, teaching things which they ought not*, as the same Apostle writes to *Titus*, whom he left at *Creet* to do this Office, *Tit.* 1.10, 11.

This is too great an Office for *one* man to exercise over the *whole* Church: as therefore Christ chose not one onely, but twelve Apostles, to whom he committed *this Office* and trust: so his Apostles, *whom he sent as his Father sent him*,[2] *i.e.* with a power to send others after them with the like power, ordained, not one Bishop onely in the City of

---

1 [Tit. 1.9.]
2 [John 20.21.]

Rome, but one in every City. But as it is too great a power and trust to be committed to *one* man over the *whole* Church, so likewise it was not for the good of unity and order that it should be committed unto every one that was fit to bear some Office in the Church. As therefore Christ, who had so many Disciples, that *the Pharisees had heard that he made more Disciples than* John,³ did not make them all Apostles; and though he gave diversity of Gifts and Graces to diverse men, yet among all these he chose but twelve Apostles: so the Apostles after him ordained Elders or Bishops, not in *every Village*, but onely in *every City*; making the Government of the Church herein conformable to that of the State, where the Prefect or Governour of a Province or Country had his residence in the *City*, but his Jurisdiction in the *Country* round about. And this *conformity* in the Government of the Church to that of the State was so much the better, because *that kind* of Government in the *State* was *best* for the State, and the like Government in the *Church* was *best* for the Church.

John Sudbury, A Sermon Preached at the Consecration of the Right Reverend Fathers in God (1660), pp. 1–2, 5–7

A BRIEF
NARRATIVE
OF
HIS MAJESTIE'S SOLEMN CORONATION.

Upon the 23rd of *April*, being Saint *George*'s Day, about seven in the Morning, the *King* took Water from the *Privy-Stairs* at *White-Hall*, and landed at the *Parliament-Stairs*: from whence He went up to the Room behind the *Lords-House*, called the *Prince*'s *Lodgings*: where, after He had reposed Himself for a while, He was arayed in Royal Robes of Crimson Velvet, furr'd with Ermine: By which time the *Nobility*, being come together in the *Lords-House*, and *Painted-Chamber*, Robed themselves.

The *Judges* also, with those of the *Long-Robe*, the *Knights* of the *Bath* (then in their Robes of Purple Satin, lined with white Taffaty) and *Gentlemen* of the *Privy-Chamber*, met in the Court of *Requests*. And, after some space, being drawn down into *Westminster-Hall*, where this great Solemnity (ordered by the Officers at Arms) began; the *Nobility*, in their proper Robes, carrying their Coronets in their Hands, proceeded according to their several Dignities, and Degrees, before His

---

3 [John 4.1.]

Majesty, up to His Throne of State; which was raised at the *West* end of that large and noble Room, and there placed themselves upon each side thereof.

The *King* being thus set in a rich Chair, under a glorious Cloth of State, Sir *Gilbert Talbot* K^t,[4] *Master* of the *Jewel-House*, presented the *Sword of State*, as also the *Sword* called *Curtana*, and two other *Swords*, to the *Lord High-Constable*; who took and delivered them to the *Lord High-Chamberlain*, and he laid them upon the Table before the *King*.

Then did he also deliver the *Spurs* to the *Lord High-Constable*; and he the same to the *Lord High-Chamberlain*, who also placed them upon the Table.

Immediately after the *Dean* and *Prebends* of *Westminster*, (by whom the *Regalia* had been brought in Procession from the *Abbey-Church* unto *Westminster-Hall*) being vested in rich Copes, came up from the lower end thereof, in the manner following:

1 The *Searjeant* of the *Vestry*, in a Scarlet Mantle.
2 Then the *Children* of the *King*'s *Chapel*, in Scarlet Mantles.
3 Then the *Quire* of *Westminster*, in Surplices.
4 Then the *Gentlemen* of the *King*'s *Chapel*, in Scarlet Mantles.
5 Next the *Pursuivants*, *Heralds*, and *Provincial* Kings of Arms.
6 Then the *Dean*, carrying Saint *Edward*'s *Crown*.

And after him five of the *Prebends* of the Church; the first carrying the *Sceptre* with the *Cross*.

The second the *Sceptre* with the *Dove*.
The third the *Orb* with the *Cross*.
The fourth King *Edward*'s *Staff*.
The fifth the *Chalice* and *Patena*.

Passing thus through the *Hall*, and making their due Reverences in three places thereof; the *Quires*, with the Officers at Arms falling off on each side, towards the upper end of the Room; the said *Dean* and *Prebends* ascended the Steps; at the top whereof *Garter, Principal King of Arms* standing, conducted them to the *Table* placed before the *Throne*, where they made their last Reverence.

Which being done, the *Dean* first presented the *Crown*, which was by the *Lord High-Constable*, and *Lord Great-Chamberlain*, set upon

---

4 Knight.

the Table; who likewise afterwards received from each of the *Prebends* that part of the *Regalia*, which they carried, and laid them also by the *Crown*: which done, they retired.

Then, the *Lord Great-Chamberlain* presenting the *Regalia* severally to the *King*, His *Majesty* thereupon disposed of them unto the *Noblemen* hereafter named, to be carried by them in the *Proceeding* to the *Abbey-Church*, viz.

> Saint *Edward*'s *Staff* to the *Earl* of *Sandwich*.
> The *Spurs* to the *Earl* of *Pembroke* and *Montgomery*.
> The *Sceptre* with the *Cross* to the *Earl* of *Bedford*.
> The *Pointed Sword* (born on the left hand of *Curtana*) to the *Earl* of *Derby*.
> The *Pointed Sword* (born on the right hand thereof) to the *Earl* of *Shrewsbury*.
> The *Sword* called *Curtana* to the *Earl* of *Oxford*.
> The *Sword* of *State* to the *Earl* of *Manchester*.
> The *Sceptre* with the *Dove* to the *Duke* of *Albe-marle*.
> The *Orb* with the *Cross* to the *Duke* of *Buckingham*.
> Saint *Edward*'s *Crown* to the *Duke* of *Ormond*.
> The *Patena* to the *Bishop* of *Exeter*; and lastly,
> The *Chalice* to the *Bishop* of *London*.

All things being thus prepared, (it being about ten a Clock,) the *Proceeding* began from the *Hall* into the *Palace-Yard*, through the *Gate-House*, and the end of *King's-street*; thence along the *Great Sanctuary*, and so to the *West-end* of the *Abbey-Church*, all upon Blew Cloth, which was spread upon the Ground, from the *Throne* in *Westminster-Hall* to the great Steps in the same *Abbey-Church*, by Sir *George Carteret* Knight, His *Majestie*'s Vice-Chamberlain; as *Almoner* for that Day by special Appointment.

THE PROCEEDING TO THE CORONATION WAS IN THIS FOLLOWING ORDER.

> The *Drums* four.
> The *Trumpets* sixteen, in four *Classis*.
> The *Six Clerks* of the *Chancery*.

Ten of the KING's *Chaplains*, having Dignities.
The *Aldermen* of LONDON.
The KING's *Learned Council* at *Law*.
The KING's *Solicitour*. The KING's *Attorney*.
The KING's eldest *Serjeant* at *Law*.
The *Esquires* of the *Body*.
The *Masters* of *Request*.
The *Gentlemen* of the *Privy-Chamber*.
The *Knights* of the *Bath*, in their *Purple Robes*.
The *Barons* of the *Exchequer*, and *Justices* of both *Benches*, two and two, in order, according to their Seniority.
The *Lord Chief-Baron*. The *Lord Chief-Justice* of the *Common-Pleas*.
The *Master* of the *Rolls*. The *Lord Chief-Justice* of the *Kings-Bench*.
The *Serjeant-Porter*. The *Serjeant* of the *Vestry*.
The *Children* of the *King*'s *Chapel*.
The *Gentlemen* of the *King*'s *Chapel*.
The *Prebends* of *Westminster*.
The *Master* of the *Jewel-House*.
The *Knights* of the *Privy-Council*.
Port-cullis, Pursuivant at Arms.
The *Barons* in their Robes, two and two, carrying their Caps of Crimson Velvet, turn'd up with Miniver, in their Hands.
The *Bishops*, two and two, according to their Dignities, and Consecrations.
Rouge-Croix, *Blew Mantle*, Pursuivants.
The *Viscounts*, two and two, in their Robes, with the Coronets in their Hands.
Somerset, *Chester*, Heralds.
The *Earls*, two and two, in their Robes, holding their Coronets in their Hands.

> John Ogilby, *The Entertainment of His Most Excellent Majestie Charles II* (1662), pp. 169–72

WHEREAS in the first year of the late Queen *Elizabeth* there was one Uniform Order of Common Service and Prayer, and of the Administration of Sacraments, Rites and Ceremonies in the Church of *England* (agreeable to the Word of God, and usage of the Primitive Church) compiled by the Reverend Bishops and Clergy, set forth in one Book, Entituled, *The Book of Common Prayer, and Administration of Sacraments, and other Rites and Ceremonies in the Church of* England, and enjoyned to be used by Act of Parliament, holden in the said First year of the said late Queen, Entituled, *An Act for the Uniformity of Common Prayer, and Service in the Church, and Administration of the Sacraments*, very comfortable to all good people desirous to live in Christian conversation, and most profitable to the Estate of this Realm, upon the which the Mercy, Favour and Blessing of Almighty God is in no wise so readily and plentifully poured, as by Common Prayers, due using of the Sacraments, and often Preaching of the Gospel, with devotion of the hearers: And yet this notwithstanding, a great number of people in diverse parts of this Realm, following their own sensuality, and living without knowledge and due fear of God, do wilfully and Schismatically abstain, and refuse to come to their Parish Churches and other Publick places where Common Prayer, Administration of the Sacraments, and Preaching of the Word of God is used upon the Sundays and other days ordained & appointed to be kept and observed as Holy days: And whereas by the great and scandalous neglect of Ministers in using the said Order, or Liturgy so set forth and enjoyned as aforesaid, great mischiefs & inconveniencies, during the times of the late unhappy troubles, have arisen and grown; and many people have been led into Factions and Schisms, to the great decay and scandal of the Reformed Religion of the Church of *England*, and to the hazard of many souls: for prevention whereof in time to come, for setling the Peace of the Church, and for allaying the present distempers, which the indisposition of the time hath contracted, The Kings Majesty (according to His Declaration of the Five and twentieth of *October*, One thousand six hundred and sixty) granted His Commission under the great Seal of *England* to several Bishops and other Divines to review the Book of Common Prayer, and to prepare such Alterations and Additions, as they thought fit to offer;

. . .

And to the end that Uniformity in the Publick Worship of God (which is so much desired) may be speedily effected, Be it further Enacted by the Authority aforesaid, That every Parson, Vicar, or other Minister whatsoever, who now hath, and enjoyeth any Ecclesiastical Benefice, or Promotion, within this Realm of *England*, or places aforesaid, shall in the Church, Chappel, or place of Publick Worship belonging to his said Benefice or Promotion, upon some Lords day before the Feast of Saint *Bartholomew*, which shall be in the year of our Lord God, One thousand six hundred sixty and two, openly, publickly, and solemnly read the Morning and Evening Prayer appointed to be read by, and according to the said Book of Common Prayer at the times thereby appointed, and after such reading thereof shall openly and publickly, before the Congregation there assembled, declare his unfeigned assent, and consent to the use of all things in the said Book contained and prescribed, in these words, and no other;

I A.B. Do here declare my unfeigned assent, and consent to all, and every thing contained, and prescribed in, and by the Book intituled, *The Book of Common Prayer and Administration of the Sacraments, and other Rites, and Ceremonies of the Church, according to the use of the Church of* England; *together with the Psalter, or Psalms of David, Pointed as they are to be sung, or said in Churches, and the form, or manner of Making, Ordaining, and Consecrating of Bishops, Priests, and Deacons*;

. . .

And be it further Enacted by the Authority aforesaid, That every Dean, Canon, and Prebendary of every Cathedral, or Collegiate Church, and all Masters, and other Heads, Fellows, Chaplains, and Tutors of, or in any Colledge, Hall, House of Learning, or Hospital, and every Publick Professor, and Reader in either of the Universities, and in every Colledge elsewhere, and every Parson, Vicar, Curate, Lecturer, and every other person in holy Orders, and every School-master keeping any publick, or private School, and every person Instructing, or Teaching any Youth in any House or private Family as a Tutor, or School-master, who upon the First day of *May*, which shall be in the year of our Lord God, One thousand six hundred sixty two, or at any time thereafter shall be Incumbent, or have possession of any Deanry, Canonry, Prebend, Mastership, Headship, Fellow-ship, Professors-place, or Readers-place, Parsonage, Vicarage, or any other Ecclesiastical Dignity or Promotion, or of any Curates place, Lecture, or School; or shall instruct or teach any Youth as Tutor, or School-master, shall before the Feast-day of Saint *Bartholomew*, which shall be in the year of our Lord One thousand six hundred sixty two, or at or before his, or their respective admission to be Incumbent, or have possession aforesaid, subscribe the Declaration or Acknowledgement following, *Scilicet,*

I A.B. Do declare that it is not lawful upon any pretence whatsoever to take Arms against the King; and that I do abhor that Traiterous Position of taking Arms by His Authority against His Person, or against those that are Commissionated by him; and that I will conform to the Liturgy of the Church of *England*, as it is now by Law established. And I do declare that I do hold, there lies no Obligation upon me, or on any other person from the Oath, commonly called the *Solemn League and Covenant*, to endeavour any change, or alteration of Government, either in Church, or State; and that the same was in it self an unlawful Oath, and imposed upon the Subjects of this Realm against the known Laws and Liberties of this Kingdom.

Excerpts from The Act of Unifomity (1662)

Liturgical reform

The Preface to the 1662 Book of Common Prayer is a positive albeit polemical statement of Anglican orthodoxy. On the one hand, it affirms Scripture and royal authority. On the other hand, because the Act of Uniformity immediately preceded the Preface, 'moderation' was also understood as imitating the 'usage of the Primitive Church'. These affirmations grounded the Preface's twofold polemic against Roman Catholicism and the various forms of Dissent.

It hath been the Wisdom of the Church of England, ever since the first compiling of her Publick Liturgy, to keep the Mean between the two Extreams, of too much Stiffness in refusing, and of too much Easiness in admitting any variation from it. For, as on the one side common Experience sheweth, that where a change hath been made of things advisedly established (no evident necessity so requiring) sundry inconveniences have thereupon ensued; and those many times more, and greater than the evils, that were intended to be remedied by such change: So on the other side, the particular Forms of Divine Worship, and the Rites, and Ceremonies appointed to be used therein, being things in their own nature Indifferent, and alterable, and so acknowledged; it is but reasonable, that upon weighty and important considerations, according to the various exigency of times and occasions, such changes and alterations should be made therein, as to those that are in place of Authority should from time to time seem either necessary or expedient. Accordingly we find, that in the Reigns of several Princes of blessed memory since the Reformation, the Church upon just and weighty considerations her thereunto moving, hath yielded to make such alterations in some particulars, as in their respective times were thought convenient: Yet so, as that the main Body and Essentials of it (as well in the chiefest materials, as in the frame and order thereof) have still continued the same unto this day, and do yet stand firm and unshaken, notwithstanding all the vain attempts and impetuous assaults made against it by such men as are given to change, and have always discovered a greater regard to their own private fancies and interests, than to that duty they owe to the publick.

By what undue means, and for what mischievous purposes the use of the Liturgy (though injoyned by the Laws of the Land, and those Laws never yet repealed) came, during the late unhappy confusions, to be discontinued, is too well known to the World, and we are not willing here to remember. But when, upon His Majesties happy Restauration it seemed probable, that, amongst other things, the use of the Liturgy also would return of course (the same having never been legally abolished) unless some timely means were used to prevent it; those men who under the late usurped powers had made it a great part of their business to render the people disaffected thereunto, saw themselves in point of reputation and interest concerned (unless they would freely acknowledge themselves to have erred, which such men are very hardly brought to do) with their utmost endeavours to hinder the restitution thereof. In order whereunto divers Pamphlets were published against the Book of Common Prayer, the old Objections mustered up, with the addition of some new ones more than formerly had been made, to make the number swell. In fine great importunities were used to His Sacred Majesty, that the said Book might be Revised, and such Alterations therein, and Additions thereunto made, as should be thought requisite for the ease of tender Consciences: Whereunto His Majesty out of His pious Inclination to give satisfaction (so far as could be reasonably expected) to all His Subjects of what perswasion soever, did graciously condescend.

In which Review we have endeavoured to observe the like Moderation, as we finde to have been used in the like case in former times. And therefore of the sundry Alterations proposed unto us, we have rejected all such as were either of dangerous consequence (as secretly striking at some established Doctrine, or laudable Practise of the Church of England, or indeed of the whole Catholick Church of Christ) or else of no consequence at all, but utterly frivolous and vain. But such Alterations as were tendred to us (by what persons, under what pretenses, or to what purpose soever so tendred) as seemed to us in any degree requisite or expedient, we have willingly, and of our own accord assented unto: Not enforced so to do by any strength of Argument, convincing us of the necessity of making the said Alterations: For we are fully perswaded in our judgments (and we here profess it to the World) that the Book, as it stood before established by Law, doth not contain in it any thing contrary to the Word of God, or *to sound Doctrine, or which a godly man may not with a good Conscience use and submit unto, or which is not fairly defensible against any that shall oppose the same; if it shall be allowed such just and favourable constructions as in Common Equity ought to be allowed to all Humane Writings, especially such as are set forth by Authority, and even to the very best Translations of the holy Scripture it self.*

Our general aim therefore in this undertaking was, not to gratifie this or that party in any their unreasonable demands; but to do that, which to our best understandings we conceived might most tend to the preservation of Peace and Unity in the Church; the procuring of Reverence, and exciting of Piety, and Devotion in the Publick Worship of God; and the cutting off occasion from them that seek occasion of cavil, or quarrel against the Liturgy of the Church. And as to the several variations from the former Book, whether by Alteration, Addition, or otherwise, it shall suffice to give this general account, That most of the Alterations were made, either first, for the better direction of them that are to officiate in any part of Divine Service; which is chiefly done in the Kalendars and Rubricks: Or secondly, for the more proper expressing of some words or phrases of ancient usage in terms more sutable to the language of the present times, and the clearer explanation of some words and phrases, that were either of doubtful signification, or otherwise liable to misconstruction: Or thirdly, for a more perfect rendring of such portions of holy Scripture, as are inserted into the Liturgy; which, in the Epistles and Gospels especially, and in sundry other places are now ordered to be read according to the last Translation:[5] And that it was thought convenient, that some Prayers and Thanksgivings, fitted to special occasions, should be added in their due places; particularly for those at Sea, together with an Office for the Baptism of such as are of riper years; which, although not so necessary when the former Book was compiled, yet by the growth of Anabaptism, through the licenciousness of the late times crept in amongst us, is now become necessary, and may be always useful for the Baptizing of Natives in our Plantations, and others converted to the Faith. If any man, who shall desire a more particular account of the several Alterations in any part of the Liturgy, shall take the pains to compare the present Book with the former; we doubt not but the reason of the change may easily appear.

And having thus endeavoured to discharge our duties in this weighty affair, as in the sight of God, and to approve our sincerity therein (so far as lay in us) to the consciences of all men; although we know it

---

5 The King James/Authorized Version.

impossible (in such variety of apprehensions, humours, and interests, as are in the world) to please all; nor can expect that men of factious, peevish, and perverse spirits should be satisfied with any thing that can be done in this kind by any other than themselves: Yet we have good hope, that what is here presented, and hath been by the Convocations of both Provinces with great diligence examined and approved, will be also well accepted and approved by all sober, peaceable, and truly conscientious sons of the Church of England.

The Church of England, Preface, *The Book of Common Prayer* (1662)

A SHORT OFFICE FOR EXPIATION & ILLUSTRATION[6] OF A CHURCH DESECRATED OR PROPHAN'D

I*F a Church hath been desecrated by murther and blood-shed, by uncleanness, or any other sort of prophanation, the Bishop attended by two Priests at least, and one Deacon, shall enter into the Church, which shall be first prepared by cleansings and washings, &c.*

The Bishop and his Clergy being vested, shall go in Procession about the Church on the inside, saying alternately the Seventh Psalm, and the ninth Psalm.

After which, the Bishop with his Clergy shall go to the Holy Table, and there kneeling down shall pray.

O Almighty God, who art of pure eyes, and canst not behold impurity, behold the Angels are not pure in thy sight, and thou hast found folly in thy Saints; have mercy upon thy servants, who with repentance and contrition of heart, return unto thee humbling our selves before thee in thy holy place. We acknowledge our selves unworthy to appear in thy glorious presence, because we are polluted in thy sight, and it is just in thee to reject our prayers, and to answer us no more from the place of thy Sanctuary; for wickedness hath entred into the Courts where thy holy feet have trod, and have defiled thy dwelling place, even unto the ground, and we by our sins have deserved this

---

6 Beautifying, illuminating.

calamity. But be thou graciously pleased to return to us as in the days of old, and remember us according to thy former loving kindnesses in the days of our Fathers. Cast out all iniquity from within us, remove the guilt of that horrible prophanation that hath been committed here, that abomination of desolation in the holy place, standing where it ought not; and grant that we may present unto thee pure Oblations, and may be accepted by the gracious interpellation of our High Priest, the most glorious Jesus. Let no prophane thing enter any more into the lot of thine inheritance; and be pleased again to accept the prayers which thy servants shall make unto thee in this place. And because holiness becometh thine house for ever, grant us thy grace to walk before thee in all holiness of conversation; that we becoming a Royal Priesthood, a chosen Generation, a people zealous of good works, thou mayest accept us according to thy own loving kindness, and the desires of our hearts. O look upon thy most holy Son, and regard the cry of his blood, and let it on our behalf speak better things than the blood of *Abel*.

O Let that sprinkling of the blood of the Holy Lamb, who was slain from the beginning of the world, make this place holy and accepted, and purifie our hands and hearts, and sanctifie our prayers and praises, and hallow all our Oblations, and preserve this house, and all the places where thy Name is invocated, from all impurity and prophanation for ever, and keep our bodies, and souls, and spirits unblameable to the coming of our Lord Jesus. Then, O blessed Father, grant that we being presented unto thee without spot or wrinkle, or any such thing, may be clothed with the righteousness of the Saints, and walk in white with the Lamb in the Kingdom of our God for ever and ever. Grant this, O Almighty God, our most gracious Father for Jesus Christ his sake, to whom with thee and the Holy Spirit, be all worship, and love, and honour, and glory from generation to generation for ever. *Amen*.

Then the Bishop and Clergy arising from their knees, shall say the Anathematism unto the εὐφημιζμός, *or Acclamation, as in the form of Consecration: After which, kneeling down shall be said the III. prayer plac'd in that Office a little before the Anathematism. And next to that, the II. Prayer which is immediately before that; and then the Prayer of S. Clement.*

The Anathematism.[7]

Ex Psalmis 79. 83. 129.[8]

---

7 Form, 21–2.
8 From the Psalms . . .

KEEP not thou silence, O God: hold not thy peace, and be not still, O God.

2. Let not thine Enemies make a tumult, and they that hate thee lift up their head.

3. Let them not come into thine inheritance to defile thy holy Temple, lest they lay waste thy dwelling places, and break down the carved work thereof with axes and hammers.

4. Make their Nobles like Oreb and Zeeb: yea, all their princes like Zeba and Zalmunna.

5. Who say, let us take to our selves the houses of God in possession.

6. O my God, make them like unto a wheel, as the stubble before the wind.

7. As the fire burneth the wood, and as the flame setteth the mountains on fire.

8. So persecute them with thy tempest, and make them afraid with thy storm.

9. Fill their faces with shame, that they may seek thy Name, O Lord.

10. That men may know, that thou, whose Name art Jehovah, art the most High over all the earth.

11. For the Lord is righteous, he will cut asunder the chords of the wicked.

12. Let them all be asham'd that hate Sion.

13. Let them be as the grass upon the house tops, which withereth before it groweth up.

14. Wherewith the mower filleth not his hand: nor he that bindeth sheaves his bosom.

15. Neither do they which go by say, The blessing of the Lord be upon you: we bless you in the name of the Lord.

III.⁹

O eternal God, who are pleas'd to manifest thy presence amongst the sons of men, by the special issues of thy favour and benediction, make our bodies and souls to be Temples pure and holy, apt for the entertainments of the Holy Jesus, and for the inhabitation of thy holy Spirit. Lord, be pleas'd, with the powers of thy grace, to cast out all impure lusts, all worldly affections, all covetous desires from these thy Temples, that they may be places of prayer and holy meditation, of godly desires, and chaste thoughts, of pure intentions, and great zeal

---

9 *Form*, 20–1.

to please thee, that we also may become Sacrifices, as well as Temples, eaten up with the zeal of thy glory, and even consumed with the fires of thy love; that not one thought may be entertain'd by us, but such as may be like perfume exhaling from the Altar of Incense; and not a word may pass from us, but may have the accent of Heaven in it, and sound pleasantly in thy ears.

O dearest God, fill every faculty of our souls with the impresses of Religion, that we loving thee above all things in the world, worshipping thee with frequent and humblest adorations, continually feeding upon the apprehensions of thy Divine sweetness, and living in a daily observation of thy Divine Commandments, and delighted with the perpetual feast of a holy Conscience, may by thy Spirit be seal'd up to the day of Redemption, and the fruition of thy glories in thine everlasting Kingdom, through Jesus Christ our Lord, to whom with thee, O Father of mercies, Father of our Lord Jesus Christ, and with thee, O blessed and Eternal Spirit the Comforter, all honour and power be ascribed from generation to generation for ever and ever. *Amen.*

II.[10]

LET this house be for the Religious uses of thy servants; let it be the abode of Angels, let it be the place of thy Name, and for the glory of thy Grace, and for the mention and honour, and the memorial of the Lord Jesus; Let no unclean thing ever enter here: Drive from hence all sacrilegious hands, all superstitious Rites, all prophane persons, all proud and unquiet Schismaticks, all misbelieving Hereticks: Let not the powers of darkness come hither, nor the secret arrow ever smite any here: Let no corrupt ayre, and no corrupt communication, no blood-shed, and no unclean action ever pollute this place dedicated to thy holiness.

By the multitudes of thy mercies and propitiations, to the visitors of this place, coming with devotion and charity, let there be peace and abundance of thy blessings. Hear them that shall call upon thee, sanctifie their Oblations, let the good Word of God come upon them, and dispense thy good things unto them. Let the title of this Church abide until the second coming of Christ, and let thy Holy Table stand prepar'd with the blessings of a Celestial Banquet. Bless the gifts and the givers, the dwellers, and the dwelling, and grant unto us here present, and to all that shall come after us, that by the participation of thy heavenly graces, we may obtain Eternal life through Jesus Christ our Lord. *Amen.*

---

10 *Form*, 19.

Restoration

The Prayer of S. Clement.[11]

GOD, the beholder and discerner of all things, the Lord of Spirits and all flesh, who hath chosen our Lord Jesus, and us through him, to be a peculiar people, grant unto every soul that calleth upon his glorious and holy Name, faith and fear, peace and patience, long-suffering and temperance, with purity and wisdom, to the well-pleasing of his Name, through our High Priest and Ruler, by whom unto him be glory and Majestie, both now and to all ages evermore. *Amen.*

After which arising from his knees, the Bishop shall say,

SEEING now, dearly beloved in the Lord, we have by humble prayer implor'd the mercy of God and his holy Spirit, to take from this place, and from our hearts, all impurity and prophanation, and that we hope by the mercies of God in our Lord Jesus Christ, he hath heard our prayers, and will grant our desires, let us give heart thanks for these mercies, and say,

Then shall be said the εὐφημιζμός, or Acclamation, as at the end of the Office of Consecration of Churches, &c.

Acclamation.[12]

The Bishop first saying.

SEEING now, dearly beloved in the Lord, that by the blessing of God, and his gracious favour, we have dedicated to God [this House of Prayer, and] these gifts for the Ministeries of Religion, let us give hearty thanks to Almighty God for these benefits, and say,

Ex Psalmis 150. 68. 87. 99. 100.

PRAISE ye the Lord: praise God in his sanctuary, praise him in the firmament of his power.
2. Blessed be the Lord who daily loadeth us with benefits: even the God of our salvation.
3. He that is our God, is the God of salvation: and unto God the Lord belong the issues from death.
4. The chariots of God are twenty thousand, even thousands of Angels: the Lord is among them as in Sinai, in the holy place.

---

11 *Form,* 21; the source is *1 Clement* 65.
12 *Form,* 23–4.

5. They have seen the goings of God, even the goings of my God, my King in the sanctuary.
6. The singers went before, the players on the instruments followed after: amongst them were the damsels playing with the timbrels.
7. Bless ye God in the congregations: even the Lord from the fountains of Israel.
8. Thy God commanded thy strength: strengthen, O God, that which thou hast wrought in us.
9. O God, thou art terrible out of thy Holy places: the God of Israel is he that giveth strength and power unto his people. Blessed be God.
10. His foundations is in the holy mountains: The Lord loveth the gates of Sion more than all the dwellings of Jacob.
11. Glorious things are spoken of thee, O thou city of God: and of Sion it shall be said, This and that man was born in her, and the highest himself shall establish her.
12. Exalt ye the Lord our God: and worship at his footstool, for he is holy.
13. Moses and Aaron among his Priests: and Samuel among them that call upon his name: they called upon his name, and he answered them.
14. Thou answeredst them, O Lord our God: thou wast a God that forgavest them, though thou didst take vengeance of their inventions.
15. Exalt the Lord our God, and worship at his holy hill: for the Lord our God is holy.
16. Enter into his gates with thanksgiving, and into his courts with praise: be thankful unto him, and bless his name.

And then shall the Priest whom the Bishop shall appoint, begin the Morning-prayer.

The Psalms for the day are Psalm 18, and Psalm 30.

The first Lesson is Zechariah 1.

The second Lesson Mark 11. unto verse 26. inclusively.

The Collect the same with that at Morning-prayer in the Consecration of Churches.

The Collect.[13]

---

13 *Form*, 26.

Restoration

O Almighty God, who dwellest amongst thy Saints, and hast plac'd thy Tabernacle in the hearts of thy servants, give thy heavenly blessings, and encrease to the place where thine honour dwelleth; that what is founded by thy Providence, and built according to thy Commandment, may be established for ever, and blessed in all things by thy Eternal goodness, through Jesus Christ our Lord. *Amen.*

If any Chalice, Paten, Font, Pulpit, or any other Oblation or Utensil for the Church, be at any time newly to be presented; the Bishop is to use the forms of Dedication of those respective gifts, which are particularly used in the dedication; and this to be done immediately after the Nicene Creed, *at the time of the Communion; ever adding the Anathematism and Acclamation.*

Te decet Hymnus.[14]

The Church of Ireland, *A Form of Consecration or Dedication of Churches and Chappels* (1666), pp. 33–6

---

14 *A hymn to you is fitting*. The opening words of the Latin translation of Psalm 51.

7

Literary Devotion

Private prayers

The seventeenth century saw the flourishing of Anglican devotional literature. Among the earliest was John Cosin's Private Devotions, *and after it followed several posthumously published devotionals, most notably the* Preces Privatae[1] *of Lancelot Andrewes.*

OF THE
ANCIENT
AND
ACCUSTOMED
Times Of Prayer
in generall.

At all times, and in all places to give thanks and praise unto Almighty God our heavenly Father, with all manner of devout *Prayer* and *Supplication,* is no more than our very meet, right, and bounden *Duety*.[2] But in as much as the common employments of most, and the naturall infirmities of all sorts of people be so great, that whiles they have this body of flesh upon them, they cannot possibly attend the heavenly Exercise of *Prayer* and *Thanks-giving* without any *Intermission* at all: it hath therefore been the custome of religious and godly persons in all ages, to appoint themselves certaine set *Times* and *Houres* of the day, wherein to performe their *Devotions*. By which meanes it came to passe, that as other [3]*carelesse people spent the whole day either in their owne affaires, or pleasures, these men bestowed it, or the chiefe and more eminent parts of it at least, in the affaires and service of God.

---

1 Private Prayers.
2 [S. *Basil* in Regu. Interr. 37.]
3 [S. *Chrysost*. hom. 59. ad. pop. Antioch.]

They that understood Christ's Parable so, as if [4]*men ought alwaies to pray, and to doe nothing else, mistooke the matter, and were put into the* [5]*Catalogue of Heretickes for their labour. They on the other side, that went about to take away all set Times of Prayer, to maintaine their affected libertie, and to doe it onely when they list, have deserved no lesse blame, and incurred no milder censure. Wise men have gone an even path, and expounding the Scripture, for continuall Prayer, by the continuall Practice of the Church, have neither one way, nor other, offered any violence to Devotion.*

The Practice then of old hath been, so to keepe up Prayer, that men might keepe up themselves withall. [6]Three *times a day to performe this Dutie; and otherwhiles* [7]Seven *times a day to doe it, was K.* Davids *sacred resolution; but* Three *times a day, howsoever,* [at Evening, & Morning, and at Noon day,] *was his custom to pray, and that* [instantly,] *in solemne and devout manner. After him, the great Prophet of God that lived in* Babylon *accustomed himself to kneele upon his knees, and in his chamber to pray* three times *a day towards* Jerusalem,[8] *(saith the story) as hee was alwaies wont to doe.*

From which holy Examples, it afterwards came to passe, that what was by them so religiously observed under the Law, three times *a day (at least) to offer up prayers and thankes-giving to Almighty God, besides the* [9]Morning *and the* Evening sacrifice, *was by Christians as piously continued and practiced under the Gospell also; both Jewes and Christians being in this duty but equall servants to the same* Trinitie, *the God both of Law and Gospell.* It is from the Prophet Daniel (*saith* S. [10]Cyprian) that we Christians have our Third, our Sixt, and our Ninth houre of Prayer, which we duly observe in reverence of the Blessed Trinitie.

Besides these (such was the ardor of ancient pietie) they added yet more,[11] *and aswell in imitation of King* Davids *holy Resolutions before mentioned, as also in honour of those times which the speciall Actions of God, and of our Saviour had in a manner made sacred unto them, they augmented their houres of Prayer, (*[12]*saith that old godly Father) and made their Devotions more frequent and fervent than they were before.*

---

4 [Luc. 18.1.]
5 [S. *Aug.* de. haeres. I.57 & epist. 121. ad Prob. *Isid.* de eccl. off. l. 1 cap. 22.]
6 [Psal. 55.18.]
7 [Psal. 119.]
8 [Dan. 6.10.]
9 [Num. 28; *Isid.* etym. lib. 6. c. ult.]
10 [S. *Cypr.* de orat. dom. in fine.]
11 [S. *Ambr.* Lib. 3. de Virgin.]
12 [S. *Cypr.* ibid.]

Such are these Houres *and* Prayers *that hereafter follow; which be not now set forth for the countenancing of their Novelties that put any trust in the bare recitall onely of a few Prayers, or place any vertue in the beadroll or certaine number of them at such and such set-houres; but for the heartie imitation of that Ancient and Christian pietie, to whom the distinction of* Houres *was but an orderly and usefull, no superstitious or wanton performance of their dueties.*

And surely, so small a part of our Time taken up from other common actions, if not perhaps from doing ill, or doing nothing; and so small a Taske, though but voluntarily imposed upon our selves for Gods service, will never undoe us, nor ever prove to be an abridgement of our Christian libertie, who say, our delight is to be [13]*numbred with the Saints of old, and professe every day, that* [14]*Gods service is perfect freedome.*

John Cosin, *A Collection of Private Devotions* (1627), pp. 3–8

THE HOURS OF PRAYER

Always. *Luc.* xviii. 1.
Without ceasing. 1 *Thess.* v. 17.
At all times. *Eph.* vi. 18.

Three times a day he was bending his knees, and he was worshiping, and he was confessing to his God, just as he was accustomed to do in previous times. *Dan.* vi. 10.

In the evening and in the morning and at noonday I will tell, and I will announce, and he will heed my voice. *Psal.* lv. 18.

Seven times a day I spoke praise to you. *Psal.* cxix. 164.

1. Greatly with the dawn. *Marc.* i. 35
2. In the morning. *Psal.* lxiii. 6.
3. In the third hour of the day. *Act.* ii. 15.
4. Around the sixth hour. *Act.* x. 9.
5. At the ninth hour of prayer. *Act.* iii. 1.
6. Now with the declining day. *Gen.* xxiv. 63.
7. In the night. *Psal.* cxxxiv. 2.

In the middle of the night. *Psal.* cxix. 62.

---

13 [In the *Te Deum*.]
14 [In the 2. Coll for Morn. Pr.]

The Places of Prayer

In every place, in which the memory of my name shall have been, I will come to you and I will bless you. *Exod.* xx. 24.

The Congregation.
In the council of the just, and with the congregation. *Psal.* cxi. [1.]

The Inner Room.
Enter into the inner room, and with the door closed, pray to your father in secret. *Matt.* vi. 6.

The Attic.
He ascended into the upper [room] so that he might pray. *Act.* x. 9.

The Temple.
They were going up into the Temple. *Act.* iii. 1.

The Shore.
On the shore. *Act.* xxi. 5.

The Garden.
In the garden. *Joan.* xviii. 2.

The Bed.
In their beds. *Psal.* cxlix. 5.

The Desert.
In the Desert. *Marc.* i. 35.

In every place lifting pure hands without anger and dispute. 1 *Tim.* ii. 8.

The Morning Hymn

Glory to God in the heights,
   and peace on earth
   on men of good will.
We praise You,
   we bless You,
   we worship You,

we glorify You,
   we give thanks to You,
   because of Your great glory,
O Lord God heavenly King,
   God the Father almighty
   O Lord the unbegotten Son,
   Jesus Christ.

O Lord God,
   Lamb of God,
   Son of the Father,
You who take away the sins of the world,
   have mercy on us.
You who take away the sins of the world,
   receive our plea for forgiveness.
You who sit at the right hand of the Father,
   Have mercy on us.
Since You alone are holy,
   You alone are the Lord,
   O Jesus Christ,
   with the Holy Spirit,
   in the Glory of God the Father. Amen.

The Evening Hymn

O gladdening light of the holy glory
   Of the immortal, heavenly,
   holy, blessed Father, O Jesus Christ;
Since we have come to the setting of the sun,
   discerning the evening light,
   we praise the Father,
   the Son,
   and the Holy Spirit of God.
You are worthy to be praised
   with holy voices at any time,
   O Son of God,
   the giver of life,
Therefore the world glorifies You.

Lancelot Andrewes, translated from *Preces Privatae* (1675),
in *Works*, Vol. 10 (1854), pp. 3, 5, 389, 391

Poetic theology

Poetry is one of the great strengths and defining features of the Anglican tradition. As it developed in the late-sixteenth and early-seventeenth centuries, a theology of poetic inspiration also developed in which the Christian poet implored the aid of the Holy Spirit.

The Printers to the Reader.

The dedication of this work having been made by the Author to the *Divine Majesty* onely, how should we now presume to interest any mortall man in the patronage of it? Much lesse think we it meet to seek the recommendation of the Muses, for that which himself was confident to have been inspired by a diviner breath then flows from *Helicon*.[15] The world therefore shall receive it in that naked simplicitie, with which he left it, without any addition either of support or ornament, more then is included in it self. We leave it free and unforestalled to every mans judgement, and to the benefit that he shall finde by perusall. Onely for the clearing of some passages, we have thought it not unfit to make the common Reader privie to some few particularities of the condition and disposition of the Person;

  Being nobly born, and as eminently endued with gifts of the minde, and having by industrie and happy education perfected them to that great height of excellencie, whereof his fellowship of Trinitie Colledge in Cambridge, and his Orator-ship in the Universitie, together with that knowledge which the Kings Court had taken of him, could make relation farre above ordinarie. Quitting both his deserts and all the opportunities that he had for worldly preferment, he betook himself to the Sanctuarie and Temple of God, choosing rather to serve at Gods Altar, then to seek the honour of State-employments. As for those inward enforcements to this course (for outward there was none) which many of these ensuing verses bear witness of, they detract not from the freedome, but adde to the honour of this resolution in him. As God had enabled him, so he accounted him meet not onely to be called, but to be compelled to this service: Wherein his faithfull discharge was such, as may make him justly a companion to the primitive Saints, and a pattern or more for the age he lived in.

---

15 In ancient Greece, sanctuaries were built on Mount Helicon to the Muses, the nine goddesses that were believed to inspire the arts.

To testifie his independencie upon all others, and to quicken his diligence in this kinde, he used in his ordinarie speech, when he made mention of the blessed name of our Lord and Saviour Jesus Christ, to adde, *My Master*.

Next God, he loved that which God himself hath magnified above all things, that is, his Word: so as he hath been heard to make solemne protestation, that he would not part with one leaf thereof for the whole world, if it were offered him in exchange.

His obedience and conformitie to the Church and the discipline thereof was singularly remarkable. Though he abounded in private devotions, yet went he every morning and evening with his familie to the Church; and by his example, exhortations, and encouragements drew the greater part of his parishioners to accompanie him daily in the publick celebration of Divine Service.

As for worldly matters, his love and esteem to them was so little, as no man can more ambitiously seek, then he did earnestly endeavour the resignation of an Ecclesiasticall dignitie, which he was possessour of. But God permitted not the accomplishment of this desire, having ordained him his instrument for reedifying of the Church belonging thereunto, that had lain ruinated almost twenty yeares. The reparation whereof, having been uneffectually attempted by publick collections, was in the end by his own and some others private free-will-offerings successfully effected. With the remembrance whereof, as of any especiall good work, when a friend went about to comfort him on his death-bed, he made answer, *It is a good work, if it be sprinkled with the bloud of Christ*: otherwise then in this respect he could finde nothing to glorie or comfort himselfe with, neither in this, nor in any other thing.

And these are but a few of many that might be said, which we have chosen to premise as a glance to some parts of the ensuing book, and for an example to the Reader. We conclude all with his own Motto, with which he used to conclude all things that might seem to tend any way to his own honour;

Lesse then the least of Gods mercies.
Nicholas Ferrar, in George Herbert, *The Temple* (1633), no pag.

LORD, *my first fruits present themselves to thee;*
Yet not mine neither: for from thee they came,
And must return. Accept of them and me,
And make us strive, who shall sing best thy Name.
   Turn their eyes hither, who shall make a gain:
   Theirs, who shall hurt themselves or me, refrain.

George Herbert, 'The Dedication', *The Temple* (1633), no pag.

G*LORIOUS and Great; whose power did divide*
The Waves, *and made them* Walls *on either side*;
That didst appeare in Cloven-tongues *of* Fyre;
Divide my thoughts: and with thy selfe, inspire
My Soule; O *cleave my* Tongue, *and make it scatter*
Various Expressions *in a various* Matter;
That like the painefull Bee, *I may derive*
From sundry Flow'rs, *to store my slender* Hive:
Yet, may my Thoughts not so divided be,
But they may mixe againe, and fixe in Thee.

Francis Quarles, 'To GOD', Divine Fancies (1633), no pag.

For Those my unbaptized Rhimes,
Writ in my wild unhallowed Times;
For every sentence, clause and word,
That's not inlaid with Thee, (my Lord)
Forgive me God, and blot each Line
Out of my Book, that is not Thine.
But if, 'mongst all, thou find'st here one
Worthy thy Benediction;
That One of all the rest, shall be
The Glory of my Work, and Me.

Robert Herrick, 'His Prayer for Absolution', His Noble Numbers (1647), A2

My God, thou that didst dye for me,
These thy deaths fruits I offer thee.
Death that to me was life, and light
But darke, and deep pangs to thy sight.
Some drops of thy all-quickning bloud
Fell on my heart, these made it bud
And put forth thus, though, Lord, before
The ground was curs'd, and void of store.
   Indeed, I had some here to hire
Which long resisted thy desire,
That ston'd thy Servants, and did move
To have thee murther'd for thy Love,
But, Lord, I have expell'd them, and so bent
Begge thou wouldst take thy Tenants Rent.

Henry Vaughan, 'The Dedication', Silex Scintillans (1650), A3

Biblical devotion

Holy Scripture was an immensely popular subject for poetic reflection. The Bible was understood as both the written medium of divine revelation and the inspired text par excellence. *Scripture was engaged in multiple poetic forms, ranging from epigrams to sonnets.*

MATT. 16.25

Whoever loses his own life for my sake, he will find it.

Go Life; Go, let me lose you: your death, O Christ, was obtained for me.
(Your death is my life; death for you, my life)

Or I myself will take you to the grave of Christ (my Life).
That third day is not so far off.

MARK 1.16

To St. Andrew the fisherman.

Of course you are able to hunt and catch fish excellently!
You, slippery man, learn to go by one hundred tricks in that place.

Hey good fisherman! Christ stretches his own nets:
Change the art, and now you also learn to be caught.

JOHN 1.23

I am the voice, &c.

I am the voice, you say: you are the voice, St. John?
If you are the voice, why was your father silent?

How amazing was that silence of your father!
Even then when he brought you forth he did not have a voice.

LUKE 14.19

I bought the team of oxen.

I call you to the supper (which the orders of the lord wanted)
You speak to me, (O foolish one) of some cows.

Indeed goodbye, you, the guest, are neither worthy nor useful to us!
The supper (I believe) may prefer to have your cows.

      Richard Crashaw, translated from *Epigrammatum*
        Sacrorum Liber[16] (1634), pp. 3, 12, 48

GODS sacred *Word* is like the *Lampe* of Day,
 Which softens *wax*, but makes obdure the *clay*;
It either melts the *Heart*, or more obdures;
It never falls in vaine; It *wounds*, or *cures*:
Lord, make my brest thy *Hive*, and then I know,
Thy Bees will bring in *Waxe* and *Honey* too.

    Francis Quarles, 'On Gods Word', *Divine Fancies* (1633), p. 61

OH Book! infinite sweetnesse! let my heart
 Suck ev'ry letter, and a honie gain,
  Precious for any grief in any part;
To clear the breast, to mollifie all pain.

Thou art all health, health thriving, till it make
 A full eternitie: thou art a masse
 Of strange delights, where we may wish & take.
Ladies, look here; this is the thankfull glasse

That mends the lookers eyes: this is the well
 That washes what it shows. Who can indeare
 Thy praise too much? Thou art heav'n's Lejger[17] here,
Working against the states of death and hell.

 Thou art joys handsell: heav'n lies flat in thee,
 Subject to ev'ry mounters bended knee.

    George Herbert, 'The H. Scriptures. I', *The Temple* (1633), p. 50

---

16 The Book of Sacred Epigrams.
17 Ledger.

> WELCOME dear book, souls Joy, and food! The feast
>   Of Spirits, Heav'n extracted lyes in thee;
>   Thou art lifes Charter, The Doves spotless neast
> Where souls are hatch'd unto Eternitie.
>
> In thee the hidden stone, the *Manna* lies,
>   Thou art the great *Elixir*, rare, and Choice;
>   The Key that opens to all Mysteries,
> The *Word* in Characters, God in the *Voice*.
>
> O that I had deep Cut in my hard heart
>   Each line in thee! Then would I plead in groans
>   Of my Lords penning, and by sweetest Art
> Return upon himself the *Law*, and *Stones*.
>   Read here, my faults are thine. This Book and I
>   Will tell thee so; *Sweet Saviour thou didst dye!*
>
>   Henry Vaughan, 'H. Scriptures', *Silex Scintillans* (1650), p. 60

Divine poems

Rewriting Scripture as poetry was one way of both celebrating and imitating biblical inspiration. The goal of such work was originally liturgical, but by the time of Charles I it had become part of literary devotion more broadly.

> THE Lord my Shepheard, me his Sheepe
>   Will from consuming Famine keepe.
> He fosters me in fragrant Meads,
> By softly-sliding waters leads;
> My Soule refresht with pleasant juice:
> And lest they should his Name traduce,
> Then when I wander in the Maze
> Of tempting Sinne, informes my wayes.
> No terrour can my courage quaile,[18]
> Though shaded in Deaths gloomy vale;
> By thy Protection fortifi'd:
> Thy Staffe my Stay, thy Rod my Guide.
> My Table thou hast furnished;

---

[18] Quell.

Powr'd[19] pretious Odors on my head:
My Mazer flowes with pleasant Wine,
While all my Foes with envy pine.
Thy Mercy and Beneficence
Shall ever joyne in my Defence;
Who in thy House will sacrifice,
Till aged Time close up mine eyes.

George Sandys, 'PSALME XXIII', A Paraphrase upon
the Divine Poems (1638), pp. 26–7

Happy me! O happy sheepe!
Whom my God vouchsafes to keepe;
Even my God, even he it is
That points me to these wayes of blisse;
On whose pastures cheerefull spring,
All the yeare doth sit and sing,
And rejoycing smiles to see
Their green backs weare his liverie:
Pleasure sings my soule to rest;
Plentie weares me at her brest,
Whose sweet temper teaches me
Nor wanton, nor in want to be.
At my feet the blubb'ring Mountaine
Weeping melts into a Fountaine,
Whose soft silver-sweating streames
Make high noone forget his beames:
When my way-ward breath is flying,
He calls home my soule from dying,
Strokes, and tames my rabid griefe,
And does wooe me into life:
When my simple weakenes strayes,
(Tangled in forbidden wayes)
He (my shepheard) is my guide,
Hee's before me, on my side,
And behind me he beguiles
Craft in all her knottie wiles:
He expounds the giddy wonder
Of my weary steps, and under

---

19 Poured.

Spreads a Path as cleare as Day,
Where no churlish rub says nay
To my joy conducted feet,
Whil'st they gladly goe to meet
Grace and Peace, to meet new laies
Tun'd to my great Shepheards praise.
Come now all ye terrors, sally,
Muster forth into the valley,
Where triumphant darknesse hovers
With a sable wing that covers
Brooding horror. Come thou Death
Let the damps of thy dull Breath
Over shadow even the shade,
And make darkenes selfe afraid;
There my feet, even there, shall find
Way for a resolved mind.
Still my Shepheard, still my God
Thou art with me, still thy Rod,
And thy staffe, whose influence
Gives direction, gives defence.
At the whisper of thy word
Crown'd abundance spreads my boord:
While I feast, my foes doe feed
Their ranck malice not their need,
So that with the self same bread
They are starv'd and I am fed.
How my head in ointment swims!
How my cup orelook's her brims!
So, even so still may I move
By the Line of thy deare love;
Still may thy sweet mercy spread
A shady arme above my head,
About my Paths, so shall I find
The faire center of my mind
Thy Temple, and those lovely walls
Bright ever with a beame that falls
Fresh from the pure glance of thine eye,
Lighting to eternity,
There I'le dwell, for ever there
Will I find a purer aire
To feed my life with, there I'le sup

Balme, and *Nectar* in my cup,
And thence my ripe soule will I breath
Warme into the Armes of Death.

Richard Crashaw, 'Psalme 23', *Steps to the Temple* (1648),
pp. 40–2

Up to those bright, and gladsome hils
   Whence flowes my weal, and mirth,
I look, and sigh for him, who fils
   (Unseen,) both heaven, and earth.

He is alone my help, and hope,
   that I shall not be moved,
His watchful Eye is ever ope,
   And guardeth his beloved;

The glorious God is my sole stay,
   He is my Sun, and shade,
The cold by night, the heat by day,
   Neither shall me invade.

He keeps me from the spite of foes,
   Doth all their plots controul,
And is a shield (not reckoning those,)
   Unto my very soul.

Whether abroad, amidst the Crowd,
   Or els within my door,
He is my Pillar, and my Cloud,
   Now, and for evermore.

Henry Vaughan, 'Psalm 121', *Silex Scintillans*[20] (1650), p. 82

---

20 The Sparkling Stone.

8

Liturgical Devotion

Eucharistic preparation and reception

In the seventeenth century, the Eucharist was received on Christmas, Easter and Pentecost. Worthy reception of it was an important facet of spiritual practice. Throughout devotional and catechetical writings of the period, high eucharistic doctrine supported an equally high valuation of the discipline of self-examination.

1 COR. XIV. 26.
Let all things be done to edifying.

When *Judas Maccabeus* had new built the Altar, and repaired the Temple at *Hierusalem*, after it had been polluted and laid waste for Three years altogether, the Church of God at that time and place rejoyced so much at it, that they kept the Dedication of it Eight days, and ordered that the same should be observed every year; 1 *Maccab.* 4.59. And so we find it was in our Saviours time, for he himself was pleased to honour that Festival, though onely of Ecclesiastical Institution, with his own presence; *Joh.* 10.22. In the like manner, we of this Parish, have cause to be transported with joy and gladness, and to spend this day in praising and adoring the most high God, for that our Church, which hath lain waste for above five times Three years, is now at last rebuilt and fitted again for his Worship and Service. For what the Altar and Temple were to the Jews then, the same will our Church be unto us now. Did they there offer up their Sacrifices to God as Types of the Death of Christ? We shall here commemorate the said Death of Christ, typified by those Sacrifices. Did they come from all parts of *Judea* to worship God there? So shall we, I hope, come from all parts of this Parish to worship God here. Was the Temple an House of Prayer to them? So is the Church to us. Was that the Place where God according to his Promise came unto his people to bless them? I do not doubt but he will do the same to us in this place, if we come unto it, and carry our selves in it as we ought to do. In short, was the Temple the place where all things were performed that could any way conduce to the Edifying of Gods people, as things then stood? The same may be said of our Church, as things now stand. For whatsoever is or can be necessary to the Edifying of our Souls here, and so to their Eternal Salvation hereafter, is clearly and fully comprehended in those several Offices, which according to the Laws of the Land, are now to be performed in this place. Neither is there any thing contained in any of them, but what doth really conduce to those great Ends and Purposes.

. . .

And now we may be well supposed to be so far edified, as to be raised up to the highest pitch of Devotion that we can arrive at in this world, and so are fit to be admitted to the highest Ordinance of the Church, the Sacrament of the Lord Supper. And therefore we now betake our selves to it. But that we may not appear before our Lord empty, we first offer up something to him of what he hath bestowed upon us, to be disposed of to pious and charitable uses; testifying thereby our acknowledgment of his goodness to us, and that we have nothing but what we receive from him. And to excite and encourage us to do this, all the while that we are offering, we have some select sentences of Scripture read to us, wherein God either commands us to be charitable, or else promiseth a blessing to those that are so. And then we pray *for Christs whole Church Militant here on earth*, whereby we profess our selves to be real Members of it, and desirous to hold Communion with it in Christs Mystical Body and Blood. And so we proceed to the Celebration of it: in which the method is so clear, so apparently edifying, that I need not say any thing of it. But shall only observe two things in general concerning it.

First, That the Sacrament of the Lords Supper, being the highest Mystery in all our Religion, as representing the death of the Son of God to us, hence that place where this Sacrament is Administred, was always made and reputed the highest place in the Church. And therefore also it was wont to be separated from the rest of the Church by a Skreen or Partition of Network in Latine *Cancelli*, and that so generally, that from thence the place it self is called the *Chancell*. That this was anciently observed in the building of all considerable Churches (for I speak not of private Oratories or Chappels) within few Centuries of the Apostles themselves, even in the days of *Constantine* the Great, as well as in all Ages since, I could easily demonstrate from the Records of those times. But having purposely waved Antiquity hitherto, I am loath to trouble you with it now. But I mention it at present, only because some perhaps may wonder why this should be observed in our Church, rather than in all the other Churches which have been lately built in this City. Whereas they should rather wonder why it was not observed in all other as well as this. For besides our Obligations to conform as much as may be to the practice of the Universal Church, and to avoid novelty and singularity in all things relating to the Worship of God; it cannot be easily imagined that the Catholick Church in all Ages and places for 13 or 1400 years together, should observe such a Custom as this, except there were great reasons for it.

...

The other thing that I would observe unto you concerning the Holy Communion, is this, that our Church requireth, or at least supposeth it to be Administered every Lords-day, and every Holy day throughout the year, as it was in the Primitive Church. For that is the reason that the *Communion Service* is appointed to be used upon all such days, and to be read at the Communion Table, that so the Minister may be there ready to Administer it unto all that desire to partake of it. Which shews the great care that our Church hath of all her Members, that they might be edified and confirmed in the Faith. To which nothing contributes more than frequent Communion at our Lords Table. Which if people could once be perswaded to, they would soon find greater benefit by it, then I can express, or they themselves, till then, imagine. I shall say no more of it at present, but only this, That I am so sensible of what I now say, that could I be sure to have a sufficient number of Communicants, I should be heartily glad to Administer this Holy Sacrament every Lords day, both for their sakes, and my own too.

Thus I have given you a short Scheme of that excellent Method wherein our Divine Service is performed: Which whosoever rightly considers, will need no other Argument to convince him, that it is according to the Apostles Rule, very *Edifying* indeed.

William Beveridge, *A Sermon Concerning the Excellency and Usefulness of the Common Prayer* (1682), pp. 1–2, 25–8

The Lords Supper.
§1. Now follows the *Reverence* due to the *Sacrament* of the *Lords Supper*; and in this I must follow my first *division*, and set down *first*, what

is to be done *before*; secondly, *at*, and thirdly, *after* the time of *receiving*; for in this *Sacrament* we cannot be excused from any one of these, though in the *former*[1] we are.

Things to be done before receiving.

2. And *first*, for that which is to be done before, *S. Paul* tells us it is *examination*, 1 Cor. 11.28. *But let a man examine himself, and so let him eat of that bread and drink of that cup.* But before I proceed to the *particulars* of this *Examination*, I must in the *general* tell you, that the *special* business we have to do in this *Sacrament*, is to *repeat* and renew that *Covenant* we make with *God* in our *Baptism*, which we having many wayes grievously *broken*, it pleases *God* in his great mercy to suffer us to come to the *renewing* of it in this *Sacrament*, which if we do in *sincerity* of heart, he hath *promised* to *accept* us, and to give us all those *benefits* in this, which he was ready to bestow in the *other Sacrament*, if we had not by our own fault *forfeited* them. Since then the *renewing* of our *Covenant* is our business of this time, it followes that these three things are necessary towards it: *First*, that we understand what the *Covenant* is; *Secondly*, that we consider, what our *breaches* of it have been; and *Thirdly*, that we resolve upon a *strict* observance of it, for the *rest* of our life. And the *trying* our selves in every one of these particulars is that *Examination* which is required of us before we come to this *Sacrament*.

3. And *first*, we are to *examine* whether we understand what this *Covenant* is; this is exceeding necessary, as being the *foundation* of both the other, for it is neither *possible* to discover our *past* sins, nor to settle *purposes* against them for the *future* without it. Let this therefore be your *first* businesse, *Try* whether you rightly understand what that *Covenant* is which you entred into at your *Baptism*, what be the *Mercies* promised on Gods part, and the *duties* on yours. And because the *Covenant* made with each of us in *Baptism* is only the applying to our *particulars*, the *Covenant* made by God in Christ with all mankinde in *general*, you are to consider whether you *understand* that; if you do not, you must immediately seek for *instruction* in it. And till you have means of gaining better, look over what is briefly said in the entrance to this Treatise, concerning the SECOND COVENANT, which is the foundation of that *Covenant* which God makes with us in our *Baptism*. And because you will there finde, that obedience to all Gods Commands is the *condition required* of us, and is also that which we

---

1 Baptism.

expresly *Vow* in our *Baptism*, it is necessary you should likewise know what those *Commands* of God are. Therefore if you finde you are ignorant of them, never be at rest till you have got your self instructed in them, and have gained such a measure of knowledge as may direct you to do that *Whole Duty of Man* which God requires. And the giving thee this instruction is the only aim of *This Book*, which the more ignorant thou art, the more earnestly I shall intreat thee diligently to read. And if thou hast heretofore approacht to this *Holy Sacrament* in utter ignorance of these *necessary* things, bewail thy sin in so doing, but presume not to come again till thou have by gaining this *necessary knowledg* fitted thy self for it, which thou must hasten to do. For though no man must come to the *Sacrament* in such *ignorance*, yet if he wilfully continue in it, that will be no *excuse* to him for keeping from this holy Table.

4. The *second* part of our *Examination* is, concerning our *breaches* of this *Covenant*; and here thou wilt finde the use of that *knowledge* I spake of. For there is no way of discovering what our *sins* have been, but by *trying* our actions by that which should be the *rule* of them, the *Law* of God. When therefore thou settest to this part of *Examination*, remember what are the several branches of thy *duty*, and then ask thy own heart in every particular, how thou hast *performed* it. And content not thy self with knowing in *general*, that thou hast broken Gods *Law*, but do thy utmost to discover in what *particulars* thou hast done so. Recall, as well as thou canst, all the passages of thy life, and in each of them consider what part of that duty hath been *transgrest* by it. And that not onely in the *grosser* act, but in *word* also, nay, even in thy most *secret thoughts*: For though mans *Law* reaches not to them, yet Gods doth; so that whatever he forbids in the act he forbids likewise in the *thoughts* and *desires*, and sees them as clearly as our most *publick acts*. This particular search is exceeding necessary; for there is no promise of *forgiveness* of any sin but only to him that confesseth and *forsaketh* it. Now to both these it is necessary that we have a *direct* and particular *knowledge* of our sins. For how can he either *confess* his Sin, that *knowes* not his guilt of it? or how can he *resolve* to *forsake* it, that discerns not himself to have formerly *cleaved* to it? Therefore we may surely conclude, that this *Examination* is not only *useful* but *necessary* towards a *full* and *compleat repentance*; for he that does not take this *particular* view of his *sins*, will be likely to *repent* but by *halves*, which will never avail him towards his *pardon*; nothing but an entire forsaking of *every evil way*, being sufficient for that. But surely of all other times it concerns us, that when we come

to the *Sacrament* our *repentance* be *full* and *compleat*; and therefore this strict search of our *own* hearts is then especially *necessary*. For although it be true, that it is not *possible* by all our *diligence* to discover or remember every sin of our whole *lives*: and though it be also true, that what is so unavoidably hid from us, may be forgiven without any more *particular* confession then that of *Davids*, Psal. 19.12. *Cleanse thou me from my secret faults*; Yet this will be no plea for us if they come to be *secret* onely because we are *negligent* in searching. Therefore take heed of *deceiving* thy self in this *weighty* business, but search thy soul to the *bottom*, without which it is impossible that the wounds thereof should ever by *thoroughly* cured.

Richard Allestree, The Whole Duty of Man (1659), pp. 67–71

The Supper of the Lord.[2]

Q. *Why was the Sacrament of the Lord's Supper ordained?*
A. *For the Continual Remembrance of the Sacrifice of the Death of Christ, and of the Benefits which we receive thereby.*
Q. *What is the outward part or Sign in the Lord's Supper?*
A. *Bread and Wine, which the Lord hath commanded to be received.*
Q. *What is the inward Part, or thing Signified?*
A. *The Body and Bloud of CHRIST, which are verily and indeed taken, and Received by the faithful in the Lord's Supper.*
Q. *What are the Benefits whereof we are made Partakers thereby?*
A. *The Strengthening and Refreshing of our Souls by the Body and Blood of Christ, as our bodies are by the Bread and Wine.*
Q. *What is required of them who come to the Lord's Supper?*
A. *To Examine themselves whether they repent them truly of their former Sins, stedfastly purposing to lead a new Life; have a lively Faith in God's Mercy through Christ, with a thankful Remembrance of His Death, and be in Charity with all men.*

Institution.
  Glory be to thee, O Crucified Love, who at thy last *Supper* didst ordain the Holy Eucharist, the Sacrament and Feast of Love.
  It was *for the continual Remembrance of the Sacrifice of* Thy *Death*, O blessed *JESU, and of the Benefits we receive thereby*, that Thou wast

---

[2] The opening questions and answers are from the 1662 catechism.

pleased to *Ordain* this Sacred and awful Rite: All Love, all Glory be to Thee.

Ah Dearest Lord, How little sensible is he of thy Love in Dying for us, who can ever forget Thee!

Ah, Wo is me, that ever a Sinner should forget his Saviour, and yet, alas, how prone we are to do it!

Glory be to Thee, O Gracious *JESU*, who to help our Memories, and to impress thy *Love* deep on our Souls, hast Instituted the Blessed Sacrament, and commanded us, *Do this in Remembrance of me.*

O Jesu, let the propitiatory Sacrifice of thy Death which thou didst offer upon the Cross for the Sins of the whole World, and particularly for my Sins, be ever fresh in my Remembrance.

O blessed Saviour, let that mighty Salvation, thy Love has wrought for us never slip out of my mind; but especially let my *Remembrance* of Thee in the Holy Sacrament be always most lively and affecting.

O Jesu, if I love Thee truly, I shall be sure to frequent thy Altar, that I may often Remember all the wonderful Loves of my crucifyed Redeemer.

I know, O my Lord and my God, that a *bare* Remembrance of Thee is not enough; O do Thou therefore fix in me *such a Remembrance* of Thee, as is suitable to the infinite Love I am to remember: Work in me all the holy and heavenly Affections, as become the Remembrance of a crucified Saviour.

Parts outward.
Glory be to Thee, O Adorable Jesus, who under the *Outward and Visible* Part, the *Bread and wine,* things obvious and easily prepared, both which thou hast *commanded to be Received,* dost communicate to our souls the Mystery of *Divine Love,* the *Inward and Invisible Grace,* thy own most blessed *Body & Blood, which are verily and indeed taken and Received by the Faithful in* thy *Supper*: for which, All Love, all Glory be to Thee.

Invisible.
O God Incarnate, How the bread and the Wine, unchanged in their Substance, become *Thy* Body and thy Blood; After what extraordinary manner Thou, who art in Heaven, art present throughout the whole Sacramental Action to every devout Receiver; how Thou canst *give us Thy Flesh to eat,* and *Thy Blood to drink*; How *Thy Flesh is Meat indeed,* and *Thy Blood is Drink indeed*; how *he that eateth Thy Flesh, & drinketh Thy Blood, dwelleth in Thee, and Thou in him*; How *he shall*

live by Thee, and be raised up by Thee to Life Eternal,[3] I can by no means comprehend; but I firmly *believe* all Thou hast said, and I firmly rely on Thy Omnipotent Love, to make good Thy Word; for which, All Love, all Glory be to Thee.

Real Presence.
I believe, O Crucified Lord, that *the Bread which we Break* in the Celebration of the Holy Mysteries, is the *Communication of Thy Body,*[4] and the *Cup of Blessing which we bless,* is the Communication of thy Blood, and that Thou dost as effectually and really conveigh thy Body and Blood to our Souls, by the Bread and Wine, as Thou didst thy holy Spirit,[5] by thy Breath to thy Disciples; for which, All Love, all Glory be to Thee.

Lord, What need I labour in vain, to search out the manner of thy mysterious Presence in the Sacrament, when my Love assures me Thou art there. All the Faithful who approach Thee with prepared Hearts, they well know thou art there, they feel the Virtue of Divine Love going out of Thee, to heal their Infirmities, and to enflame their Affections, for which, All Love, all Glory be to Thee.

O holy JESU, when at thy Altar I see the *Bread* broken, and the *Wine* poured out, O teach me to *discern thy Body* there,[6] O let those Sacred and significant Actions, Create in me a most lively Remembrance of thy Sufferings, how thy most blessed Body was Scourged, and Wounded, and Bruised, and Tormented; how thy most precious Blood was shed, for my sins; and set all my powers on work to Love Thee, and to celebrate thy Love in thus Dying for me.

Thomas Ken, *An Exposition on the Church Catechism* (1685), pp. 94–7

Of *Communicating* upon a short Advertisement.

I was only this Morning, informed of an occasion to partake of the Blessed Sacrament. Though I rejoiced to hear of such a desireable opportunity, and earnestly desired to lay hold on it; yet I began to debate with my self, whither I durst go to that Holy Ordinance, with so short a Preparation, as the morning could affoord: I knew that after the

---

3 [*Joh.* 6.54. &c.]
4 [1 *Cor.* 10.16.]
5 [*Joh.* 22.22.]
6 [1 *Cor.* 11.29.]

exactest preparation, I would be unfit and unworthy, to intertain so great a Guest, or to be receaved and intertained by him: with tears therefore and fervent prayers, I begged of God to direct me, to that which was most aggreeable to his Divine Majesty; That I might not offend him either by approaching to, or withdrawing from that Heavenly Banquet. I considered that it was not length of time, so much as sincerity, that made a due preparation. And that the Primitive Christians, (as we are Informed) Communicated every day, and yet no doubt, they neglected not, the duties of their several stations and occupations.

I had heard it recommended in order to a due preparation for the Sacrament, to do on that occasion whatever was fit to be done, if one were going to die. I was conscious, that, Blessed be God, it is the desire of my Soul, That all my thoughts and words and actions and the continual frame and Temper of my heart may be such, as that they may not unfit me for approaches unto God; and my endeavour is, so to live, as to be dayly prepared for death; And therefore I hoped, that I might venture to present my self before the Lord.

I examined my Repentance for all my Sins, and my Sincere endeavours to be conformed to the whole will of God: My Charity extended to the whole World, and I heartily forgave all that had ever wronged me, wishing them the same mercy I desired to my self. I did firmly and steadfastly believe that our Lord Jesus Christ came into the World to save Sinners, of whom I looked on my self as one of the greatest.[7] And the sense of this, made me humble and more sensible, of my need of, and desireous to obtain the mercy and Grace offered: And all these, encouraged and confirmed my resolution of going to that Holy Sacrament.

And for the Peace, Joy and Consolation, I had at that Holy Ordinance, May the God of peace for ever be exalted; And O Holy and Eternal Lord God, keep for ever in my heart, the thoughts and resolutions which thy Grace hath imprinted there, let them never be defaced, but increased more and more, till I grow to the perfect stature of one in Christ Jesus, and advance from strength to strength, till I appear before Thee in thy Heavenly Sion: And may this Heavenly repast, which I have now twise of late been partaker of, be unto me as the food brought by the Angel to *Elias*; that in the strength thereof I may go unto *Horeb* the mount of God.[8]

May the remainder of my Life, be a continual waiting for the Bridegroom, to whom I am espoused, with Oil in my Lamp, that I may enter

---

7 1 Timothy 1.15.
8 1 Kings 19.4–8.

with him unto the marriage Chamber, where, all that Faith believes, Hope expects, and Charity rejoiceth in, shall be eternaly consummated. *Amen.*

Anne Halkett, *Meditations upon the Seven Gifts of the Holy Spirit* (1702), pp. 4–8[9]

The liturgical year

Observance of the liturgical year set Anglicans apart from Dissenters in the British Isles. Sparrow's Rationale, *like Beveridge's sermon above, relies heavily upon typology. The poetry that follows is a small sampling of a much larger literary expression of popular devotion.*

Of HOLY-DAYES.

Holy in Scripture phrase is all one with separate or set a part to God, and is opposed to common. *What God hath cleans'd, that call not thou common, Acts* 10.15. Holy dayes then are those which are taken out of common dayes, and separated to Gods holy service and worship, either by Gods own appointment, or by holy Churches Dedication. And these are either Fasting and Penitential dayes (for there is a holy Fast, *Joel* 2. as well as a holy Feast, *Nehem.* 8.10.) such as are *Ash-Wednesday, Good-Friday,* and the whole week before *Easter* commonly called the *Holy-week,* which dayes holy Church hath dedicated to Gods solemn worship, in religious fastings and prayers. Or else holy Festivals which are set apart to the solemn and religious commemoration of some eminent mercies & blessings of God. And amongst these Holy-dayes, some are higher days then other, in regard of the greatnesse of the blessing commemorated, and of the solemnity of the service appointed to them. So we read, *Lev.* 23.34. &c. The Feast of *Tabernacles* was to continue seven dayes, but the *first* and the *eight* were the highest dayes, because then were the most solemn Assemblies.

This sanctification or setting apart of *Festival-dayes,* is a token of that thankfulnesse, and a part of that publick honour which we owe to God for admirable benefits; and these days or Feasts so set apart are of excellent use, being, as learned *Hooker* observes,[10] the

---

9 Original Source British Library (RB.23.a.9741).
10 Richard Hooker, *Of the Lawes of Ecclesiasticall Politie,* Book V (1597), Chs 71–2.

1. Splendor and outward dignity of our Religion.
2. Forcible witnesses of ancient truth.
3. Provocations to the exercise of all piety.
4. Shadows of our endlesse felicity in heaven.
5. On earth, everlasting records, teaching by the eye in a manner, whatsoever we beleeve.

And concerning particulars. As the *Jewes* had their *Sabbath*, which did continually bring to minde the former World finished by Creation; so the *Christian* Church hath her *Lords* dayes or *Sundayes* to keep us in perpetual remembrance of a far better World begun by him, who came to restore all things to make Heaven and Earth new. The rest of the holy Festivals which we celebrate have relation all to one Head CHRIST. We begin therefore our Ecclesiastical year (as to some accounts, though not as to the order of our service) with the glorious *Annunciation* of his Birth by angelical message. Hereunto are added his blessed *Nativity* it self, the mystery of his *legal Circumcision*, the Testification of his true Incarnation by the *Purification* of his blessed Mother the Virgin *Mary*: his glorious *Resurrection* and *Ascension* into Heaven, the admirable sending down of his *Spirit* upon his chosen.

Again, for as much as we know that CHRIST hath not only been manifested *great in himself*, but *great* in other *his Saints also*; the days of whose departure out of this world are to the Church of Christ, as the birth & coronation-dayes of Kings or Emperours; therefore especial choice being made of the very flower of all occasions in this kinde, there are annual selected times to meditate of Christ glorified in *them*, which had the honour to suffer for his sake, before they had age and ability to know him, namely, the blessed *Innocents*: glorified in them which knowing him as *S. Stephen*, had the sight of that before death, whereinto such acceptable death doth lead: glorified in those *Sages of the East*, that came from far to adore him, & were conducted by *strange light*: glorified in the second *Elias* of the World, sent before him to prepare his way: glorified in every of those *Apostles* whom it pleased him to use as founders of his kingdom here: glorified in the Angels, as in S. *Michael*: glorified in *all* those *happy souls* that are already possest of blisse.

Besides these, be four dayes annext to the Feasts of *Easter* and *Whitsunday*, for the more honour and enlargement of those high Solemnities. These being the dayes which the Lord hath made glorious, *Let us rejoice and be glad in them*.[11] These dayes we keep not in a secret

---

[11] Psalm. 118.24.

Calendar, taking thereby our private occasions as we list our selves, to think how much God hath done for all men: but they are chosen out to serve as publick memorials of such mercies, and are therefore clothed with those outward robes of holiness, whereby their difference from other dayes may be made sensible, having by holy Church a solemn Service appointed to them.

>   Anthony Sparrow, *A Rationale upon the Book of Common-Prayer of the Church of England* (1657), pp. 104–8

Sunday

COME Ravisht souls with high Delight;
    In sweet immortal Verse,
To crown the day, and welcome night;
    Jehovahs praise Reherse.

O sing the Glories of our Lord,
    His Grace and Truth resound.
And his stupendious acts Record,
    Whose mercies have no bound.

He made the All informing Light,
    And hosts of Angels fair:
'Tis he with shadows cloaths the night,
    He clouds or clears the air.

Those restless skies with stars enchaste
    He on firm hindges set:
The wave embraced earth he plac'd
    His hanging Cabinet.

Wherein for us all things comply
    Which he hath so decreed.
That each in order faithfully
    Shall evermore proceed.

We in his Sommer sun-shine stand,
    And by his favour grow,
We gather what his bounteous hand
    Is pleased to bestow.

When he contracts his brow we mourn,
And all our strength is vain,
To former dust in death we turn,
Till he inspire again.

Then to this mighty Lord give praise
And all our voices prove.
The Glory of his name to raise,
The God of Peace and Love.

Thomas Pestell, 'A Psalm for Sunday Nights', *Sermons and Devotions* (1659), no pag.

Annunciation

Haile most high, most *humble One*!
Above the *World*, below the *Son*,
Whose blush the *Moone* beauteously marres,
And staines the timerous light of starres;
He that made all things had not done
Till he had made himselfe thy Son;
The whole Worlds *Host* would be thy Guest,
And boord himself at thy Rich *Brest*.
O boundlesse Hospitalitie,
The *Feast* of all things *feeds* on *thee*,
The first *Eve*, *Mother* of our *fall*,
E're she bore any one flew *All*.
Of her unkind Gift might we have
Th' Inheritance of a hastie *Grave*.
Quick buried in the wanton *Tomb*
   Of one forbidden bitt,
Had not a better fruit forbidden it:
   Had not thy healthfull *wombe*
The world's new *Eastern Window* been,
And given us Heav'n again, in giving *Him*;
Thine was the *Rosie-Dawn*, that *Spring* the *Day*
Which renders all the *Starres* she stole away.
Let then the aged world be wise; And all
Prove *nobly*, here, *unnaturall*;
'Tis *Gratitude* to forget that other,
And call the *Maiden Eve* your mother.

Yet redeem'd Nations farre and neere,
Applaud your happie-selves in *Her*
(All you to whom this Love belongs)
And keep't alive with lasting songs.
Let *Hearts*, and *Lippes* speake lowd and say,
Haile, *Doore of life*; and *Sourse*[12] *of Day*.
The *Doore* was shut, the *Fountain* seal'd,
Yet *Light* was seen, and *Life* reveal'd;
The *Doore* was shut, yet let in day,
The *Fountain* seal'd, yet life found way.
Glory to thee, Great *Virgins Son*,
In bosome of thy *Father's* blisse,
The same to *Thee* sweet *Spirit* be done,
As ever shall be, was and is.
Amen.

    Richard Crashaw, 'The Virgin-Mother', *Steps to the Temple* (1648),
                       pp. 109–10

Christmas

RUNNE (Sheepheards) run where *Bethleme* blest appears,
Wee bring the best of newes, bee not dismay'd,
A Saviour there is borne, more olde than yeares,
Amidst Heavens rolling hights this Earth who stay'd;
In a poore Cotage Inn'd, a Virgine Maide
A weakling did him beare, who all upbeares,
There is hee poorelie swadl'd, in Manger lai'd,
To whom too narrow Swadlings are our Spheares:
Runne (Sheepheards) runne, and solemnize his Birth,
This is that Night, no, Day growne great with Blisse,
In which the power of *Sathan* broken is,
In Heaven bee glorie, Peace unto the Earth.
Thus singing through the Aire the Angels swame,
And Cope of Starres re-echoed the same.

   William Drummond, 'Runne Sheepe-heardes runne where Bethleme blest
             appears', *Flowres of Sion* (1630), p. 5

---

12 Source.

Purification

Pure and spotless was the Maid
  That to the Temple came,
A pair of Turtle doves she paid,
  Although she brought the Lamb.
Pure and spotless though she were,
Her body chaste, and her soul faire,
        She to the Temple went
            To be purifi'd
            And try'd,
That she was spotless and obedient.
O make us to follow so blest Precedent,
  And purifie our souls, for we
  Are cloth'd with sin and misery.
    From our conception
    One imperfection,
And a continued state of sin,
Hath sullied all our faculties within.
  We present our souls to thee
  Full of need and misery:
And for Redemption a Lamb
The purest, whitest that e're came
        A Sacrifice to thee,
Even he that bled upon the Tree.

> Jeremy Taylor, 'On the Purification of the Blessed Virgin', *Golden Grove* (1654), pp. 152–3

Epiphany

Great, without controversie great,
  They that do know it will confesse
  The mysterie of godlinesse;
Whereof the Gospel doth intreat.

God in the flesh is manifest,
  And that, which hath for ever been
  Invisible, may now be seen,
Th' eternal deitie new drest.

Angels to shepherds brought the news,
  And wise-men guided by a star,
  To seek the sunn are come from far.
  Gentiles have got the start of Jews.

The stable and the manger hide
  His glory from his own: but these,
  Though strangers, his resplendent rayes
  Of majestie divine have spy'd.

Gold, frankincense, and myrrhe, they give,
  And worshipping him plainly show,
  That unto him they all things owe,
  By whose free gift it is they live.

Though clowded in a vaile of flesh,
  The sunne of righteousnesse appears,
  Melting cold cares, and frosty fears,
  And making joyes spring up afresh.

O that his light and influence,
  Would work effectually in me
  Another new Epiphany,
  Exhale, and elevate me hence:

That, as my calling doth require,
  Star-like I may to others shine,
  And guid them to that sunne divine,
  Whose daylight never shall expire.

           Christopher Harvey, 'The Epiphanie', *The Synagogue* (1647),
                                                            pp. 38–9

Lent

WELCOME deare feast of Lent: who loves not thee,
  He loves not Temperance, or Authoritie,
  But is compos'd of passion.
The Scriptures bid us *fast*; the Church says, *Now*:
Give to thy Mother, what thou wouldst allow
  To ev'ry Corporation.

The humble soul, compos'd of love and fear,
Begins at home, and layes the burden there,
   When doctrines disagree.
He says, in things which use hath justly got,
I am a scandall to the Church, and not
   The Church is so to me.

True Christians should be glad of an occasion
To use their temperance, seeking no evasion,
   When good is seasonable;
Unlesse Authoritie, which should increase
The obligation in us, make it lesse,
   And Power it self disable.

Besides the cleannesse of sweet abstinence,
Quick thoughts and motions at a small expense,
   A face not fearing light:
Whereas in fulnesse there are sluttish fumes
Sowre[13] exhalations, and dishonest rheumes,
   Revenging the delight.

Then those same pendent profits, which the spring
And Easter intimate, enlarge the thing,
   And goodnesse of the deed.
Neither ought other mens abuse of Lent
Spoil the good use; lest by that argument
   We forfeit all our Creed.

It's true, we cannot reach Christs fortieth day;
Yet to go part of that religious way,
   Is better then to rest:
We cannot reach our Saviours puritie;
Yet are we bid, *Be holy ev'n as he.*
   In both let's do our best.

Who goeth in the way which Christ hath gone,
Is much more sure to meet with him, then one
   That travelleth by-wayes:
Perhaps my God, though he be farre before,

---

13 Sour.

May turn, and take me by the hand, and more
   May strengthen my decayes.

Yet Lord instruct us to improve our fast
By starving sinne, and taking such repast,
   As may our faults controll:
That ev'ry man may revell at his doore,
Not in his parlour; banquetting the poore,
   And among those his soul.

               George Herbert, 'Lent', *The Temple* (1633), pp. 78–80

Easter

        1.
RISE heire of fresh eternity
   From thy virgin Tombe,
Rise mighty man of wonders, and thy world with thee,
   Thy Tombe the universall East
      Natures new wombe,
Thy tombe faire immortalities presumed Nest.

        2.
Of all the glories make Noone gay,
   This is the Morne,
This Rock bud's forth the fountain of the streames of Day,
   In joyes white annalls lives this howre
      When life was borne,
No cloud scoule[14] on his radiant lids, no tempest lower.

        3.
Life, by this light's Nativity
   All creatures have,
Death onely by this Dayes just doome is forc't to Dye
   Nor is Death forc't; for may he ly
      Thron'd in thy Grave
Death will on this condition be content to dye.

   Richard Crashaw, 'Upon Easter Day', *Steps to the Temple* (1648), pp. 56–7

---

14 Scowl.

Ascension

To day white Saints and holy Angels sing
 To that pure Lamb some new triumphant thing.
Whereat the whole frame of the world ascends,
Each Bird on wings across his Journey bends
Upright, and from the most exalted twist
His voice proclaims, his Joyes above consist.
Earth swels to rise, and heaves her Issue fair,
In swift perfumes to latch the mounting Air.
Rise then my soul, and every power awake!
Can wals of Dust so strong Resistance make?
Lo! Thy Redeemer, that brave Eagle flies
With Cage and all, breaking the marble skies.
His way to climb, was first to be deprest,
Lay then his bloody Cross upon thy brest.
Which will be such a load as birds wings are
To bear thee where his pleading wounds prepare
A Crown of Glory made by conquest thine,
Was his by Nature, where he will refine
Thee and thy case of clay bright as his own,
When join'd in Glory, both ascend one Throne.

Thomas Pestell, 'First on Ascension Day', *Sermons and Devotions* (1659),
no pag.

Pentecost

LISTEN sweet Dove unto my song,
 And spread thy golden wings in me;
  Hatching my tender heart so long,
Till it get wing, and flie away with thee.

  Where is that fire which once descended
   On thy Apostles? thou didst then
  Keep open house, richly attended,
Feasting all comers by twelve chosen men.

  Such glorious gifts thou didst bestow,
   That th' earth did like a heav'n appeare;
  The starres were coming down to know
If they might mend their wages, and serve here.

> The sunne, which once did shine alone,
> Hung down his head, and wisht for night,
> When he beheld twelve Sunnes for one
> Going about the world, and giving light.
>
> But since those pipes of gold, which brought
> That cordiall water to our ground,
> Were cut and martyr'd by the fault
> Of those, who did themselves through their side wound.
>
> Thou shutt'st the doore, and keep'st within;
> Scarce a good joy creeps through the chink:
> And if the braves of conqu'ring sinne
> Did not excite thee, we should wholly sink.
>
> Lord, though we change, thou art the same;
> The same sweet God of love and light:
> Restore this day, for thy great Name,
> Unto his ancient and miraculous right.
>
> George Herbert, 'Whitsunday', *The Temple* (1633), pp. 51–2

Trinity Sunday

> O HOLY, blessed, glorious three,
> Eternall witnesses that be
> In heaven, one God in trinitie!
>
> As here on earth (when men with-stood)
> The Spirit, Water, and the Blood,
> Made my Lords Incarnation good:
>
> So let the *Anty-types* in me
> Elected, bought and seal'd for free,
> Be own'd, sav'd, *Sainted* by you three!
>
> Henry Vaughan, *Silex Scintillans* (1655), Book II, p. 17

Liturgical hymnody

If use is indicative of popularity, then Ken's Three Hymns *are, arguably, the most popular hymns ever written in the Anglican tradition. Still today, the final stanza is sung in Anglican and other churches throughout the world during the offertory.*

AWAKE my Soul, and with the Sun
Thy dayly Stage of Duty run:
Shake off dull Sloth and early rise,
To pay thy Morning Sacrifice.

Redeem thy mispent Time that's past,
Live this Day as if 'twere thy last:
T' improve thy Talent take due care,
'Gainst the *Great Day* thy self prepare.

Let all thy Converse be sincere,
Thy Conscience as the Noon-Day clear;
Think how All-seing GOD thy Ways,
And all thy secret Thoughts surveys.

Influenc'd by the Light Divine,
Let thy own Light in good works shine:
Reflect all Heavens propitious ways,
In ardent love and chearful Praise.

Wake and lift up thy self, my Heart,
And with the Angels bear thy part,
Who all Night long unwearied sing,
Glory to the Eternal King.

I wake, I wake, ye Heavenly Choire,
May your Devotion me inspire,
That I like you my Age may spend,
Like you may on my GOD attend.

May I like you in GOD delight,
Have all day long my God in sight,
Perform like you my Maker's Will,
O may I never more do ill.

Had I your Wings, to Heaven I'd fly,
But GOD shall that defect supply,
And my Soul wing'd with warm desire
Shall all day long to Heav'n aspire.

Glory to thee who safe hast keept,
And hast refresh me whilst I sleept.
Grant Lord, when I from Death shall wake,
I may of endless Light partake.

I would not wake, nor rise again,
Ev'n Heaven it self I would disdain,
Wer't not thou there to be enjoy'd
And I in Hymns to be imploy'd.

Heav'n is dear Lord where e'r thou art
O! never then from me depart;
For to my Soul, 'tis Hell to be
But for one Moment without Thee.

Lord! I my Vows to thee renew:
Scatter my Sins as Morning-Dew,
Guard my first springs of thought & will
And with thy self my Spirit fill.

Direct control, suggest this day,
All I design, or do or say;
That all my Powers, with all their might
In thy sole Glory may unite.

Praise GOD, from whom all Blessings flow,
Praise him all creatures here below;
Praise him above y' Angelick host:
Praise Father, Son, and Holy-Ghost.

An Evening HYMN.

GLORY to Thee, my God this Night
For all the Blessings of the Light
Keep me, O keep me! King of Kings
Under thy own Almighty Wings,

Forgive me Lord, for thy dear Son,
The ill that I this day have done,
That with the World, my self and Thee,
I, e'r I sleep, at peace may be.

Teach me to live, that I may dread
The Grave as little as my Bed.
Teach me to die, that so I may
Triumphing rise at the last day.

O may my Soul on the repose,
And with sweet sleep mine eye lids close
Sleep that may me more vig'rous make
To serve my GOD when I awake.

When in the Night I sleeplessly,
My Soul with Heav'nly thoughts supply
Let no ill Dreams disturb my rest,
No powers of darkness me molest.

Dull sleep of sense me to deprive,
I am but half my days alive;
Thy faithful Lovers, Lord, are griev'd
To ly so long of the bereav'd,

But tho sleep o'r my frailty reigns,
Let it not hold me long in Chains,
And now and then let loose my Heart,
Till it an *Hallelujah* dart.

The faster sleep the sense doth bind,
The more unfetter'd is the Mind;
O may my Soul, from matter free,
Thy unvail'd Goodness waking see,

O! when shall I in endless day,
For ever chase dark sleep away,
And endless Praise with th' Heavenly Choire
Incessant sing and never tire?

You my blest Guardians whilst I sleep
Close to my Bed your Vigils keep;
Divine Love into me instill,
Stop all the Avenues of ill.

Thought to thought with my Soul converse,
Celestial Joyes to me rehearse;
And in my stead, all the Night long,
Sing to my GOD a gratefull Song.

Praise GOD, from whom all Blessings flow,
Praise him all creatures here below;
Praise him above y' Angelick host:
Praise Father, Son, *and* Holy-Ghost.

A *Mid Night* HYMN.

LORD, now my sleep does me forsake,
The sole Possession of me take,
Let no vain fancy me illude,
No one impure desire intrude.

Blest Angels while we silent ly,
You *Hallelujahs* sing on high;
You, ever wakeful near the Throne,
Prostrate adore the Three in One,

I now awake do with you joyn
To praise our God in Hymns Divine:
With you in Heaven I hope to dwell,
And bid the Night & World Farewell.

My Soul when I shake off this dust
Lord in thy Arms I will entrust:
O make me thy peculiar care?
Some Heav'nly Mansion me prepare!

Give me a place at thy Saints feet,
Or some fall'n Angel's vacant seat;
I'll strive to sing as loud as they.
Who sit above in brighter day.

O may I always ready stand
With my Lamp burning in my hand,
May I in sight of Heav'n rejoyce,
When e're I hear the Bridegrooms voice

Glory to thee in light aray'd,
Who light thy dwelling place hast made
An immense Ocean of bright beams,
From thy All-glorious Godhead streams

The Sun in its Meridian height,
Is very darkness in thy sight:
My Soul, O lighten, and enflame,
With thought & love of thy great Name

Blest Jesus thou on Heav'n intent,
Whole Nights hast in Devotion spent
But I frail creature, soon am tir'd
And all my Zeal is soon expir'd.

My Soul how canst thou wearie grow,
Of Antedating Heav'n below,
In sacred Hymns, and Divine Love,
Which will eternal be above?

Shine on me Lord new Life impart,
Fresh ardours kindle in my heart;
One ray of thy All-quickning light,
Dispels the sloth and clouds of night.

Lord, lest the tempter me surprize,
Watch over thine own Sacrifice.
All loose, all idle thoughts cast out,
And make my very Dreams devout.

Praise GOD, from whom all Blessings flow,
Praise him all creatures here below;
Praise him above y' Angelick host:
Praise Father, Son, and Holy-Ghost.

Thomas Ken, Three Hymns (1700)

9

The Book of Nature

Wonder

The central half of the seventeenth century saw the growth of what is now considered modern science. A sense of surprise at the strangeness of creation pervaded much literature of the period. Brown's Religio Medici[1] *is a collection of personal meditations; Walton's* Compleat Angler *is in the form of a Platonic dialogue.*

Thus there are two Books from whence I collect my Divinity; besides that written one of God, another of his servant Nature, that universal and publick Manuscript, that lies expans'd unto the Eyes of all, those that never saw him in the one, have discovered him in the other: this was the Scripture and Theology of the Heathens; the natural motion of the Sun made them more admire him, than its supernatural station did the Children of *Israel*;[2] the ordinary effects of nature wrought more admiration in them, than in the other all his Miracles; surely the Heathens knew better how to joyn and read these mystical Letters, than we Christians, who cast a more careless Eye on these common Hieroglyphicks, and disdain to suck Divinity from the flowers of Nature. Nor do I so forget God as to adore the name of Nature; which I define not with the Schools, to be the principle of motion and rest, but that streight and regular line, that settled and constant course the wisdom of God hath ordained the actions of his creatures, according to their several kinds. To make a revolution every day, is the Nature of the Sun, because of that necessary course which God hath ordained it, from which it cannot swerve, by a faculty from that voice which first did give it motion. Now this course of Nature God seldome alters or perverts, but like an excellent Artist hath so contrived his work, that with the self same instrument, without a new creation, he may effect his obscurest designs.

---

1 The Religion of a Doctor.
2 Joshua 10.13.

Thus he sweetneth the Water with a Word, preserveth the Creatures in the Ark, which the blast of his mouth might have as easily created; for God is like a skilful Geometrician, who when more easily, and with one stroak of his Compass he might describe or divide a right line, had yet rather do this in a circle or longer way; according to the constituted and fore-laid principles of his Art: yet this rule of his he doth sometimes pervert, to acquaint the World with his Prerogative, lest the arrogancy of our reason should question his power, and conclude he could not: and thus I call the effects of Nature the works of God, whose hand and instrument she only is; and therefore to ascribe his actions unto her, is to devolve the honour of the principal agent, upon the instrument; which if with reason we may do, then let our hammers rise up and boast they have built our houses, and our pens receive the honour of our writing. I hold there is a general beauty in the works of God, and therefore no deformity in any kind or species of creature whatsoever: I cannot tell by what Logick we call a *Toad*, a *Bear*, or an *Elephant* ugly, they being created in those outward shapes and figures which best express those actions of their inward forms. And having past that general Visitation of God, who saw that all that he had made was good, that is, conformable to his Will, which abhors deformity, and is the rule of order and beauty; there is no deformity but in Monstrosity, wherein notwithstanding there is a kind of Beauty. Nature so ingeniously contriving the irregular parts, as they become sometimes more remarkable than the principal Fabrick. To speak yet more narrowly, there was never any thing ugly or mis-shapen, but the Chaos; wherein notwithstanding, to speak strictly, there was no deformity, because no form, nor was it yet impregnant by the voice of God; Now nature is not at variance with Art, nor art with Nature; they being both servants of his providence: Art is the perfection of Nature: were the World now as it was the sixth day, there were yet a Chaos: Nature hath made one World, and Art another. In brief, all things are artificial; for Nature is the Art of God.

Thomas Browne, *Religio Medici* (1642), pp. 33–7

[*Pisc.*] But I will lay aside my Discourse of Rivers and tell you some things of the Monsters, or Fish, call them what you will, that they breed and feed in them. *Pliny* the Philosopher says, (in the third Chapter of his ninth Book)[3] that in the *Indian Sea*, the fish call'd the *Balaena* or *Whirle-Pool* is so long and broad, as to take up more in length and

---

3 Pliny the Elder's *Natural History*, written in the first century AD.

bredth than two Acres of ground, and of other fish of two hundred cubits long; and that in the River *Ganges*, there be Eeles of thirty foot long. He says there, that these Monsters appear in that Sea only, when the tempestuous winds oppose the Torrents of Waters falling from the Rocks into it, and so turning what lay at the bottom to be seen on the waters top. And he says, that the people of *Cadara* (an Island near this place) make the Timber for their houses of those Fish-bones. He there tells us, that there are sometimes a thousand of these great Eeles found wrapt, or interwoven together. He tells us there, that it appears that Dolphins love musick, and will come, when call'd for, by some men or boys, that know and use to feed them, and that they can swim as swift as an Arrow can be shot out of a Bow, and much of this is spoken concerning the *Dolphin*, and other Fish, as may be found also in learned Dr. *Casaubons* Discourse of Credulity, and Incredulity, printed by him about the year 1670.

I know, we Islanders are averse to the belief of these wonders: but, there be so many strange Creatures to be now seen (many collected by *John Tredescant*, and others added by my friend *Elias Ashmole* Esq;[4] who now keeps them carefully and methodically at his house near to *Lambeth* near *London*) as may get some belief of some of the other wonders I mentioned. I will tell you some of the wonders that you may now see, and not till then believe, unless you think fit.

You may see there the *Hog-fish*, the *Dog-fish*, the *Dolphin*, the *Cony-Fish*, the *Parrot-fish*, the *Shark*, the *Poyson-fish*, *Sword-fish*, and not only other incredible fish! but you may there see the *Salamander*, several sorts of *Barnacles*, of *Solan Geese*, the *bird* of *Paradise*, such sort of *Snakes*, and such *birds-nests*, and of so various forms, and so wonderfully made, as may beget wonder and amusement in any beholder: and so many hundreds of other rarities in that Collection, as will make the other wonders I spake of, the less incredible; for, you may note, that the waters are natures store-house, in which she locks up her wonders.

Walton later offers a brief discourse about environmental ethics.

Venat. Why, Sir, what be those that you call the Fence months?
Pisc. Sir, they be principally three, namely, *March*, *April*, and *May*, for these be the usual months that *Salmon* come out of the Sea to spawn in most fresh Rivers, and their Fry would about a certain time return back to the salt water, if they were not hindred by *wires* and *unlawful*

---

4 Founders of the Ashmolean Museum.

gins, which the greedy Fisher-men set, and so destroy them by thousands, as they would (being so taught by nature) change the *fresh* for *salt water*. He that shall view the wise Statutes made in the 13 of *Edw. the I.* and the like in *Rich. the III.* may see several provisions made against the destruction of Fish: and though I profess no knowledg of the Law, yet I am sure the regulation of these defects might be easily mended. But I remember that a wise friend of mine did usually say, *That which is every bodies business, is no bodies business*. If it were otherwise, there could not be so many Nets and Fish that are under the Statute size, sold daily amongst us, and of which the *conservators* of the waters should be ashamed.

But above all, the taking Fish in Spawning time, may be said to be against nature; it is like the taking the dam on the nest when she hatches her young: a sin so against nature, that Almighty God hath in Levitical Law made a Law against it.[5]

Izaak Walton, *The Compleat Angler* (1676), pp. 30–2, 54–5

Finitude and discovery

Early modern science was variously termed natural philosophy, mechanical philosophy and experimental philosophy. On the one hand, recognizing this allows us to note the continued influence of ancient philosophy upon seventeenth-century scientific study. For example, Hooke depends entirely upon Aristotle, who claimed in his Metaphysics *that all knowledge comes through the senses, particularly sight, and then imprints itself upon the memory. From this perspective, the best way to improve knowledge is to improve sight – and Hooke's* Micrographia *was a record of experiments conducted with magnifying glasses. On the other hand, uncovering this philosophical foundation helps us to better understand why Anglican 'scientists' such as Robert Boyle took human finitude so seriously; they reflected upon the human inclination to err and misperceive as a given fact, and this in turn grounded a strong sense of humility.*

It is the great prerogative of Mankind above other Creatures, that we are not only able to behold *the works of Nature, or barely to* sustein *our lives by them, but we have also the power of* considering, comparing, altering, assisting, *and* improving *them to various uses. And as this is the peculiar priviledge of humane Nature in general, so is it capable of*

---

5 Deuteronomy 22.6.

The Book of Nature

being so far advanced by the helps of Art, *and* Experience, *as to make some Men excel others in their* Observations, *and* Deductions, *almost as much as they do Beasts. By the addition of such* artificial Instruments *and* methods, *there may be, in some manner, a reparation made for the mischiefs, and imperfection, mankind has drawn upon it self, by negligence, and intemperance, and a wilful and superstitious deserting the Prescripts and Rules of Nature, whereby every man, both from a deriv'd corruption, innate and born with him, and from his breeding and converse with men, is very subject to slip into all sorts of errors.*

The only way which now remains for us to recover some degree of those former perfections, seems to be, by rectifying the operations of the Sense, *the* Memory, *and* Reason, *since upon the evidence, the* strength, *the* integrity, *and the* right correspondence *of all these, all the light, by which our actions are to be guided, is to be renewed, and all our command over things is to be establisht.*

It is therefore most worthy of our consideration, to recollect their several defects, that so we may the better understand how to supply them, and by what assistances we may inlarge *their power, and* secure *them in performing their particular duties.*

As for the actions of our Senses, *we cannot but observe them to be in many particulars much outdone by those of other Creatures, and when at best, to be far short of the perfection they seem capable of: And these infirmities of the Senses arise from a double cause, either from the* disproportion of the Object to the Organ, *whereby an infinite number of things can never enter into them, or else from* error in the Perception, *that many things, which come within their reach, are not received in a right manner.*

The like frailties are to be found in the Memory; *we often let many things* slip away *from us, which deserve to be retain'd; and of those which we treasure up, a great part is either* frivolous or false; *and if good, and substantial, either in tract of time* obliterated, *or at best so overwhelmed and buried under more frothy notions, that when there is need of them, they are in vain sought for.*

The two main foundations being so deceivable, it is no wonder, that all the succeeding works which we build upon them, of arguing, concluding, defining, judging, and all the other degrees of Reason, are liable to the same imperfection, being, at best, either vain, or uncertain: So that the errors of the understanding *are answerable to the two other, being defective both in the quantity and goodness of its knowledge; for the limits, to which our thoughts are confind, are small in respect of the vast extent of Nature it self; some parts of it are* too large to be *comprehended, and some too little to be perceived. And from thence it must follow, that not having a full sensation of the Object, we must be very lame and imperfect in our conceptions about it, and in all the propositions which we build upon it; hence we often take the shadow of things for the substance, small appearances for good similitudes, similitudes for definitions; and even many of those, which we think to be the most solid definitions, are rather expressions of our misguided apprehensions then of the true nature of the things themselves.*

The effects of these imperfections are manifested in different ways, according to the temper and disposition of the several minds of men, some they incline to gross ignorance and stupidity, and others to a presumptuous imposing on other mens Opinions, and a confident dogmatizing on matters, whereof there is no assurance to be given.

Thus all the uncertainty, and mistakes of humane actions, proceed either from the narrowness and wandring of our Senses, from the slipperiness or delusion of our Memory, from the confinement or rashness of our Understanding, so that 'tis no wonder, that our power over natural causes and effects is so slowly improv'd, seeing we are not only to contend with the obscurity and difficulty of the things whereon we work and think, but even the forces of our own minds conspire to betray us.

These being the dangers in the process of humane Reason, the remedies of them all can only proceed from the real, the mechanical, the experimental Philosophy, which has this advantage over the Philosophy of discourse and disputation, that whereas that chiefly aims at the subtilty of its Deductions and Conclusions, without much regard to the first ground-work, which ought to be well laid on the Sense and Memory; so this intends the right ordering of them all, and the making them serviceable to each other.

Robert Hooke, *Micrographia* (1667), pp. 1–3

Sophr. I was just going to say, *Eugenius*, that after what I have premised, I hope it may now be seasonable to apply the newly delivered Notions to the three sorts of things that I formerly represented as being in some sence *above reason*. For I consider, that there are some objects of so immense and peculiar a nature, that (if I may so speak) by an easie view of the mind, that is without any subtle and laborious disquisition, the Soul discerns, and as it were feels the Object to be disproportionate to her powers: And accordingly if she thinks fit to try, she quickly finds her self unable to frame conceptions of them fit to be acquiesc'd in, and this sort of Objects I do upon that account call inconceivable, or (on some occasions) *supra-intellectual*.

But when by attentively considering the attributes and operations of things, we sometimes find that a thing hath some property belonging to it, or doth perform somewhat, which by reflecting on the beings and ways of working that we know already, we cannot discern to be reducible to them or derivable from them, we then conclude this property or this operation to be *inexplicable*; that is, such as that it cannot so much as in a general way be intelligibly accounted for, and this makes the second sort of our things above Reason. But this is not all, for the Rational Soul that is already furnished with innate, or at least primitive *Ideas* and Rules of true and false, when she comes to examine certain things and make successive inferences about them, she finds (sometimes to her wonder as well as trouble) that she cannot avoid admitting some consequences as true & good which she is not able to reconcile to some other manifest Truth or acknowledged Proposition: And whereas other Truths are so harmonious, that there is not disagreement between any two of them, the Heteroclite Truths I speak of appear not symmetrical with the rest of the body Truths, and we see not how we can at once embrace these and the rest, without admitting that grand absurdity which subverts the very foundation of our reasonings, *That Contradictories may both be true.* As in the controversie about the endless divisibility of a strait line, since 'tis manifest that a line of three foot for instance is thrice as long as a line of one foot, so that the shorter line is but the third of the longer, it would follow that a part of a line may contain as many parts as a whole, since each of them is divisible into infinite parts, which seems repugnant to common sence, and to contradict one of those common Notions in *Euclid*, whereon Geometry it self is built. Upon which account I have ventured to call this third sort of things above Reason *Asymmetrical* or *Unsociable*, of which eminent instances are afforded us by those controversies (such as that of the *compositio continui*[6]) wherein which side soever of the question you take, you will be unable *directly* and truly to answer the objections that may be urged to show that you contradict some primitive or some other acknowledged truth.

These, *Eugenius*, are some of the considerations by which I have been induced to distinguish the things that to me seem to overmatch our Reason, into three kinds. For of those things I have stil'd

---

6 The composition of the continuum. Here this refers to the geometric concern with the division of lines, which can continue infinitely and thus surpasses what might otherwise seem reasonable.

Unconceivable, our *Ideas* are but such as a moderate attention suffices to make the mind sensible that she wants either light or extent enough to have a clear and full comprehension of them: And those things that I have called *Inexplicable*, are those which we cannot perceive to depend upon the *Ideas* we are furnished with, and to resemble in their manner of working any of the Agents whose nature we are acquainted with: And lastly, those things which I have named *Unsociable*, are such as have Notions belonging to them, or have conclusions deducible from them, that are (for ought we can discern) *either* incongruous to our primitive *Ideas*, *or* when they are driven home, inconsistent with the manifest Rules we are furnished with, to judge of True and False.

Robert Boyle, *A Discourse of Things above Reason* (1681), pp. 72–6

Defending the New Philosophy

As we have seen with predestinarian debates, many people considered it impious to inquire into the secrets of God. The secrets of Nature were held in a similar reverence because they too belonged to God. Those engaged in scientific study had to defend the orthodoxy of their actions. Patrick's Brief Account *was an early defence; he noted that the 'Latitude-Men', who were not 'latitudinarian' in their theology, embraced the Creeds, the Articles of Religion, the Prayer Book, the Book of Homilies, episcopacy, lawfully constituted authority, and the Church Fathers. New 'philosophy' – science – need not undermine orthodox divinity. Sprat took a different approach, arguing that Jesus Christ was the first natural philosopher. The study of nature underscores that Christian faith is based upon evidence, even as it allows us to imitate Jesus' miraculous benevolence.*

But me thinks I hear some men say, all innovations are dangerous; *Philosophy* and *Divinity* are so inter-woven by the School-men, that it cannot be safe to separate them; *new Philosophy* will bring in *new Divinity*; and freedom in the one will make men desire a liberty in the other. The very same argumentation the Presbyterians used, when they bore rule in the University, and the *new Philosophy* was interdicted in some Colledges upon that account. But what was the event? it was so much the more eagerly studied and embraced; there was a time when all Learning was upon the same pretence discountenanced; *Graece nosse suspectum erat, Hebraice plane haereticum;*[7] and there was a

---

7 To have known Greek was suspect, and Hebrew clearly heretical.

Colledge in *Cambridge* that shut their Gates against the *Greek Testament*: but all their endeavours were but vain; they might as well have hindred the Sun from rising, or being up, from filling the whole *Horizon* with light; Learning and Knowledge will breake forth like fire, and pierce like Lightning through all impediments; politeness and elegancy hath long ago subdued Monastick barbarism; *Erasmus* and *Melancthon* with the rest of those restorers of Learning have made *Holcot* and *Bricot*[8] quite out of fashion; and the inquisitive *Genius* of latter years, like a mighty wind hath brushed down all the Schoolmens Cobwebs. There is an infinite desire of knowledge broken forth in the world, and men may as well hope to stop the tide, or bind the Ocean with Chains, as hinder free *Philosophy* from overflowing: it will be as easie to satisfie mens corporal appetites with chaff and straw, as the desires of their minds with empty words and terms; the Church of *Rome* quickly saw her error in this point, and forbore to strive against the stream; for when she perceived that Learning would be in fashion, she presently set her children to School; and who so great Schollars in all kinds as they? and she hath been so wise ever since, that there shall be no piece of Learning but some of her sons shall be masters of it: and if they will but give her respectfull words, they may be as free Philosophers as they please; and I dare say she would take it very ill, if any one should deny *Descartes* or *Gassendus*[9] to be hers. *Galileo* indeed fell under her correction for holding the motion of the Earth, but the true crime was his abusing his Holiness in his Dialogues under the name of *Simplicius*; For others have with impunity adventured on as great *Paradoxes*, but they had the good manners to make a legg[10] and say, *Omnia Ecclesiae authoritati submittimus.*[11]

I will never therefore believe, that the Church of *England* can be more stingy than the Beldame of *Rome*, but will do that of choice, that the other doth of necessity. True *Philosophy* can never hurt sound *Divinity*. Christian Religion was never bred up in the *Peripatetick School*,[12] but spent her best and heathfullest years in the more Religious *Academy*,[13] amongst the primitive Fathers; but the Schoolmen afterwards ravished

---

8 Robert Holcot (d. 1349), English Dominican, and Thomas Bricot (d. 1516), French scholastic.

9 Pierre Gassendi (d. 1655), French Roman Catholic priest, humanist and experimental philosopher whose empiricism was highly influential.

10 Bow.

11 Every one of us submits to the authority of the Church.

12 Followers of Aristotle.

13 Plato's school.

her thence, and shut her up in the decayed ruines of *Lyceum*,[14] where she served an hard servitude, and contracted many distempers: why should she not at last be set at liberty, and suffered to breath in a free air? let her alone be Mistress, and choose her Servants where she best likes; let her old loving Nurse the *Platonick Philosophy* be admitted again into her family; nor is there any cause to doubt but that the Mechanick[15] also will be faithful to her, no less against the open violence of *Atheisme*, than the secret treachery of *Enthusiasm* and *Superstition*, as the excellent works of a late learned Author have abundantly demonstrated. Nor will it be possible otherwise to free Religion from scorn and contempt, if her Priests be not as well skilled in nature as the people, and her Champions furnished with as good Artillery as her enemies. How shall the Clergy be able to maintain their credit with the ingenuous Gentry, who begin generally to be acquainted with the *atomical Hypothesis*, and know how to distinguish between a true Gemme and a *Bristol*-Diamond? or how shall they encounter with the witts (as they are called) of the age, that assault Religion with new kind of weapons? will they acquiesce in the authority of *Aristotle* or St. *Thomas*? Or be put off with *contra negantem principia*?[16] let not the Church send out her Souldiers armed with Dock-leaves and Bullrushes, to encounter swords and Guns, but let them wear as good brass and steel as their enemyes, and fight with them at their own weapons; and then having Truth and Right on their side, let them never despair of victory.

Simon Patrick, *A Brief Account of the New Sect of Latitude-Men* (1662), pp. 22–4

Sect. XIV. *Experiments not dangerous to the Christian Religion.*

I will now proceed to the weightiest, and most solemn part of my whole *undertaking*; to make a defence of the *Royal Society*, and this new *Experimental Learning*, in respect of the *Christian Faith*. I am not ignorant, in what a slippery place I now stand; and what a tender matter I am enter'd upon. I know that it is almost impossible without offence, to speak of things of this Nature, in which all *Mankind*, each *Country*, and now almost every *Family*, do so widely disagree among themselves. I cannot expect that what I shall say will escape misinterpretation, though it be spoken with the greatest simplicity, and submission, while

---

14 Aristotle's school.

15 The mechanical philosophy.

16 An abbreviation for 'Contra principia negantem non est disputandum' (There is no disputing against one denying first principles).

I behold that most men do rather value themselves, and others, on the little differences of *Religion*, than the main substance itself; and while the will of *God* is so variously distracted, and what appears to be *Piety* to some *Christians*, is abhorr'd as the greatest superstition, and heresy by others.

However to smooth my way as much as I can, and to prepare all our several *Spiritual Interests*, to read this part with some tolerable *moderation*; I do here in the beginning most sincerely declare, that if this design should in the least diminish the *Reverence*, that is due to the *Doctrine of Jesus Christ*, it were so far from deserving *protection*, that it ought to be abhorr'd by all the *Politic*, and *Prudent*; as well as by the devout Part of Christendom. And this I profess, I think they were bound to do, not only from a just dread of the *Being*, the *Worship*, the *Omnipotence*, the *Love of God*, all which are to be held in the highest veneration: but also out of a regard to the peace, and prosperity of men. In matters that concern our *opinions* of another *World*, the least alterations are of wonderful hazard: how mischievous then would that enterprise be, whose effects would abolish the *command of Conscience*, the belief of a *future life*; or any of those Hevenly *Doctrines*, by which not only the *eternal condition* of men is secur'd, but their *natural Reason*, and their *Temporal safety* advanc'd? Whoever shall impiously attempt to subvert the Authority of the *Divine Power*, on false pretences to better *Knowledge*, he will unsettle the strongest foundations of our *hopes*: he will make a terrible confusion in all the offices, and opinions of men: he will destroy the most prevailing *Argument* to *virtu*: he will remove all *human Actions*, from their firmest center: he will even deprive himself, of the prerogative of his *Immortal Soul*; and will have the same success, that the *Antient Fables* make those to have had, who contended with their *Gods*, of whom they report, that many were immediately turn'd into *Beasts*.

With these apprehensions I come to examin the *Objections*, which I am now to satisfy: and having calmly compar'd the *Arguments* of some devout men against *Knowledge*, and chiefly that of *Experiments*; I must pronounce them both, to be altogether inoffensive. I did before affirm, that the *Royal Society* is abundantly cautious, not to intermeddle in *Spiritual things*: But that being only a general plea, and the question not lying so much on what they do at present, as upon the probable effects of their Enterprise; I will bring it to the test through the chief Parts of *Christianity*; and shew that it will be found as much avers from *Atheism*, in its issue and consequences, as it was in its original purpose.

The public Declaration of the *Christian Religion*, is to propose to mankind, an infallible way to *Salvation*. Towards the performance of this happy end, besides the *Principles* of *Natural Religion*, which consists in the acknowledgment and Worship of a *Deity*: It has offer'd us the merits of a glorious *Saviour*: By him, and his *Apostles Ministry*, it has given us sufficient *Examples*, and *Doctrines* to acquaint us with *divine things*, and carry us to *Heven*. In every one of these, the *Experiments* of *Natural things*, do neither darken our eyes, nor deceive our minds, nor deprave our hearts.

Sect. XVII. *Experiments not prejudicial to the doctrine of the Gospel.*

But the chief part of our *Religion*, on which the certainty of all the rest depends, is the *Evangelical Doctrine* of *Salvation* by *Jesus Christ*. In this there is nothing, from which he that converses much with *Nature*, can be thought to be more avers than others; nay, to which he may not be concluded to be more inclinable, on this very account; seing it has all been prov'd to him his own way. Had not the appearance of *Christ* been strengthen'd by undeniable signs of *almighty Power*, no age nor place had been oblig'd to believe his Message. And these *Miracles* with which he asserted the *Truths* that he taught (if I might be allow'd this boldness in a matter so sacred) I would even venture to call *Divine Experiments* of his *Godhead*.

What then can there be in all this *Doctrine*, at which a Real and impartial *Inquirer* into *Natural Things*, should be offended? Does he demand a Testimony from *Heven*? he has it: He reads effects produc'd, that did exceed all mortal skill and force: And of this he himself is a better judge than others: For to understand aright what is *supernatural*, it is a good step first to *know* what is according to *Nature*.

Does he require that this should be testified, not by men of *Craft* or *Speculation*; but rather by men of *Honesty*, *Trades*, and *Business*? The *Apostles* were such. Will he not consent to any mans *Opinions*, unless he sees the *operations* of his hands agree with them? *Christ* himself requires no more of any of his *Followers*: For he commanded his *Disciples* not to believe him, but the *Works* that he did. Does he think that it is the most honorable Labor to study the benefit of Mankind? to help their infirmities? to supply their wants? to ease their burdens? He here may behold the whole *Doctrine* of *Future Happiness*, introduc'd by the same means; by feeding the Hungry, by curing the Lame, and by opening the eyes of the Blind: All which may be call'd *Philosophical Works*, perform'd by an *Almighty hand*.

What then can hinder him from loving and admiring this *Saviour*, whose *Design* is so conformable to his own, but his *Ability* so much greater? What jealousie can he have of an imposture in this *Messias*? Who though his *Doctrine* was so pure and venerable, though his *Life* was so blameless, though he had the power of *Heaven* and *Earth* in his hands, though he knew the thoughts of men, and might have touch'd and mov'd them as he pleas'd; did yet not rely on his *Doctrine*, on his *Life*, on the irresistible assistance of *Angels*, or on his own *Divinity* alone; but stoop'd to convince men by their *Senses*, and by the very same cours by which they receive all their *Natural Knowledge*.

Thomas Sprat, *The History of the Royal-Society of London* (1667), pp. 345–7, 351–3

10

Christian Ethics

Duty

Few themes from antiquity remained as vitally important in the seventeenth century as duty. It was given its classical exposition in Marcus Tullius Cicero's De Officiis, *translated as* Offices *by L'Estrange and his contemporaries but today translated as* On Duties. *Cicero was also known as Tully, a tradition that extends back to the medieval era. Duty was a central topic in popular devotional writing, too, and was the driving theme of Allestree's great work, where it is contextualized by the relationship between nature and grace.*

The *Benefits* purchased for us by *Christ*, are such as will undoubtedly make the Soul *Happy*, for *Eternal* Happiness it self is one of them; but because these *Benefits* belong not to us till we perform the *Condition* required of us; whoever desires the *happiness* of his Soul, must set himself to the performing of that *Condition*; what that is, I have already mentioned in the *General*, *That it is the hearty, honest endeavour of obeying the whole Will of God*. But then that *Will of God* containing under it many particulars, it is necessary we should also know what those are; that is, what are the *several* things, that God now requires of us, our performance whereof will bring us to everlasting happiness, and the neglect to endless misery.

Of the Light of NATURE.

2. Of these things there are some which God hath so stamp'd upon our souls, that we *Naturally* knew them; that is, we should have known them to be our Duty, though we had never been told so by the Scripture. That this is so, we may see by those *Heathens*, who having never heard of either *Old* or *New Testament*, do yet acknowledge themselves

bound to some *General* Duties, as to *Worship God,* to be *Just,* to *Honour* their *Parents,* and the like. And as *S. Paul* saith, *Rom.* 2. 15. *Their consciences do in those things accuse or excuse them*; That is, tell them, whether they have done what they should, in those particulars, or no.

3. Now though *Christ* have brought greater Light into the world, yet he never meant by it to put out any of that *Natural* light, which God hath set up in our *Souls*: Therefore let me here by the way, advise you not to walk contrary even to this *lesser* light, I mean, not to venture on any of those Acts, which meer *Natural Conscience* will tell you are Sins.

4. It is just matter of sadness to any Christian heart, to see some in these dayes, who profess much of *Religion,* and yet live in such sins, as a meer *heathen* would *abhor*; men that pretending to higher degrees of *Light,* and *holiness,* then their *brethren* do, yet *practice* contrary to all Rules of *common honesty,* and make it part of their Christian liberty so to do; of whose Seducement it concerns all that love their *Souls* to beware: and for that purpose let this be laid as a Foundation, *That that Religion or Opinion cannot be of God, which allows men in any wickedness.*

5. But though we must not put out this *light* which God hath thus put into our Souls, yet this is not the onely way whereby God hath revealed his will, and therefore we are not to rest here, but proceed to the knowledg of those other things which God hath by other means revealed.

The light of SCRIPTURES.

6. The way for us to come to know them is by the SCRIPTURES, wherein are set down those several commands of God which he hath given to be the Rule of our *Duty*.

7. Of those, some were given before *Christ* came into the world, such are those precepts we finde scattered throughout the *Old Testament,* but especially contained in the *Ten Commandements,* and that excellent book of *Deuteronomy*; others were given by *Christ,* who added much, both to the *Law* implanted in us by *Nature,* and that of the *Old Testament,* and those you shall find in the *New Testament,* in the several precepts given by him and his *Apostles,* but especially in that *Divine Sermon* on the Mount, set down in the fifth, sixth and seventh Chapters of *S. Matthews* Gospel.

Richard Allestree, *The Whole Duty of Man* (1659), pp. 1–3

To come now to the Reasons *that induced me to the* Translating *of This Little Book; I shall* Begin *with the* Excellency *of the* Work it Self; *which has ever been* Esteemed, *both for the* Method, *and* Matter *of it, as one of the most* Exact Pieces *of the Kind that ever was written, and the most* Instructive *of* Human Life. *In so much that* Cicero *himself valu'd himself upon This Tract of* Morals, *as his* Master-Piece; *and accordingly recommended the Study of it to his Beloved Son, under That Illustrious Character.* Secondly, *as it was Composed in a* Loose, *and* Troublesome Age, *so was it accommodated also to the Circumstances of Those Times; for the asserting of the* Force, *and* Efficacy *of* Virtue *against the utmost* Rigour, *and* Iniquity *of* Fortune. *Upon which Consideration likewise, I have now turn'd it into* English *with a regard to a* Place, *and* Season, *that extreamly* needs *it. I do not speak This, as if at any time it would have been* Superfluous; *but that* Desperate Diseases *require the most* Powerful Remedies.

To give you the Sum of it in a few Words; It is a Manual of Precepts *for the Government of our Selves, in all the Offices, Actions, and Conditions of Human Life; and tending, not only to the Comfort of Men in Society, but to the Conducting of* Particulars *also, into a State of* Felicity, *and* Virtue. *It is a Lesson that serves us from the very* Cradle, *to the* Grave. *It teaches us what we* Owe *to* Mankind; *to our* Country; *to our* Parents; *to our* Friends; *to our* Selves; *what we are to do as* Children; *what, as* Men; *what, as* Citizens: *It* sets, *and it* keeps *us* Right *in all the Duties of* Prudence, Moderation, Resolution, *and* Justice. *It Forms our* Manners; *Purges our* Affections; *enlightens our* Understandings; *and leads us, through the* Knowledge, *and the* Love *of* Virtue, *to the* Practice, *and* Habit *of it.*

This Treatise of Offices, *I find to be one of the Commonest* School-Books *that we have; and as it is the* Best *of* Books; *so it is apply'd to the* Best *of* Purposes; *that is to say, to the* Training up *of* Youth, *in the* Study *and* Exercise *of* Virtue. *The* Foundations *of an* Honorable, *and a* Blessed Life, *are laid in the very* Cradle; *and we suck in the* Tincture *of* Generous, *or* Perverse Inclinations, *even with* our Mothers Milk: *Insomuch that we may date the greater part of our greatest Miscarriages, from the* Errors, *and* Infelicities *of our* First Institution, *and* Education.

Roger L'Estrange, To the Reader, *Tully's Offices* (1680), no pag.

Conscience

Conscience was a topic of continued interest and reflection. Sanderson and Taylor wrote the two most important works on this point; each assumes a broadly Aristotelian psychology, with its firm belief that humanity can and therefore must be educated into virtue.

XVII. I do therefore thus state it. The Conscience *properly*, and *formally* and by a *direct predication* is a Habit, yet not withstanding it may be a *Potentia*,[1] and that two ways, first *materially*, because it is in the *Potentia* as in the Subject, that is to say *in which*; Secondly by *approximation*, for being placed as it were in the midst, betwixt *Habitum acquisitum*, and *puram potentiam* a Habit acquired, and a *pure potentia*, it can assume the name of either, as the *Mediums* do participate of either of the Extreams; And hereupon it is that Conscience is found in little Children, who are not capable of *acquired Habits*; Neither is it altogether necessary that the *mind*, and the *Conscience*, in *Tit.* 1. be contradistinct as *bare Potentia*'s, but it seems rather that both words are there taken by a *Synecdoche*; the *mind* for *the speculative Intellect with all its pertinences*, as the Schoolmen speak it, and the *Conscience* for the *practicall Intellect* with all its *pertinences*, that is, with all the *faculties*, *Habits*, and *Acts*, and what do respectively pertain to any of them.

XVIII. In the *Definition of Conscience*, I have placed the word *Faculty*, which in some measure doth seem to me to be common to the *Potentia*'s and *Habits*, and is very proper to signifie *Habits innate*. Peradventure you will object, that every *Habit* is acquired by often actings, and therefore this doth so appertain to the essence of a *Habit* that *Habits* are especially to be known from *Potentia*'s by it, as by a *specifical difference*, to wit, that the *Potentia*'s are acquired, and the *Habits* natural, therefore unless a man will maintain meet contradictions, he ought not to say that Conscience is a *Habit innate*. To this I answer, that it must be indeed confessed that all *Habits* whatsoever, both are, and ought to be called *acquired*, nay even those *Habits* which seem to be most *natural*, and for this cause, because they want the assistance of the *sences*, and many previous sensible actions that so the *Species* of things sensible (in respect whereof the Soul of it self is like a clear table-Book) may be conveyed into the Phantasy, and become at last intelligible; Neverthelesse some *Habits* may be called, and with great reason too *innate*, for as much as the mind by an *inbred-light* doth immediately give an assent to the thing propounded, without any fear of the *opposite* to it, only the *Apprehension of Terms* being supposed; neither to procure its assent, doth it want the helps of internal *study* of external *institution*. For example, *The Intellective Habit* of this Principle, *Omne totum est majus qualibet sui parte*, Every thing that is whole is greater

---

1 Potency. In Aristotelian thought, *potentia* refers to both the ability to acquire a skill and the ability to use a skill already acquired.

then any part of it, is a *Habit innate* so far as by the force of the light of Nature, and only out of the apprehension of the Terms, the truth thereof of its own accord doth enter into the mind, without any study or Teacher; And yet nevertheless this *Habit* is acquired, so far as it needeth the assistance of the sences, that so by *often actions* in sensible things, one may arrive unto the *knowledge of the Terms*, that is to say, what belongeth to the whole, and what unto the parts.

XIX. If it may be yet objected that the *Conscience* cannot be called an *Innate Habit*, for those things which are *Innate*, are not capable of errour, neither can they be defective, and they are the same in all, in whomsoever they are, but the *Conscience* can erre, and be evil, neither is it the same in all men, I make answer, that it doth indeed follow from this that the *Conscience* is not a *Habit simply innate* which no reasonable man will affirm, for it is repugnant to Nature, but as partly (as before mentioned) it is *innate*, so also it is partly *acquired*. The Soul of man doth bring with it as it were, some seeds of knowledge of *good*, and *evil*, which grow up and are perfected by *study* and *institution*; In the same manner, *natural agility* is compleated by *Exercise*, and *natural Logick*, by *Logick artificial*; the Conscience therefore in respect of those morall *Agibles*,[2] which as the School-men speak, are of the first *Dictates* of Nature, and are its *primary objects*, is a natural or an *innate Habit*, and is alike in all men, and is always *right*, without any *errour* or *depravation*; but in respect of those things which are afterwards learned and come close up unto those first principles, whether it be by an *internal* and *proper meditation*, or an *external institution*, it is a *Habit* acquired, and may be erronious, and defective.

Robert Sanderson, *Ten Lectures on the Obligation of Human Conscience* (1647), pp. 20–3

RULE III.

Be careful that prejudice or passion, fancy and affection, error or illusion, be not mistaken for Conscience.

. . .

2. But by this Rule it is intended that we should observe the strict measures of Conscience. For an illusion may make a Conscience, that

---

2 Things which can be done.

is, may oblige by its directive and compulsive power. Conscience is like a King whose power and authority is regular, whatsoever counsel he follows. And although he may command fond things, being abused by flatterers, or misinformation, yet the commandment issues from a just authority, and therefore equally passes into a law; so it is in Conscience. If error, or passion dictates, the King is mis-inform'd, but the inferiors are bound to obey; and we may no more disobey our Conscience commanding of evil things, than we may disobey our King injoyning things imprudent and inconvenient. But therefore this Rule gives caution to observe the information and inducement, and if we can discern the abuse, then the evil is avoided. For this Governor [*Conscience*] is tied to Laws, as Kings are to the Laws of God and Nations, to Justice and Charity; and a Man's Conscience cannot be malicious: his *Will* may, but if the error be discovered, *the Conscience*, that is, *the practical understanding* cannot. For it is impossible for a man to believe what himself finds to be an error: and when we perceive our Conscience to be misguided, the deception is at an end. And therefore to make up this Rule compleat, *we ought to be strict and united to our rule*, for by that only we can be guided, and by the proportions to it we can discern *right* and *wrong*, when we walk safely, & when we walk by false fires. Concerning which, besides the direct survey of the rule and action, and the comparing each other, we may in cases of doubt & suspicion be helped by the following measures.

Advices for the practice of the former Rule.

3. We are to suspect our Conscience to be mis-informed when we are not willing to enquire into the particulars. He that searches, desires to find, and so far takes the right course; for truth can never hurt a man, though it may prejudice his vice, and his affected folly. In the inquiries after truth, every man should have a travellers indifferency, wholly careless whether this or that be the right way, so he may find it. For we are not to choose the way because it looks fair, but because it leads surely. And to this purpose, the most hearty and particular inquest is most prudent and affective. But we are afraid of truth when we will not enquire, that is, when the truth is against our interest and passion, our lust or folly, that is, seemingly against us, in the present indisposition of our affairs.

4. He that resolves upon the conclusion before the premises, inquiring into particulars to confirm his opinion at aventures,[3] not to shake

---

3 An error, possibly deadly.

it if it be false, or to establish it only in case it be true, unless he be defended by chance, is sure to mistake, or at least can never be sure whether he does or no.

This is to be understood in all cases to be so unless the *particular unknown* be secured by a *general* that is *known*. He that believes Christs advocation and intercession for us in Heaven upon the stock of Scripture, cannot be prejudic'd by this rule, although in the inquiries of probation, and arguments of the doctrine, he resolve to believe nothing that shall make against his Conclusion; because he is ascertain'd by a proposition that cannot fail him. The reason of this exception is this, because in all discourses which are not perfectly demonstrative, there is one lame supporter, which must be help'd out by the better leg; and the weaker part does its office well enough, if it can bring us to a place where we may rest our selves and rely. He that cannot choose for himself, hath chosen well enough if he can choose one that can choose for him; and when he hath, he may prudently rely upon such a person in all particulars: where he himself cannot judge, and the other can, or he thinks he can, and cannot well know the contrary. It is easier to judge of the general lines of duty, than of minutes, and particulars: and Travellers that are not well skill'd in all the little turnings of the ways, may confidently rely upon a Guide whom they choose out of the natives of the place; and if he understands the coast of the Country, he may well harden his face against any vile Person that goes about wittily to perswade him he must go the contrary way, though he cannot answer his arguments to the contrary. A man may prudently and piously hold a conclusion which he cannot defend against a witty adversary, if he have one strong hold upon which he may rely for the whole question; because he derives his conclusion from the best ground he hath, and takes the wisest course he can, and uses the best means he can get, and chooses the safest ways that are in his power. No man is bound to do better than his best.

5. Illusion cannot be distinguished from the Conscience, if in our search we take a wrong course and use incompetent instruments. He that will choose to follow the multitude which easily erres rather than the wise Guides of souls; and a Man that is his partner in the Question rather than him that is dis-interess'd, and them that speak by chance, rather than them who have studied the Question, and a man of another Profession, rather than him whose office and imployment is to answer, hath no reason to be confident he shall be well instructed.

Jeremy Taylor, *Ductor Dubitantium, Or, The Rule of Conscience* (1660), pp. 20–2

Deification

Like the early Greek Fathers, Anglican divines understood deification as a gift of grace and as a moral imperative. To share in the divine life, one must imitate God. The deified life is an intentional life, an active pursuit which begins with moral goodness, thereby exceeding natural goodness while striving for divine goodness.

GOODNESS is a vertue of the first Estate, a Divine Perfection in GOD by which he is, and enjoys his Blessedness. In Men it is an Habit or an Act of the Soul, by force of which they Love, and delight in all that is Blessed. Tis that by which all Creatures Communicate themselves to others Benefit, all Living Creatures affect others, and delight in doing Good unto them. In GOD it is that infinite and Eternal Act from which all other Goodnesses spring, and on which they depend. The Nature of Goodness is founded in a *Convenience*, between that which is Good, and that to which it is profitable. If we consult its several Kinds, there is a *Natural* Goodness, a *Moral*, and a *Divine*.

NATURAL Goodness is the Aptitude of Corporeal Beings, to produce such profitable and healing Effects as the enjoyer desires. The Nutritive Power in Aliment, the Medicinal Vertue in Herbs, the Pleasing Quality in Perfumes, the Grateful Lustre in Precious Stones, the Comfortable Heat in fire, the Beautiful splendor in the Sun, the Refreshing Moisture in the Sea, the Reviving Nature of the Air, the solid Convenience and fertility of the Ground, all these are *Physically* Good. But this is Goodness in the meanest Degree, being no more then the natural fitness of Dead Agents that are made to act by a *Fatal* Necessity, without sence or Desire; tho their Action be answerable to the several Exigencies of other Creatures.

MORAL Goodness includeth all the Perfections of the former, and something more. For *Life* and *Liberty* enter its Existence; and it is *Wisely* exercised in *Love* and *Vertue*. A clear Understanding and a free will are the principles of those Actions that are *Morally* Good: they must flow from *Ingenuity* and *Desire*; tho the Person doing them be subject to anothers Empire, and made to give Account of his Actions. The Nature of its Excellence is very deep and retired, because it consists more in the *Principal* and *Manner* of its Operation, than the *Thing* that is *Done*; and is measured more by the *Intention*, then the *Benefit*. A mad man, or a fool, may by accident save a mans Life, or preserve an Empire, yet be far from that Goodness which is seated in the Will and Understanding. Which plainly shews, that the *Goodness* chiefly regarded is in the *Soul* of him that does any thing convenient, not in the *Benefit* received, but in the *Mind* of the Benefactor. And the Truth is that the *External Benefit*, tho it saves the Lives, and the Souls, and Estates, and Liberties, and Riches, and Pleasures, and Honors, of all mankind, acts but *Physically* by a Dead or passive Application, the root of its influence and value is seated in another place, in the Soul of him whose Goodness was so Great as to sacrifice his Honor, and Felicity for the Preservation and Welfare of those whom he *intended* to save. It is seated in the *Counsel* and *Design* of the Actor. It is a hard matter to define it, but it is something like *a willing Conformity to the Interests and Affections of his fellow Creatures*, attended with a voluntary Convenience in a person Obliged and subject to Laws, to all those Obligations that are laid upon him, & to all the Rewards that are set before him, but especially to the Desires and Commands of his Superior, to whom he Naturally owes himself and desires to be pleasing. To Act upon Great and Mighty Principles, in a vigorous free and Generous Manner, for the sake of those that obliged him, and for the sake of those to whom his Kindness is shewn, increases the *Measure* of Moral Goodness: but its Perfection is seated in a Loyal Respect, and Perfect Gratitude to GOD Almighty. Who, by being infinitely Good to us, has infused and created such a Goodness in the Soul, that its principal Joy and Delight is to please him. For tho all Creatures consult themselves & their own Preservation, yet the force of Gratitude upon an Ingenuous Soul is very powerful. Moral Goodness is an Alacrity and Readiness of the Will, to sacrifice it self, upon consideration of the Benefits a Man hath received, to anothers Benefit, Enjoyment, Comfort, Satisfaction.

DIVINE Goodness is an Active and Eternal Principle, stirring up it self without Obligation or reward, to the best and most excellent Things in an Eternal manner. It is proper only to GOD; Its Excellency is Supreme, its Beauty infinite, its Measure endless, its Nature ineffable, its Perfection unconceiveable. It hath no Cause, but it is the Cause of all other Things whatsoever. It is a *Living* and *Eternal Act* of free and undeserved Love, an indeficient Ocean of Bounty, which can never be fathomed, or (by finite Degrees be) wholy received. It is *Invisible* in its Essence, but *Apparent* in its effects; Incomprehensible, but manifest enough, to be *believed* and *adored*. It is an infinite and Eternal Essence, which is Good to it self, by being Good to all, infinitely Good to it self, by being without Bound or Measure Good to all its Objects. It is an infinite and Eternal Act, which continually ponders, and intirely intends the Welfare of others, and establishes its own (in a voluntary manner) by that intention: An Act whose Essence is seated in the Preparation of all Delights and the Communication of all its Glories. Its Felicity is

Eternal and Infinite, yet seated intirely in the Felicity of others. It doth infinite Good, to all its Recipients Meerly for the sake of the Excellency of the Act of *Doing Good*. It delighteth in the Excellency of that Act, and useth all its power in doing Good, that the Act in which it delighteth might be infinitely perfect. And the perfect Act in which it finally resteth is the Goodness which all adore and desire. Its Sovereign Joy and Pleasure, is to be delightful to others. All its Creatures are Delightful to it self, only as they imitate, and receive its Goodness. Should we run into its Properties, they are innumerable and Endless; but as infinite in Beauty, as variety and greatness. It is the utmost Height of all Goodness as well as the Original, and end of all. It exceedeth Moral Goodness, as much as that exceedeth Natural, and infinitely more. In Physical Goodness there is a Mechanical fitness, and Dead Convenience: but all it can pretend to, is the Benefit and Pleasure of Moral Agents. For the Sun and Moon, and Stars, and Trees, and Seas, and Minerals are made for Men. Whereas Moral Goodness is made to enjoy all Physical Goodness, that in a higher sphere it might be pleasing to GOD and is immediately subservient to his Divine & Essential Goodness.

. . .

TO be made Partaker of the Divine Nature, without having the Goodness of Almighty GOD is impossible. Nor can we enjoy his Goodness, or bear the similitude of his Glory, unless we are good in like Manner. We enjoy the Goodness of GOD, and may be said to have it, either when we have its *Similitude* in our selves, or the *Pleasure* of it in others. Since the Goodness of GOD is the great Object of our Joy, its Enlargment is our Interest; and the more there are to whom he is Good, and the more he communicates his Felicity to every one the Great Pleasures he prepares for us, and the more is our goodness therein delighted. To see innumerable Millions in Communion with him, and all of them made Glorious and Blessed, and every one seated in his throne, is the greatest Elevation of our Souls, and the highest Satisfaction in the World. When our Goodness meeteth his in all Places, and congratulates the Felicity of every person, we may then use the Words of our Saviour, because we are endued with the same *Mind* and Affection: And as he accepts all the Good that is done to his Members as done to himself, saying *Inasmuch as ye have done it to the least of these my Brethren, ye have done it to me.*[4] Our Souls will reply, *Inasmuch as thou hast*

---
4 Matthew 25.40.

done all this to the least of these my Brethren, thou hast done it to me, for loving our Neighbours as ourselves, all Angels and Men will be our fellow Members, our Brethren, our other selves! As we delight in all Acts of Goodness for their own sakes, that are done to us, so shall we delight in all the Bounties of GOD for theirs, who are the partakers of them, and in GOD for this very reason, *Because he is good to all*. We shall be as Happy in others, as in our selves; and Esteem the Goodness of GOD our Felicity, because it hath prevented[5] our Goodness, and done all for them, which were it undone, we should desire to do our selves, because our Goodness is a principle that carries us to delight in their perfect Felicity. Which that we may do the more Sweetly, and with more full Satisfaction and perfect Reason, his Goodness to all others is but the Perfection of Goodness to us, for they are all made Blessed for our fuller and greater Felicity.

Thomas Traherne, *Christian Ethicks: Or, Divine Morality* (1675), pp. 143–9, 152–4

Let us consider; That nothing is more conformable to Gods nature, or renders us more like to him, than beneficence and mercy; and that consequently nothing can be more grateful to him; that nothing is more disagreeable and contrary to the essential disposition of God, than illiberality and unmercifulness, and therefore that nothing can be more distasteful to him. What is any being in the world, but an efflux of his bounty, and an argument of his liberality? Look every where about Nature, consider the whole tenour of Providence; survey all the works, and scan all the actions of God, you will find them all conspiring in attestation to those sweet Characters and Elogies, which the holy Scripture ascribeth to God, representing him to be *Merciful and gracious, long-suffering, and abundant in goodness;*[6] to be *sorry for evil*,[7] (incident or inflicted upon any Creature) to *delight in mercy*,[8] to *wait that he may be gracious*;[9] stiling him the *God of love, of peace, of hope, of patience, of all grace, and of all consolation;*[10] *the Father of pities, rich in mercy, and full of bowels;*[11] affirming of him, and by manifold evident evidences demonstrating, that he is *benign even unto*

---

5 Come before.
6 [Exod. 34.6.]
7 [Joel 2.13.]
8 [Mic. 7.18.]
9 [Isai. 30.18.]
10 [Rom. 5.33. 13.5. Ephes. 2.4. 2 Cor. 13.11. 1.3.]
11 [Jam. 5.11. 1 Pet. 5.10.]

the ingrateful and evil;[12] that *He is good to all, and his tender mercies are over all his works.*[13] Nature, (I say) Providence and Revelation, do all concur in testifying this, that there is nothing in God so peculiarly admirable, nothing (as it were) so God-like; that is, so highly venerable and amiable, as to do good and shew mercy.[14] We therefore by liberal communication to the needy, do most approach to the nature of God, and most exactly imitate his practise;[15] acquiring to ourselves thereby somewhat of Divinity, and becoming little Gods to our Neighbour: *Nothing* (saith St. *Chrysostome*) *maketh us near equal to God, as beneficence*;[16] and, *Be* (saith St. *Gregory Nazianzen*) *a God to the unfortunate, imitating the mercy of God; for a man hath nothing of God so much as to do good.*[17] That such hath always been the common apprehension of men, the practice of all times sheweth, in that men have been ever apt to place their Benefactors among their Gods, deferring that love and veneration unto them in degree, which in perfection do appertain to the supreme Benefactor. *Be merciful, as your heavenly Father is merciful*;[18] so our Saviour proposeth Gods mercy to us, both as a pattern directing, and as an argument inducing us to mercifulness; implying it also to be a good sign declaring us the children of God; the genuine off-spring of the all-good and all-merciful Father; yea, that it even renders and constitutes us such, (we thereby coming most truly to represent, and most nearly to resemble him.) Our Lord farther teaches us, saying, *Love your enemies, bless them that curse you, do good to those that hate you – that you may be the sons of your Father which is in heaven.*[19] And they who thus are Gods children, must consequently be very dear to him, and most gracious in his sight; he cannot but greatly like and love himself (the best of himself) in them; he cannot but cherish and treat them well, who are the fairest and truest images of himself; no spectacle can be so pleasant to him, as to see us in our practise to act himself, doing good to one another; *as the elect of God, holy and beloved, putting on bowels of mercies and kindness, humbleness of mind, meekness, long-suffering; forbearing one another, and*

---

12 [Luk. 6.35.]
13 [Psal. 145.9.]
14 [Naz. Orat. 26.] cf. Micah 6.8.
15 [Plin. Nat. H. lib. 2.]
16 [Chrys. in Mat. Orat. 35.]
17 [Naz. Orat. 16.]
18 [Luk. 6.35, 36.]
19 [Matt. 5.44, 45.]

forgiving one another, even as Christ forgave us,[20] being *followers of God as dear children, and walking in love, even as Christ also loved us.*[21] But on the other side, there is not in Nature any thing so remotely distant from God, or so extreamly opposite to him, as a greedy and griping Niggard; Hell is scarce so contrary to Heaven, as such a mans disposition to the nature of God; for 'tis *goodness* which sits gloriously triumphant at the top of Heaven; and *uncharitableness* lieth miserably grovelling under the bottom of Hell: Heaven descends from the one, as its principal cause; Hell is built on the other, as its main foundation: as the one approximates the blessed Angels to God, and beatifies them; so the other removeth the cursed Fiends to such a distance from God and happiness: not to wish, not to do any good, is that which renders them both so bad, and so wretched; and whoever in his conditions is so like to them, and in his practise so agrees with them, cannot but also be very odious to God, and extreamly unhappy; God cannot but abhor so base a degeneration from his likeness in those, who by nature are his children, and should be farther such according to his gracious design; neither can any thing more offend his eyes, than seeing them to use one another unkindly: so that if obtaining the certain favour of the great God, with all the benefits attending it, seem considerable to us; or if we think it adviseable to shun his displeasure, with its sad effects; it concerns us to practice these duties.

Isaac Barrow, *The Duty and Reward of Bounty to the Poor* (1671), pp. 105–13

---

20 [Colos. 3.12.]
21 [Ephes. 5.1, 2.]

11

The Kingdom

The body politic

Peace, monarchy and law were themes central to every consideration of the state in the seventeenth century. Laud's sermon is a classic political application of biblical typology, while Charles I's discourse to his son partook of the long, Renaissance tradition of advice books for kings.

PSAL. 122. V. 3, 4, 5.

Jerusalem *is builded as a* Citie *that is at* unitie *in it selfe*, (or compacted together). *For thither the* Tribes *goe up, even the* Tribes *of the Lord, to the* Testimony of Israel, *to give thankes unto the Name of the Lord. For there are the* Seats (*or the* Thrones) *of Judgement; even the* Thrones *of the house of* David.

Some are of opinion this *Psalme* was made by *David*, and delivered to the Church to be sung, when the *Arke* of God was carried up to *Jerusalem*; when *Jerusalem* was setled by *David*, to bee the special Seate both of *Religion* and the *Kingdome*. The people were bound thrice a yeere, at *Easter*, *Pentecost*, and the *Feast of Tabernacles*, to come up and worship at *Jerusalem. Deut.* 16.[1] And some thinke this *Psalme* was prophetically made to sing by the way; to sing when they went up by the steps to the Temple. And t'was fit. For they came up with joy. And joy is apt to set men a singing. And at joy the Psalme begins. *I was glad when they said unto mee, We will goe into the house of the Lord.*[2]

But whatsoever the use of this *Psalme* was in any speciall Service, certaine it is, that *Jerusalem* stands here in the letter for the *Citie*, and in type and figure for the *State, and the Church of Christ*. My Text lookes upon both; and upon the duetie which the *Jewes* did then, and which *wee* now doe owe to both. The *Temple* the Type of the *Church*, that's

---

1 [*Deut.* 16.16.]
2 [Vers. 1.]

for God's service. No Temple but for that. The *Citie* the Type of the *State*, that's for the peoples peace. No happy *State* but in that.

Both the *Temple* and the *State*, *God's* house and the *Kings*, both, are built upon *Pillars*. And it is not long since I told you out of *Psalm*. 75.[3] that there are many times of exigence, in which if God doe not beare up the *Pillars*, no strength which the *Pillars* have in and of themselves can support the weight that lies upon them: Be they *Pillars* of the *Temple*; or *Pillars* of the *State*. Therefore here to ease the *Pillars* God hath built up *Buttresses* (if men doe not pull them downe) to stay the maine walles of both buildings. The *Buttresse* and support of the *Temple* is *Religion*. God will not blesse the house, if men doe not honour and serve him in it. The *Buttresse* and stay of the *Kingdome* is *Justice*. God will not blesse the State, if *Kings* and Magistrates doe not execute judgement; If the widdow and the fatherlesse have cause to crie out against the Thrones of Justice.

So the *Church*, and the *Commonwealth*, *Gods* house, the Temple, and the *Kings* house, the house of *David*, are met in my Text. And they would ever meet, and in love no question, did not some distempered spirits breathe sour upon them. For the *Church* cannot dwell but in the *State*. Ye never read that she fled out of the State into the wildernesse, but when some *Dragon* persecuted her. *Revel*. 12.[4] And the *Commonwealth* cannot flourish without the *Church*. For where the Church is not to teach true Religion, States are enforced, out of necessitie of some, to imbrace a false. And a false is not a helpe to make a Kingdome flourish. But when they dwell together; when the Church, the *House of Grace* is a welcome inmate to the State, which is a *wise fabricke of Nature*; then in the Temple there's meeting: The people go up to blesse, and praise the Name of the Lord. And then in the State there's meeting: To settle the Thrones of Judgement, to make firme the house of *David*. And then, and never but then, *Jerusalem*, that is, both State and Church *is as a Citie that is at unitie in it selfe.*

William Laud, First Sermon (1625), pp. 1–5

XXVII. *To the Prince of Wales.*

I had rather You should be *Charls le bon*, than *le Grand*, Good, than Great; I hope God hath designed You to be both, having so early put You into that exercise of his Graces, and Gifts bestowed upon You, which may best weed out all vicious inclinations, and dispose You to

---

3 [*Psalm*. 75.4.]
4 [Apoc. 12.6.]

those Princely endowments, and employments which will most gain the love, and intend the welfare of those, over whom God shall place you.

With God I would have You begin and end, who is King of Kings; the Soveraign Disposer of the Kingdoms of the world, who pulleth down one, and setteth up another.

The best Government, and highest Soveraignty You can attain to, is, to be subject to him, that the Sceptre of his Word and Spirit may rule in Your heart.

The true glory of Princes consists in advancing Gods glory in the maintenance of true Religion, and the Churches good; also in the dispensation of Civil Power, with Justice and Honour to the Publique Peace.

Piety will make You prosperous; at least it will keep You from being miserable; nor is he much a loser, that loseth all, yet saveth his own soul at last.

To which Center of true happiness, God (I trust) hath, and will graciously direct all these black lines of affliction, which he hath been pleased to draw on Me, and by which he hath (I hope) drawn Me nearer to himself. You have already tasted of that Cup, whereof I have liberally drank, which I look upon as Gods physic, having that in healthfulness which it wants in pleasure.

Above all, I would have You, as I hope you are already, well-grounded and setled in Your Religion: The best profession of which, I have ever esteemed that of *the Church of England*, in which You have been educated; yet I would have Your own Judgement and Reason now seal to that sacred Bond, which education hath written, that it may be judiciously Your own Religion, and not other mens custom or tradition, which You profess.

In this I charge You to persevere, as coming nearest to Gods Word for Doctrine, and to the Primitive examples for Government,[5] with some little amendment, which I have otherwhere expressed, and often offered, though in vain. Your fixation in matters of Religion, will not be not more necessary for Your Soul's, than Your Kingdoms Peace, when God shall bring You to them.

For I have observed, that the Devil of Rebellion, doth commonly turn himself into an Angel of Reformation, and the old Serpent can pretend new Lights: When some mens Consciences accuse them for Sedition and Faction, they stop its mouth with the name and noise of Religion; when Piety pleads for peace and patience, they cry out Zeal.

So that, unless in this point You be well setled, You shall never want temptations to destroy You and Yours, under pretensions of Reforming

---

5 Episcopacy.

matters of Religion; for that seems, even to worst men, as the best and most auspicious beginning of their worst designs.

Charles I, *Eikon Basilike* (1649), in *Reliquae Sacrae Carolinae* (1650), Part II, pp. 210–12

Against fatalism

Due in large part to the experience of civil war, Anglicans became convinced that fatalism, whether theological, philosophical or scientific, led to immorality and, above all, to violence. The freedom of the individual was located in their reason, which could be educated with Christian principles. Theological rationalism is a bright line of conviction here.

For the interest of the republique, and the well being of bodies politick is not to depend upon the nicety of our imaginations, or the fancies of any peevish or mistaken Priests, and there is no reason a Prince should ask *John-a-Brunck*,[6] whether his understanding will give him leave to raign, and be a King: Nay, suppose there were divers places of Scripture which did seemingly restraine the Politicall use of the Sword, yet since the avoyding a personall inconvenience, hath by all men been accounted sufficient reason to expound Scripture to any sense rather then the literall, which inferres an unreasonable inconvenience, (and therefore the *pulling out of an eye, and the cutting off a hand*, is expounded by mortifying a vice, and killing a criminall habit) much rather must the Allegations against the power of the Sword endure any sence rather then it should be thought that Christianity should destroy that which is the only instrument of Justice, the restraint of vice and support of bodies politick. It is certain that Christ and his Apostles, and Christian Religion did comply with the most absolute Government, and the most imperiall that was then in the world; and it could not have been at all indured in the world if it had not; for indeed the world it selfe could not last in regular and orderly communities of men, but be a perpetuall confusion, if Princes and the Supreme Power in Bodies Politick, were not armed with a coercive power to punish Malefactors: The publike necessity and universall experience of all the world convinces those men of being most unreasonable, that make such pretences which destroy all Lawes, and all Communities, and the bands of civill

---

6 This is most likely a nonsense name, equivalent to 'John Doe'. It is unique to this particular work by Taylor.

Societies, and leave it arbitrary to every vaine or vitious person whether men shall be safe, or Lawes be established, or a Murderer hang'd, or Princes Rule. So that in this case men are not so much to Dispute with particular Arguments, as to consider the Interest and concernment of Kingdomes and Publick Societies: For the Religion of Jesus Christ is the best establisher of the felicity of private persons, and of publick Communities; it is a Religion that is prudent and innocent, humane, and reasonable, and brought infinite advantages to mankind, but no inconvenience, nothing that is unnaturall, or unsociable, or unjust. And if it be certain that this world cannot be governed without Lawes, and Lawes without a compulsory signifie nothing, then it is certain, that it is no good Religion that teaches Doctrine whose consequents will destroy all Government; and therefore it is as much to be rooted out, as any thing that is the greatest pest and nuisance to the publick interest: And that we may guesse at the purposes of the men, and the inconvenience of such Doctrine; these men that did first intend by their Doctrine to disarme all Princes, and bodies Politick, did themselves take up armes to establish their wild, and impious fancie; and indeed that Prince or Common-wealth that should be perswaded by them, would be exposed to all the insolencies of forraigners, and all mutinies of the teachers themselves, and the Governours of the people could not doe that duty they owe to their people of protecting them from the rapine and malice which will be in the world as long as the world is. And therefore, here they are to be restrained from preaching such Doctrine, if they mean to preserve their Government, and the necessity of the thing will justifie the lawfulnesse of the thing: If they think it to themselves, that cannot be helped; so long it is innocent as much as concernes the Publick; but if they preach it, they may be accounted Authors of all the consequent inconveniences, and punisht accordingly: *No Doctrine that destroyes Government is to be endured*; For although those Doctrines are not alwayes good that serve the private ends of Princes, or the secret designes of State, which by reason of some accidents or imperfections of men may be promoted by that which is false and pretending, yet no Doctrine can be good that does not comply with the formality of Government it selfe, and the well being of bodies Politick.

Jeremy Taylor, *A Discourse of the Liberty of Prophesying* (1647), pp. 246–8

But his[7] greatest errour is that which I touched before, to make Justice to be the proper result of Power. Power doth not measure and

---

7 Thomas Hobbes, identified by his initials *T. H.* in what follows.

regulate Justice, but Justice measures and regulates Power. The will of God, and the eternal Law which is in God himself, is properly the rule and measure of Justice. As all goodness whether Natural or Moral, is a participation of Divine goodness, and all created rectitude is but a participation of Divine rectitude, so all Laws are but participations of the eternal Law, from whence they derive their Power. The rule of Justice then is the same both in God and us, but it is in God, as in him that doth regulate and measure; in us, as in those who are regulated and measured. As the will of God is immutable, always willing what is just and right and good; So his justice likewise is immutable. And that individual action which is justly punished as sinful in us, cannot possibly proceed from the special influence and determinative power of a just cause. See then how grossly T. H. doth understand that old and true principle, that *the will of God is the rule of justice*, as if by willing things in themselves unjust, he did render them just, by reason of his absolute dominion and irresistible power. As fire doth assimilate other things to it self, and convert them into the nature of fire. This were to make the eternal Law a *Lesbian* rule.[8] Sin is defined to be *that which is done, or said, or thought contrary to the eternal Law*. But by this doctrine[9] nothing is done, nor said, nor thought contrary to the will of God. St. *Anselm* said most truly, *then the will of man is good and just and right, when he wills that which God would have him to will*: but according to this Doctrine every man always wills that which God would have him to will. If this be true, we need not pray, *Thy will be done in earth as it is in Heaven*: T. H. hath devised a new kind of Heaven upon Earth. The worst is, it is an Heaven without Justice. Justice is a constant and perpetual act of the will, to give every one his own; but to inflict punishment for those things which the Judge himself did determine and necessitate to be done, is not to give every one his own; right punitive Justice is a relation of equality and proportion, between the demerit and the punishment; but supposing this opinion of absolute and universal necessity, there is no demerit in the World. We used to say, that right springs from Law and fact, as in this Syllogism, every Thief ought to be punished, there's the Law; but such an one is a Thief, there's the fact, therefore he ought to be punished, there is right. But this opinion of T. H. grounds the right to be punished, neither upon Law, nor upon Fact, but upon the irresistible power of God. Yea, it overturneth as much as in it lies all Law; First, the eternal Law, which is the

---

8 Not a reference to sexuality, but a shifting standard.
9 Hobbesian fatalism.

Ordination of Divine Wisdom, by which all creatures are directed to that end which is convenient for them. That is, not to necessitate them to eternal flames. Then, the Law participated, which is the Ordination of right reason, instituted for the common good, to shew unto man, what he ought to do, and what he ought not to do. To what purpose is it to shew the right way to him, who is drawn and held a contrary way by Adamantine bonds of inevitable necessity?

> John Bramhall, *A Vindication of True Liberty* (1655), in *Works* (1676), pp. 675–6

1 COR. 10.13.

There hath no Temptation taken you, but such as is common to man: but God is faithful, who will not suffer you to be tempted above that ye are able; but will with the Temptation also make a way to escape, that you may be able to bear it.

And thus, I hope, I have said enough to confirm and illustrate this great Truth, having prov'd it both by *Authority* and *Reason*; and charg'd the contrary error (or Blasphemy shall I say) with such absur'd and damnable Consequences, as may justly make any Man, that is not desperate, both asham'd and afraid to assert it in the presence of God, and reasonable Men. But we live (*God knows*) in a Nation and Age, wherein Sin and Nonsense are Presumptuous, and wherein 'tis long since become fashionable and gentile to question Principles, and deny all those fundamental Truths of natural and revealed Divinity, which neither *Heathens* nor *Christians* ever Questioned before. This is the reason, why Divines, whom God hath set for the service and defence of the Gospel, have of late been fain to lay the Foundations again, and Preach up such Doctrins as sober Men, not acquainted enough with the iniquity of the Times, have judged at first hearing, to need no proof: Such as the *being and providence of God, the immortality of the Soul,* and *the necessity of good works*; to which I may add the Subject of this Discourse, which hath been to prove, that no Temptations which God suffers to fall upon *Christians* are irresistible, or that no thinking, circumspect, vigilant Man, that's true to his own Reason, and careful to make use of the promised assistance of God, can be over-matched by any Trial, though never so sharp, nor meet with any Temptation too strong to be withstood, how delightful or charming soever it be.

And this Doctrin being proved by so many undeniable *experiments*, and *reasons*, I hope may be sufficient to demonstrate the Folly, and chastise the Insolence and Impiety of those Prophane Men, who, because they have enslaved themselves to their own Passions, affect to make Man like a Beast, (that is, like themselves) all Sense and Appetite, and represent him as determin'd in all his actions by outward objects, and unable to moderate his Lusts, and Fears. But had these Men but common Reverence for God, or Man, they would not so Libel the Nature of the latter, which is the workmanship of the former; they would be more modest and civil, than to define Humane Nature by their own Corruptions, or pretend to judge of the Thoughts, Actions, and Inclinations of all other men by their own; they would be more considerate and reserv'd, and not take a Pride to maintain and propagate an Opinion which is chargeable with such foul and absurd conclusions, and which shews them to be an inconsiderate sort of Men, that Think little, and Talk much, and makes them obnoxious to that dreadful curse pronounced by the Prophet against those, that *call good evil, and evil good; that put light for darkness, and darkness for light; that put bitter for sweet, and sweet for bitter.*[10]

'Twould be very seasonable for these Licentious Times, that such Blasphemers Tongues were restrained by severe Laws, that they might only discourse these, and their other pernicious Doctrins in their own *Cabals*, and not dare to divulge them, and corrupt and trouble the company of civil, and sober Men, with such damnable confident talk. But since these Mens Tongues are their own, and in this great defect of Civil and Ecclesiastical Censures, they take the liberty to speak of God and Man as they please, 'tis more necessary that they should be rebuk'd, and their horrid Opinions expos'd and confuted in the Pulpit, lest their Devilish Doctrin should spread, and corrupt the World like a Canker, while the Ministers of the Gospel hold their Peace.

As for this Opinion, it divests Man, as you have heard, of his better part, *viz.* his free and rational Nature, wherein the Image of God consists; it proves all Laws and Orders of Societies to be useless, insignificant, and unnatural Institutions; and so makes the Legislative Power, whether invested in God, or the King, to be Tyranny and Violence; and Men that live under Government to be worse Slaves, than the Children of *Israel* in *Ægypt*, where they were commanded make *Brick, when they had no Straw.*[11] It contradicts the Doctrinal and Historical parts of Scripture, and with unparallel'd Impudence, gives the Lie to the *Martyrologies* both of the *Jewish* and *Christian* Church. It contradicts the

---

10 Isaiah 5.20.
11 Exodus 5.16.

Definitions of Virtue and Grace; in particular, it makes *Fortitude, Temperance, Self-denial, Patience, Sobriety, Chastity*, and all other infus'd and acquir'd Habits of resisting Sin, to be idle Fictitious notions; and so makes all the Divines and Philosophers that have ever been, to have been Imposters or Fools. Furthermore, it is inconsistent with the Doctrin of Repentance, and destroys the Goodness and Wisdom of God, who, upon the supposition that the Scriptures are true, hath exhorted his People to the practice of such Duties, which he knew before, they could not do. To conclude, it overthrows the Catholick Hypothesis of assisting Grace, dissolves the Obligation of our Sacramental Vows, disarms Hell of the most exquisit part of its Torments, and confounds the notion of Good and Evil, by making it Lawful, in supposing it sometimes necessary for all Men to commit the most heinous Sins. All which absurd and detestable Consequences, I hope, you now hear with *Christian* Indignation, and will remember hereafter with horrour and disdain, when ever you shall hear these sensual Men, like those that were sent to spy out the Holy Land, represent themselves and their Brethren, as *Grasshoppers*; but their Spiritual Adversaries, the Temptors and Temptations with which they ought to conflict, as insuperable *Anakims*, as enemies of a prodigious stature, greater, and taller, and stronger than themselves.[12] But these are usually Men, that have *turn'd the grace of God into lasciviousness, whose glory is their shame, whose God is their belly, who mind earthly things*.[13] And because they have debauch'd themselves into Brute Beasts, or at least have a mind to do so, therefore (as St. *Jude* Speaks) they *foam out their shame*[14] and infidelity in slandering the rational nature of Man, exploding the Doctrin of assisting Grace, Drolling upon Godly Men, and discrediting, as much as they can, the Authority of the Gospel, because it thwarts their Lusts, and disturbs their sensual repose, by Teaching, that men by the grace of God have power to *overcome the World, resist the Devil*, and *deny all ungodliness and worldly Lusts*;[15] and because it exhorts Men in Gods name to be *patient, vigilant,* and *stedfast*; to be *sober, temperate,* and *chaste*; to *fight the good fight*; to *finish the course*; and *persevere unto the end.*[16] Lastly, because it assures us that God assists us in all our Spiritual Combats, supports us in all our Trials, and will make us

---

12 Numbers 13.32–33.
13 Philippians 3.19.
14 Jude 1.13.
15 Titus 2.12.
16 Matthew 24.13.

more than Conquerours through Christ that loveth us; nay, *that Christ himself, who hath suffered and been tempted, is able to succor them that are tempted;*[17] and that no Temptation hath taken us, but such as is moderate and common to Man; because God is faithful to his Promises, and will not suffer us to be Tempted above our strength, but will with the Temptation make a gracious way to escape, that we may be able to bear it.

>George Hickes, *A Discourse to Prove that the Strongest Temptations are Conquerable by Christians* (1677), pp. 29–34

---

17 Hebrews 2.18.

12

The Church

Churches

The Church of England defined itself in relation to Roman Catholics, the reformed churches (both Lutheran and Reformed) in Europe and Separatists in England. Self-definition, as the following readings show, oscillated between the positive and the polemical.

Now, one Thing *more let me be bold to Observe to* Your Majesty *in particular, concerning Your Great Charge, the* Church of England. *'Tis in a hard Condition. Shee professes the* Ancient Catholike Faith; *And yet the* Romanist *condemnes Her of* Novelty in her Doctrine. *Shee practices* Church Government, *as it hath beene in use in all* Ages, *and all* Places, *where the* Church of Christ *hath taken any Rooting, both in, and ever since the* Apostles Times; *And yet the* Separatist *condemnes Her for* Antichristianisme *in her Discipline. The plaine truth is, She is between these two Factions, as betweene two* Milstones, *and unlesse* Your Majesty *looke to it, to* Whose Trust *She is committed, Shee'll be grownd to* powder, *to an irrepairable both Dishonour, and losse to this* Kingdome. *And 'tis very Remarkeable, that while both these presse hard upon the* Church of England, *both of them Crye out upon* Persecution, *like froward Children, which scratch, and kicke, and bite, and yet crye out all the while, as if themselves were killed. Now to the* Romanist *I shall say this; The* Errors *of the* Church of Rome *are growne now (many of them) very* Old. *And when* Errors *are growne by Age, and Continuance to* strength, *they which speake for the* Truth, *though it be farre* Older, *are ordinarily challenged for the Bringers in of* New Opinions. *And there is no* Greater Absurdity *stirring this day in* Christendome *then that the* Reformation of an Old Corrupted Church, *will we, nill wee, must be taken for the* Building of a New. *And were not this so, we should never be troubled with that idle and impertinent* Question *of theirs:* Where was your Church before *Luther? For it was just there, where their's is now.*[1] *One, and the* same *Church still, no doubt of that.* One in Substance, *but not one in* Condition of state and purity; *Their part of the same Church remaining* in Corruption: *and Our part of the same Church under* Reformation. *The same* Naaman, *and he a* Syrian *still, but* Leprous *with them, and* Cleansed *with us; The same man still.*[2] *And for the* Seperatist, *and him that layes his* Grounds *for* Separation *or* Change of Discipline, *though all hee sayes, or can say, be in* Truth *of* Divinity, *and among* Learned Men *little better then ridiculous: yet since these* fond Opinions *have gain'd some ground among your people; to such among them as are* wilfully *set to follow their blinde Guides, through thicke and thin, till* [3]*they fall into the Ditch together, I shall say nothing. But for so many of them, as meane well, and are onely* misled by Artifice and Cunning; *Concerning them, I shall say thus much only.* They are Bells *of passing good* mettle, *and tuneable enough of themselves, and in their owne disposition; and a world of pity it is, that they are* Rung *so miserably out of* Tune, *as they are, by them which have gotten power in and over their* Consciences. *And for this there is yet* Remedy *enough; but how long there will bee, I know not.*

Much talking *there is (*Bragging, Your Majesty *may call it) on both sides. And when they are in their* ruffe, *they both exceed all* Moderation, *and* Truth *too; So farre till both* Lips *and* Penns *open for all the World like a* Purse without money; *Nothing comes out of this, and that which is worth nothing out of them. And yet this* nothing *is made so great, as if the* Salvation of Soules *that Great worke of the* Redeemer of the World, the Sonne of God, *could not be effected without it. And while the one faction cryes up the* Church *above the* Scripture: *and the other the* Scripture *to the neglect and* Contempt *of the* Church, *which the* Scripture *it selfe teaches men both to* honour, *and* obey: *They have so farre endangered the* Beliefe *of the One, and the* Authority *of the Other, as that neither hath its* Due *from a great part of Men. Whereas according to* Christs Institution, *The* Scripture, *where 'tis plaine, should guide the* Church: *and the* Church, *where there's Doubt or Difficulty,*

---

1 [There is no other difference betweene Us & *Rome,* then betwixt a Church miserably corrupted, and happily purged. &c. *Jos. Hall. B.* of *Exon.* In his Apologeticall Advertisement to the Reader. *p.* 192. Approved by *Tho. Morton. B.* then of *Cov. & Lich.* now of *Duresme.* in the Letters printed by the *B.* of *Exeter.* in his Treatise called, The Reconciler. *p.* 68 And *D. Field.* In his Appen. to the third *part. c.*2. where he cites Calv. to the same purpose *L.*4. *Inst. c.*2. §.11.]
2 2 Kings 5.1–14.
3 [S. Matth. 15.14.]

The Church

should expound the Scripture; *Yet so, as neither the* Scripture *should be forced, nor the* Church *so bound up, as that upon* Just *and farther* Evidence, Shee *may not revise that which in any* Case *hath slipt by Her. What Successe this* Great Distemper, *caused by the* Collision *of two such* Factions, *may have, I know not, I cannot* Prophesie. *This I know, That the use which* Wise men *should make of other mens falles, is not to fall with them; And the use, which* Pious and Religious men *should make of these great* Flawes in Christianity, *is not to* Joyne *with them that make them, nor to helpe to dislocate those maine* Bones *in the* Body, *which being once put out of* Joynt, *will not be easily set againe. And though I cannot* Prophesie, *yet I feare That* Atheisme, *and* Irreligion *gather strength, while the* Truth *is thus weakned by an* Unworthy *way of* Contending *for it. And while they thus* Contend, *neither part* Consider, *that they are in a way, to induce upon themselves, and others, that* Contrary Extreame, *which they seeme most both to* feare, *and* oppose.

Besides: *This I have ever Observed, That many* Rigid Professors *have turn'd* Roman Catholikes, *and in that Turne have beene* more Jesuited *then any other: and such* Romanists *as have chang'd from them, have for the most part quite leaped over the* Meane, *and beene as* Rigid *the other way as* Extremity *itself. And this, if there be not both* Grace, *and* Wisdome *to governe it, is a very* Naturall Motion. *For a Man is apt to thinke he can never runne farre enough from that, which he once begins to hate; And doth not Consider therewhile, That where* Religion Corrupted *is the thing he hates, a* Fallacy *may easily be put upon him. For he ought to hate the* Corruption *which depraves* Religion, *and to runne from* it; *but from* no part of Religion *it selfe, which he ought to Love, and Reverence, ought hee to depart. And this I have* Observed *farther: That no* One thing hath made Conscientious men *more wavering in their owne mindes, or more apt, and easie to be drawne aside from the sincerity of* Religion professed in the Church of England, *then the* Want of Uniforme *and* Decent Order *in too many Churches of the* Kingdome. *And the* Romanists *have beene apt to say,* The Houses of God *could not be suffer'd to lie so* Nastily *(as in some places they have done) were the* True worship of God *observed in them: Or did the People thinke that such it were. 'Tis true, the* Inward Worship *of the Heart, is the* Great Service of God, *and no Service acceptable without it: But the* Externall worship of God *in his Church is the* Great Witnesse *to the World, that Our heart stands right in that Service of God. Take this away, or bring it into Contempt, and* what Light is there left to shine before men, that they may see our Devotion, and glorifie our Father which is in Heaven? *And to deale clearely with Your Majesty, These Thoughts are they, and no other, which have made me labour so much, as I have done, for Decency and an Orderly settlement of the Externall Worship of God in the Church. For of that which is Inward there can be no Witnesse among men, nor no Example for men. Now no Externall Action in the world can be Uniforme without some Ceremonies. And these in Religion, the Ancienter they bee, the better, so they may fit Time and Place. Too many Over-burden the Service of God; And too few leave it naked. And scarce any Thing hath hurt Religion more in these broken Times, than an Opinion in too many men, That because Rome had thrust some Unnecessary, and many Superstitious Ceremonies upon the Church, therefore the Reformation must have none at all; Not considering therewhile, That Ceremonies are the Hedge that fence the Substance of Religion from all the Indignities, which Prophanenesse and Sacriledge too Commonly put upon it. And a Great Weaknesse it is, not to see the strength which Ceremonies (Things weake enough in themselves, God knowes) adde even to Religion it selfe; But a farre greater to see it, and yet to Cry Them downe, all, and without Choyce, by which their most hated Adversaries climb'd up, and could not crie up themselves, and their cause, as they doe, but by them. And Divines of all the rest might learne, and teach this Wisdome if they would, since they see all other Professions*[4], *which helpe to beare downe their Ceremonies, keepe up their owne therewhile, and that to the highest.*

William Laud, Dedicatory Epistle to Charles I, *The Conference with Fisher the Jesuite* (1639), no pag.

The differences, in the chief points of religion, between the Roman Catholics and us of the Church of England; together with the agreements, which we for our parts profess, and are ready to embrace, if they for theirs were as ready to accord with us in the same.

The Differences.

We that profess the Catholic Faith and Religion in the Church of England do not agree with the Roman Catholics in any thing whereunto they now endeavor to convert us. But we totally differ from them (as they do from the ancient Catholic Church) in these points:

1. That the Church of Rome is the mother and mistress of all other Churches in the world:

---

4 Christian professions, which we now term denominations.

2. That the Pope of Rome is the vicar-general of Christ; or that he hath an universal jurisdiction over all Christians that shall be saved:

3. That either the synod of Trent was a general council, or that all the canons thereof are to be received as matters of Catholic Faith under pain of damnation:

4. That Christ hath instituted seven true and proper Sacraments in the New Testament, neither more nor less, all conferring grace, and all necessary to salvation:

5. That the Priests offer up our Saviour in the mass, as a real, proper, and propitiatory sacrifice for the quick and the dead; and that whosoever believes it not is eternally damned:

6. That, in the Sacrament of the Eucharist, the whole substance of bread is converted into the substance of Christ's Body, and the whole substance of wine into His Blood, so truly and properly, as that after consecration there is neither any bread nor wine remaining there; which they call transubstantiation, and impose upon all persons under pain of damnation to be believed:

7. That the communion under one kind is sufficient and lawful, (notwithstanding the institution of Christ under both;) and that whosoever believes or holds otherwise is damned:

8. That there is a purgatory after this life, wherein the souls of the dead are punished, and from whence they are fetched out by the prayers and offerings of the living; and that there is no salvation possibly to be had by any that will not believe as much:

9. That all the old saints departed, and all those dead men and women, whom the Pope hath of late canonized for saints, or shall hereafter do so, whosoever they be, are and ought to be invocated by the religious prayers and devotions of all persons; and that they who do not believe this as an article of the Catholic Faith cannot be saved:

10. That the relics of all these true or reputed saints ought to be religious worshipped; and that whosoever holdeth the contrary is damned:

11. That the images of Christ, and the blessed Virgin, and of the other saints, ought not only to be had and retained, but likewise to be honoured and worshipped, according to the use and practices of the Roman Church; and that this is to be believed as of necessity to salvation:

12. That the power and use of indulgences, as they are now practised in the Church of Rome, both for the living and the dead, is to be received and held of all, under pain of eternal perdition:

13. That all the ceremonies used by the Roman Church in the administration of the Sacraments, (such as are spittle and salt at Baptism, the five crosses upon the Altar and Sacrament of the Eucharist, the holding of that Sacrament over the Priest's head to be adored, the exposing of it in their churches to be worshipped by the people, the circumgestation and carrying of it abroad in procession upon their Corpus Christi day, and to their sick for the same, the oil and chrism in confirmation, the anointing of the ears, the eyes, and noses, the hands, and reins,[5] of those that are ready to die, the giving of an empty chalice and paten to them that are to be ordained Priests, and many others of this nature now in use with them,) are of necessity to salvation, to be approved and admitted by all other churches:

14. That all the ecclesiastical observations and constitutions of the same Church, (such as are their laws of forbidding all Priests to marry, the appointing several orders of monks, friars, and nuns, in the Church, the service of God in an unknown tongue, the saying of a number of Ave-Marias by tale upon their chaplets, the sprinkling of themselves and the dead bodies with holy water, as operative and effectual to the remission of venial sins, the distinctions of meats to be held for true fasting, the religious consecration and incensing of images, the baptizing of bells, the dedicating of divers holidays for the immaculate conception and the bodily assumption of the blessed Virgin, and for Corpus Christi or transubstantiation in the Sacrament, the making of the Apocryphal books to be as canonical as any of the rest of the holy and undoubted Scriptures, the keeping of those Scriptures from the free use and reading of the people, the approving of their own Latin translation only, and divers other matters of the like nature,) are to be approved, held, and believed, as needful for salvation; and that whoever approves them not is out of the Catholic Church, and must be damned:

All which, in their several respects, we hold, some to be pernicious, some unnecessary, many false, and many fond, and none of them to be imposed upon any Church, or any Christian, as the Roman Catholics do upon all Christians and all Churches whatsoever, for matters needful to be approved for eternal salvation.

Our Agreements.

If the Roman Catholics would make the essence of their Church (as we do ours) to consist in these following points, we are at accord with them in the reception and believing of:

---

5 Other relevant parts of the body.

1. All the two and twenty canonical books of the Old Testament, and the twenty-seven of the New, as the only foundation and perfect rule of our faith:

2. All the apostolical and ancient Creeds, especially those which are commonly called the Apostles' Creed, the Nicene Creed, and the Creed of S. Athanasius; all which are clearly deduced out of the Scriptures:

3. All the Decrees of faith and doctrine set forth, as well in the first four general councils, as in all other councils, which those first four approved and confirmed, and in the fifth and sixth general councils besides, (than which we find no more to be general,) and in all the following councils that be thereunto agreeable, and in all the anathemas and condemnations given out by those councils against heretics, for the defence of the Catholic Faith:

4. The unanimous and general consent of the ancient Catholic Fathers and the universal Church of Christ in the interpretation of the Holy Scriptures, and the collection of all necessary matters of Faith from them during the first six hundred years, and downwards to our own days:

5. In acknowledgment of the Bishop of Rome, if he would rule and be ruled by the ancient canons of the Church, to be the Patriarch of the West, by right of ecclesiastical and imperial constitution, in such places where the kings and governors of those places had received him, and found it behooveful for them to make use of his jurisdiction, without any necessary dependence upon him by divine right:

6. In the reception and use of the two blessed Sacraments of our Savior; in the confirmation of those persons that are to be strengthened in their Christian Faith, by prayer and imposition of hands, according to the examples of the holy Apostles and ancient Bishops of the Catholic Church; in the public and solemn benediction of persons that are to be joined together in holy matrimony; in public or private absolution of penitent sinners; in the consecrating of Bishops, and the ordaining of Priests and Deacons, for the service of God in His Church by a lawful succession; and in visiting the sick, by praying for them, and administering the blessed Sacrament to them, together with a final absolution of them from their repented sins:

7. In commemorating at the Eucharist the Sacrifice of Christ's Body and Blood once truly offered for us:

8. In acknowledging His sacramental, spiritual, true, and real Presence there to the souls of all them that come faithfully and devoutly to receive Him according to His own institution in that holy Sacrament:

9. In giving thanks to God for them that are departed out of this life in the true Faith of Christ's Catholic Church; and in praying to God, that they may have a joyful resurrection, and a perfect consummation of bliss, both in their bodies and souls, in His eternal kingdom of glory:

10. In the historical and moderate use of painted and true stories, either for memory or ornament, where there is no danger to have them abused or worshipped with religious honour:

11. In the use of indulgences, or abating the rigour of the canons imposed upon offenders, according to their repentance, and their want of ability to undergo them:

12. In the administration of the two Sacraments, and other rites of the Church, with ceremonies of decency and order, according to the precept of the Apostle, and the free practice of the ancient Christians:

13. In observing such holy days, and times of fasting, as were in use in the first ages of the Church, or afterwards received upon just grounds, by public or lawful authority:

14. Finally, in the reception of all ecclesiastical constitutions and canons made for the ordering of our Church; or others which are not repugnant either to the Word of God, or the power of kings, or the laws established by right authority in any nation.

The State of Us who Adhere to the Church of England

THE ROMAN CATHOLICS:	THE REFORMED CHURCHES:
1. SAY and believe (as by the articles of their new creed they are bound to believe) that we are all damned, and accursed persons.	1. SAY and believe (as we do) that we profess and believe whatsoever is necessary to salvation; and that it is an accursed belief which the Roman Catholics have of us.
2. They call us heretics.	2. These acknowledge us to be true Catholics.
3. They excommunicate us, and abhor to join with us in any sacred action either of prayer or sacraments.	3. They do most willingly receive us into their churches, and frequently repair to ours, joining with us both in prayers and sacraments.

4. Not long since, they burned us (both alive and dead) at their stakes; and, where the edicts of princes restrain them not, they do so still, as by their own laws they have obliged themselves to do; which laws (if civil respects suspend them not for the time) they can put in execution at an hour's warning, when they please.

4. These men, (whose predecessors were burned up and martyred, as ours have been,) being in such times of persecution received and harboured in our Churches, gave us the like relief in theirs, both in Germany and France; where, when at any time we come, they have obtained freedom for us from this kind of persecution, under which we might otherwise suffer and be in continual danger to lose our lives.

5. They will allow us no other burial of our dead, than the burial of a dog; accounting their churches and their churchyards to be polluted, if any of our people be there put into a grave; and whoever it is among them, (be it a son that shall bury his father, or a wife her husband, that die in our religion,) if they venture to make a grave there, and put the dead corpse either of a father, or a husband, or other the like into it, they are bound to scrape up that corpse again with their own fingers, and carry it away to be buried in a ditch, or a dunghill, or where else they can find room for it: prince or peasant are herein alike: if they be not Roman Catholics, they shall be used no better.

5. They allow us, not only to bury our dead among theirs in the churchyards which they have purchased and peculiarly set apart for that purpose, but they give us leave also to use our own Office and Order of Burial, (at least they hinder us not to do it, if the Roman Catholics permit it,) and to set up our monuments and inscriptions over the graves, hereby professing unity with us both alive and dead.

In all which regards we ought no less acknowledge them, and to make no schism between our Churches and theirs, however we approve not some defects that may be seen among them.

John Cosin, 'A Paper Concerning the Differences in the Chief Points of Religion Betwixt the Church of Rome and the Church of England' and 'The State of Us who Adhere to the Church of England', in *Works*, vol. 4, pp. 332–8.

The Church in space and time

Despite polemics such as those above, much writing about the Church continued in a strongly catechetical vein, emphasizing shared principles and the unity which all Christians share across space and time, with the living no less than the dead.

The necessity of the belief of this Communion of Saints appeareth, first, in that it is proper to excite and encourage us to holinesse of life. *If we walk in the light, as God is in the light, we have fellowship one with another.*[6] But *if we say that we have fellowship with him, and walk in darknesse, we lie, and do not the truth. For what fellowship hath righteousnesse with unrighteousnesse? and what communion hath light with darknesse? and what concord hath Christ with Belial?*[7] When Christ sent S. *Paul* to the Gentiles, it was *to open their eyes, and to turn them from darkness to light, and from the power of Satan unto God, that they might receive forgivenesse of sins, and inheritance among them which are sanctified by faith that is in Christ.*[8] Except we be turned from darknesse, except we be taken out of the power of Satan, which is the dominion of sin, we cannot receive the inheritance among them which are sanctified, we cannot be thought *meet to be partakers of the inheritance of the Saints in light.*[9] Indeed there can be no communion where there is no similitude, no fellowship with God without some sanctity; because his nature is infinitely holy, and his actions are not subject to the least iniquity.

Secondly, the belief of *the Communion of Saints* is necessary to stir us up to a proportionate gratitude unto God, and an humble and cheerfull acknowledgement of so great a benefit. We cannot but acknowledge that they are *exceeding great and precious promises*, by which we become *partakers of the divine nature.*[10] *What am I?* said David, *and what is my life that I should be son in law to the King?*[11] What are we the sons of men, what are they which are called to be Saints, that they should have fellowship with God the Father? S. *Philip* the Apostle said unto our Saviour, *Lord, shew us the Father and it sufficeth;*[12] whereas

---

6 [1 Joh. 1.6, 7.]
7 [2 Cor. 6.14, 15.]
8 [Act. 26.18.]
9 [Col. 1.12.]
10 [2 Pet. 1.4.]
11 [1 Sam. 18.18.]
12 [Joh. 14.8.]

he hath not onely shewn us, but come unto us with the Father, and dwelt within us by his holy Spirit; he hath called us to the fellowship of Angels and Archangels, of the Cherubins and Seraphins, to the glorious company of the Apostles, to the goodly fellowship of the Prophets, to the noble Army of Martyrs, to the holy Church militant in earth, and triumphant in heaven.

Thirdly, the belief of *the Communion of Saints* is necessary to inflame our hearts with an ardent affection towards those which live, and a reverent respect towards those which are departed and are now with God. Nearnesse of relation requireth affection, and that man is unnaturall who loveth not those persons which nature hath more immediately conjoyned to him. Now no conjunction naturall can be compared with that which is spirituall, no temporall relation with that which is eternall. If similitude of shape and feature will create a kindesse, if congruity of manners and disposition will conjoyn affections; what should be the mutuall love of those who have the image of the same God renewed within them, of those who are endued with the gracious influences of the same Spirit? And if all the Saints of God living in communion of the Church deserve the best of our affections here on earth: certainly when they are dissolved and with Christ, when they have been blessed with a sight of God, and rewarded with a Crown of glory, they may challenge some respect from us, who are here to wait upon the will of God expecting when such a happy change shall come.

To conclude, every one may learn from hence what he is to understand by this part of the Article, in which he professeth to believe *the Communion of Saints*; for thereby he is conceived to express thus much; I am fully perswaded of this as of a necessary and infallible truth, that such persons as are truly sanctified in the Church of Christ, while they live among the crooked generations of men, and struggle with all the miseries of this world, have fellowship with God the Father, God the Son, and God the Holy Ghost, as dwelling with them, and taking up their habitations in them: that they partake of the care and kindnesse of the blessed Angels, who take delight in the ministration for their benefit: that beside the externall fellowship which they have in the Word and Sacraments with all the members of the Church, they have an intimate union and conjunction with all the Saints on earth as the living members of Christ; nor is this union separated by the death of any, but as Christ in whome they live, is the Lamb slain from the foundation of the world, so have they fellowship with all the Saints which from the death of *Abel* have ever departed in the true faith and fear of God, and now enjoy the presence of the Father, and follow the Lamb whithersoever he goeth. And thus I believe *the Communion of Saints*.

John Pearson, *An Exposition of the Apostles Creed* (1659), pp. 717–19

That we reverently receive also the unanimous *Tradition* or Doctrine of the Church in all ages, which determines the *meaning* of the holy Scripture; and makes it more clear and unquestionable in any point of Faith, wherein we can find it hath declared its sense. For we look upon this *Tradition* as nothing else but the *Scripture unfolded*: not a new thing, which is not in the Scripture; but the Scripture explained and made more evident.

And thus some part of the *Nicene Creed* may be called a *Tradition*; as it hath expresly delivered unto us the sense of the Church of God, concerning that great Article of our Faith; that Jesus Christ is *the Son of God*. Which they teach us was always thus understood; the Son of God, *begotten of his Father before all worlds, and of the same substance with the Father*.

But this Tradition supposes the Scripture for its ground; and delivers nothing but what the Fathers, assembled at *Nicaea*, believed to be contained there; and was first fetch'd from thence. For we find in *Theodoret* (L.I. C.6) that the famous Emperour *Constantine*, admonished those Fathers, in all their questions and debates to consult onely with these heavenly inspired Writings: *because the Evangelical, and Apostolical Books, and the Oracles of the old Prophets, do evidently instruct us what to think in Divine matters*. This is so clear a Testimony, that in those days, they made this the complete Rule of their Faith, whereby they ended Controversies (which was the reason that in several other Synods we find they were wont to lay the Bible before them) and that there is nothing in the *Nicene Creed*, but what is to be found in the Bible; that Cardinal *Bellarmine*[13] hath nothing to reply to it, but this: *Constantine was indeed a great Emperour, but no great Doctour*. Which is rather a scoff, than an Answer: and casts a scorn not onely upon him, but upon that great Council, who, as the same *Theodoret*, witnesseth, assented unto that Speech of *Constantine*. So it there follows in these words, *the most of the Synod were obedient to what he had discoursed; and embraced both mutual Concord, and sound Doctrine*.

And accordingly S. *Hilary* a little after extols his Son *Constantius* for this, that he adhered to the Scriptures; and blames him onely for not attending to the true Catholick sense of them. His words are these, (in his little book, which he delivered to *Constantius*) *I truly admire thee, O*

---

13 Roberto Bellarmino (d. 1621), Roman Catholic controversialist.

The Church

Lord Constantius the Emperour, who desirest a Faith according to what is written. They pretended to no other in those days; but, (as he speaks a little after) look'd upon him *that refused this, as Antichrist.* It was onely required that they should receive their Faith out of *God's Books,* not merely according to the *words* of them, but according to their true *meaning* (because many *spake Scripture without Scripture, and pretended to Faith without Faith,* as his words are) and herein Catholick and constant Tradition was to guide them. For whatsoever was contrary, to what the whole Church had received and held from the beginning, could not in reason be thought to be the meaning of that Scripture, which was alleged to prove it. And, on the other side, the Church pretended to no more than to be a Witness of the received sense of the Scriptures: which were the bottom upon which they built this Faith.

Thus I observe *Hegesippus* saith (in *Euseb.* his History, L.IV. C.22) that when he was at *Rome* he met with a great many Bishops, and that he *received the very same Doctrine from them all.* And then, a little after, tells us what that was, and whence they derived it, saying, *that in every succession of Bishops, and in every City, so they held; as the Law preached, and as the Prophets, and as the Lord.* That is, according to the Doctrine of the Old and New Testament.

I shall conclude this particular, with a pregnant passage, which I remember in a famous Divine of our Church (D. *Jackson,* in his Treatise of the Catholick Church, *Chap.* 22.) who writes to this effect,

That Tradition, which was of so much use in the Primitive Church, was not *unwritten Traditions* or customs, commended or ratified by the supposed infallibility of any visible Church, but did especially consist in the *Confessions,* or *Registers* of particular Churches. And the unanimous consent of so many several Churches, as exhibited their confessions to the *Nicene* Council, out of such Forms as had been framed, and taught before this Controversie arose, about the Divinity of Christ; and that voluntarily and freely (these Churches being not dependent one upon another; nor overswayed by any Authority over them; nor misled by faction to frame their confessions of Faith by imitation, or according to some pattern set them) was a pregnant argument, that this Faith wherein they all agreed, had been delivered to them by the Apostles and their followers, and was the true meaning of the holy Writings, in this great Article: and evidently proved, that *Arius* did obtrude such interpretations of Scripture, as had not been heard of before; or were but the sense of some private persons in the Church, and not of the generality of Believers.

In short the unanimous consent of so many distinct visible Churches, as exhibited their several Confessions, Catechisms, or Testimonies, of their own or Forefathers Faith unto the Council of *Nicaea*, was an argument of the same force and efficacy against *Arius* and his partakers, as the General consent and practice of all Nations, in worshipping a Divine Power in all ages, is against *Atheists*. Nothing but the ingrafted notion of a Deity, could have induced so many several Nations, so much different in natural disposition, in civil disposition and education, to affect or practise the duty of Adoration. And nothing but the evidence of *the ingrafted word* (as Saint *James* calls the Gospel) delivered by Christ and his Apostles in the holy Scriptures, could have kept so many several Churches, as communicated their Confessions unto that Council, in the unity of the same Faith.

The like may be said of the rest of the *four first General Councils*; whose Decrees are a great confirmation of our belief: because they deliver to us, the consent of the Churches of Christ, in those great Truths, which they assert out of the holy Scriptures.

And could there any *Traditive* Interpretation of the whole Scripture be produced, upon the Authority of such *Original Tradition*, as that now named; we would most thankfully and joyfully receive it. But there never was any such pretended; no, not by the Roman Church: whose Doctours differ among themselves, about the meaning of hundreds of places in the Bible. Which they would not doe sure, nor spend their time unprofitably, in making the best conjectures they are able; if they knew of any exposition of those places, in which all Christian Doctours had agreed from the beginning.

Simon Patrick, *A Discourse about Tradition* (1683), pp. 18–22

13

From Dust to Dust

Birth, childhood, marriage and death were topics of reflection in numerous literary genres, from poetry to devotional prayers, from catechetical manuals to liturgical commentaries. Although the Book of Common Prayer provided a shared framework for the human experience, the historical realities of civil war and military rule sometimes invested the very discussion of major life events with strong political overtones. Robert Herrick's poetic encomium on the Churching of women celebrated a service that dissenters hated. Jeremy Taylor's sermon on the marriage ring was printed in 1653 when Christian weddings had been outlawed. Archbishop Laud's prayers on death were composed shortly before he was beheaded. The following selections offer a window on to the Anglican experience from dust to dust, an experience that was hardened by the fires of persecution and religious violence.

Birth

A Prayer to be used by a Woman with CHILD.

O God, the Author of our being, the Fountain of life, and all other good; who hast begun an excellent work in me, which no eye but thine sees, and no hand but thy Almighty power can finish. I adore thy great and glorious Majesty in this and in all other thy works of wonder. *Thou dost great things without number:*[1] but art more particularly to be acknowledged in the formation of mankind, who *are fearfully and wonderfully made*,[2] after thy own image and likeness.

Be pleased, O Lord, in thy infinite goodness to perfect and compleat that which thou hast begun. Preserve the smallest degree of life, which

---

1 Job 5.9.
2 Psalm 139.14.

thou hast inspired. Bestow upon it intireness of all its parts: and prepare a convenient habitation for an understanding spirit, capable of the best wisdom, and inclinable to vertue and goodness. Prevent, good Lord, the miscarriage of my hopes; and ripen them to a good issue. And the nearer they come to their full growth; strengthen the more my humble trust in thee, and submission to thee, and hearty desires to encrease the number of thy faithful people, together with my own Family.

That ought to be the chiefest desire of my soul, to be formed my self in all things, according to the mind and will of thee, my God; that so I may be an instrument of doing good to others. O thou who hast wrought many holy purposes and resolutions in my heart, preserve and confirm them, that they may not prove abortive; but bring forth continually the fruit of good living. Perfect me in Knowledge, in Faith, in Love, and in Obedience. Enable me so discreetly and carefully to discharge the duties of all the Relations wherein I at present, or shall hereafter, stand: that I may be a comfort to them, and a credit to Religion. And howsoever thou disposest of me or them, Lord, make me well contented, and in every condition to give thanks unto thee, and rejoyce in thy holy Name and in the hope of eternal life; through Christ Jesus my most blessed Lord and Saviour. *Amen.*

Simon Patrick, *The Devout Christian Instructed* (1674), pp. 356–8

Put on thy *Holy Fillitings*,[3] and so
To th' Temple with the sober *Midwife* go.
Attended thus (in a most solemn wise)
By those who serve the Child-bed misteries.
Burn first thine incense; next, when as thou see'st
The candid Stole thrown ore the *Pious Priest*:
With reverend Curtsies come, and to him bring
Thy free (and not decurted[4]) offering.
All Rites well ended, with faire Auspice come
(As to the breaking of a Bride-Cake) home:
Where ceremonious *Hymen* shall for thee
Provide a second *Epithalimie.*
*She who keeps chastely to her husbands side
Is not for one, but every night his Bride:*

---

3 Veil.
4 Reduced.

And stealing still with love, and feare to Bed,
Brings him not one, but many a Maiden-head.

Robert Herrick, 'Julia's Churching, or Purification', *Hesperides* (1648),
p. 339

BLEST Infant Bud, whose Blossome-life
Did only look about, and fal,
Wearyed out in a harmles strife
Of tears, and milk, the food of all;

Sweetly didst thou expire: Thy soul
Flew home unstain'd by his new kin,
For ere thou knew'st how to be foul,
Death *wean'd* thee from the world, and sin.

Softly rest all thy Virgin-crumbs!
Lapt in the sweets of thy young breath,
Expecting till thy Saviour Comes
To *dresse* them, and *unswaddle* death.

Henry Vaughan, 'The Burial of an Infant', *Silex Scintillans* (1650), p. 71

First, there is a great difference to be made, between the sole want of baptism upon invincible necessity, and the contempt or wilful neglect of Baptism when it may be had. The latter we acknowledge to be a damnable sin and without repentance and Gods extraordinary mercy, to exclude a man from all hope of salvation. But yet if such a person, before his death, shall repent and deplore his neglect of the means of grace, from his heart, and desire with all his Soul to be Baptised, but is debarred from it invincibly, we do not, we dare not pass sentence of condemnation upon him; nor yet the Roman Catholicks themselves. The question then is, whether the want of baptism upon invincible necessity, do evermore infallibly exclude from heaven?

Secondly, We distinguish between the Visible sign, and the Invisible Grace; between the exterior sacramentall Ablution, and the grace of the sacrament, that is interior Regeneration. We believe, that whosoever hath the former hath the latter also, so that he do not put a barr against the efficacy of the sacrament by his infidelity or Hypocrisy, of which a Child is not capable. And therefore our very Liturgy doth teach, that a Child baptised, dying before the commission of actual sin is undoubtedly saved. Secondly, We believe that without baptismal grace, that is regeneration, no man can enter into the Kingdom of God. But whether God hath so tied and bound himself to his ordinances and sacraments that he doth not or cannot conferr the grace of the sacraments, extraordinarily, where it seemeth good in his eyes, without the outward element, This is the question between us.

Thirdly, We teach that the case is not alike with little infants born of Christian Parents, who die unbaptised, without their own fault, and men of age and discretion such as *Nicodemus* was, to whom Christ said, *Except ye be born again of water and of the spirit ye cannot enter, into the Kingdom of Heaven*.[5] These latter can have no hope of salvation in an ordinary way, except they be baptised either in deed or desire. But we dare not pass a definitive sentence against the former, whose want of Baptism is not their own fault, but the fault of their Parents, seing that God hath said, that *As he lives the son shall not bear the iniquity of his father*.[6] Yet do we not believe, that the Children of Christian parents do derive any inward or inherent sanctity by propagation (as is by some imputed to us, amiss). We know well that a Christian begets not a Christian. But that holiness, which saint *Paul* ascribes to the Children of believing parents, *if the root be Holy, so are the Branches*,[7] we expound of an exterior or ecclesiastical sanctity, or a right to the Sacrament of Baptism by the priviledge of their birth, being not born forreiners, but natives and free-men of the Church. And for as much as they have a right to the sacrament, but are defrauded of it without their own defaults, we believe, that God, who hath not limited his grace to his outward ordinances, may and doth many times according to his good pleasure supply the defect of others, and operate in them the grace of the Sacrament by his Holy Spirit.

John Bramhall, 'Of Persons Dying Without Baptism', *Works* (1677), pp. 979–80

Childhood

I exhort all you who are parents, to instil good things into your Children, as soon as ever they begin to speak; let the first words they utter, if possible, be these, *Glory be to God*. Accustom them to repeat these words on their knees, as soon as they Rise, and when they go to bed, and oft times in the day; and let them not eat or drink, without saying, *Glory be to God*.

---

5 John 3.5.
6 Ezekiel 18.20.
7 Romans 11.16.

As their Speech grows more plain and easie to them, Teach them who Made, and Redeem'd, and Sanctified them, and for what End, Namely, to Glorifie and to Love GOD; and withal, teach them some of the shortest Ejaculations[8] you can, such as these;

Lord help me, Lord save me.
Lord have Mercy upon me.
All Love, all Glory be to God, who first loved me.
Lord keep me in Thy love.

Within a little time you may teach them the Lord's Prayer, and hear them say it every day, Morning and Evening, on their knees, with some one or more of the fore-going Ejaculations; and by degrees as they grow up, they will learn the Creed, and the whole Catechism.

Be sure to teach your Children with all the sweetness and gentleness you can, lest if you should be severe, or should over-task them, Religion should seem to them, rather a Burden than a Blessing.

As their Knowledge encreases, so let their Prayers encrease also, and teach them as they go to turn their Catechism in Prayers, after the manner which I shall shew you, and to Confirm and improve their Knowledge, bring them duly to the Church to be Catechised by the parish Priest, that by his familiar and devout Explications of the Catechism, they may learn to understand it, and may be capable of Reading the Exposition on it, and other Books of Piety.

Take conscientious Care to Season your Children as early as you can, with the Love of GOD, which is *the first and great Commandment,*[9] and with *the Fear of God* which *is the Beginning of wisdom;*[10] for the awful Love, and the Filial Fear of God, must always go together.

Thomas Ken, *An Exposition on the Church Catechism* (1685), pp. 108–9

A short Prayer for the use of a little CHILD.

O Lord, my most loving Saviour and merciful Redeemer; who commandedst that the little children should come unto thee, and didst take them up in thine arms, lay thy hands upon them, & bless them: Look graciously upon me, I humbly beseech thee, and bless me; who am one

---

8 Short prayers.
9 [Matth. 22.38.]
10 [Psal. 111.10.]

of thy children, dedicated to thy service. Pitty the weakness of my tender age, and prevent[11] me betimes with thy grace. Make me seriously to remember my Creator in the days of my youth.[12] Endue me with the fear of my God: and make me always mindful of the Vow and Promise that was made in my name, when I was baptized; *to forsake the Devil and all his works, to believe in God and to serve him.*

Make me dutiful (as thou O Lord Jesus wast) unto my Parents [*loving to my Brethren and Sisters*] obedient to my Instructors: thankful for the good counsel of my Friends: humble and reverent to my betters: and meek and gentle to all men. That as I grow in years, so I may grow in wisdom and favour with thee, and with all those who are good.

Preserve me from all dangers; let thy good Angels be my keepers and defenders; and guide me by thy holy Spirit; that the longer I live, the better I may be: to the comfort of my Parents, and the honor and glory of my God, and my own happiness, here and for ever. *Amen.*

A shorter.

Heavenly Father, who despisest nothing that thou hast made, but takest care of the beasts of the Earth, and of the fowls of the Air: bless me thy child, whom thou hast made in thy own Image. Preserve me this day from all evil, both in soul and body. Give me what thou seest good for me. Especially an heart to know thee early, to be thankful to thee, to love thee, and to do thy will, as well as I am able. Bless my Father and my Mother, and all my friends: and make me a follower of those who are good; for the sake of my Saviour Christ Jesus the Lord. *Amen.*

Simon Patrick, *The Devout Christian Instructed* (1674), pp. 399–401

The imposition of Hands is one of the most antient Ceremonies in the World, observed by *Jacob* in the giving of his blessing, *Gen.* 48.14. and by his Example ever practised among the Jews in Benedictions, in conferring of all holy Offices, *Numb.* 27.18. and to many other purposes in their Religion; whereupon our Lord Jesus used it also when he blessed little Children, *Math.* 19.13. as well as when he healed the sick, *Math.* 8.15. and the Apostles adopted it to be the Rite, for Communicating the Spirit in Confirmation, *Acts* 8.17. which was so regularly observed, that it gave name to the whole Office, which is called, *Laying on of Hands, Hebrews*

---

11 Go before.
12 Ecclesiastes 12.1.

6.2. as we noted before, and not only St. *Augustine*,[13] but most of the Latine writers call it usually Imposition of Hands; nor was Confirmation ever Ministred without Laying on of Hands. The Roman Church of late hath left it out, and instead thereof use anointing and giving the party a Box on the Ear: But our Church hath restored this Essential and Apostolick Rite; and as upon *Moses* laying his Hands upon the Seventy Elders, God put his Spirit upon them, *Numb.* 11.17. so we hope he will impart it to us when the Bishop lays his hand upon us, see *Numb.* 6.27. and therefore we kneel most humbly when we receive it. It was antiently the manner for the Bishop to lay both his hands a-cross on the head of the confirmed, not only in imitation of *Jacob, Gen.* 48. but with allusion to the Death of Christ in whom we believe, and from whom we receive the Holy Ghost. But this is now laid aside. It may seem more strange to some, how our Reformers came to omit the Ceremony of anointing with Oyl, used so antiently in the Latine Church, and in the Greek also, that it hath caused the whole Office to be called Chrism, or Anointing, and by that name it is called in some very antient Canons: But it must be considered, that this Oyl or Chrism is not of Apostolical Institution, nor use in *Confirmation*, but was added after their times in allusion to that Oyl unto which the Holy Spirit is compared, for its healing and flaming qualities: and I am apt to believe this anointing was first added to the office of Baptism, but not used in Confirmation till afterwards, which hath occasioned divers to mistake, who apply many places of Antiquity where the Baptismal anointing is mentioned, as if they belonged to Confirmation . . . our Reformation hath restored the Primitive Ceremony, and rejected the Anointing, well-knowing it was not essential to this Office, nor used by the Apostles, so that if any shall object there is a deficiency in our Confirmation, he may say there was a defect in that of the Apostles also, since we do all that it is recorded they did.

Thomas Comber, 'The Laying on of Hands',
A Brief Discourse upon the Offices of Baptism and Confirmation (1674),
pp. 446–8

Marriage and household

A Prayer to be used by any Married Person.

O Most holy Father, who in Paradise didst appoint and consecrate the conjugal State, bless thy Servant to whom that holy state has obliged me

---

13 [August. in Donat. de Baptis. Lib.3. Cap.16.]

in the Sacred Tyes of Love and Duty: Teach us mutual Forbearance, and Tenderness, and Kindness to one another; and let a perfect Harmony and Agreement of our Affections, be the Evidence, that by that holy State thou hast made us one: Bless us together with all Spiritual and Temporal Blessings; forgive all our Failings and Infirmities, and let the most sincere and sacred Love sweeten and endear the Cares that attend that state of Life, and fit us to be ever happy with the God of Peace and Love, through Jesus Christ our most Blessed Lord and Savior. *Amen.*

Benjamin Whichcote, *A Compendium of Devotion* (1697), p. 283

Family. Home.

Visit, I ask, my dwelling O Lord, and drive far from her all the traps of the enemy; let Your holy angels dwell in her, and let them guard us in peace and health, and may Your blessing be upon us always through Jesus Christ our Lord. Amen.

The Kingdom of England.

Bless, O Lord God almighty, this kingdom, that health, fidelity, victory, all virtue may be in it, and thanksgiving to God the Father, and to the Son, and to the Holy Spirit: and let this blessing remain upon this kingdom, and upon those dwelling in it, through Jesus Christ our Lord. Amen.

William Laud, translated from *A Summarie of Devotions* (1667), in *Works*, Vol. 3 (1853), pp. 44, 69

Single life makes men in one instance to be like Angels, but marriage in very many things makes the chast pair to be like to Christ. *This is a great mystery,*[14] but it is the symbolicall and sacramentall representment of the greatest mysteries of our Religion. Christ descended from his Fathers bosome, and contracted his divinity with flesh and bloud, and married our Nature, and we became a Church, the spouse of the bridegroom, which he cleansed with his bloud, and gave her his holy Spirit for a dowry, and heaven for a joynture; begetting children unto God by the Gospel; this spouse he hath joyn'd to himself by an excellent charity, he feeds her at his own table, and lodges her nigh his own heart, provides for all her necessities, relieves her sorrowes, determines her doubts, guides her wandrings, he is become her head, and she as a signet upon his right hand . . . Here is the eternall conjunction, the

---

14 Ephesians 5.32.

indissoluble knot, the exceeding love of Christ, the obedience of the Spouse, the communicating of goods, the uniting of interests, the fruit of marriage, a celestiall generation, a new creature; *Sacramentum hoc magnum est*,[15] this is the sacramentall mystery represented by the holy rite of marriage; so that marriage is divine in its institution, sacred in its union, holy in the mystery, sacramentall in its signification, honourable in its appellative, religious in its imployments: It is advantage to the societies of men, and it is *holinesse to the Lord. Dico autem in Christo & Ecclesia*, It must be in Christ and the Church.

If this be not observed, marriage loses its mysteriousnesse: but because it is to effect much of that which it signifies, it concerns all that enter into those golden fetters to see that Christ and his Church be in at every of its periods, and that it be intirely conducted and over-rul'd by Religion; for so the Apostle passes from the sacramentall rite to the reall duty; *Neverthelesse*, that is, although the former discourse were wholly to explicate the conjunction of Christ and his Church by this similitude, yet it hath in it this reall duty, *that the man love his wife, and the wife reverence her husband.*

Jeremy Taylor, Sermon XVII: The Marriage Ring,
A Course of Sermons (1653), pp. 223–4

Sleeping in Christ

A Prayer.

O Lord Jesus Christ, Son of the living God, interpose I pray thee, thine owne pretious death, thy Crosse and Passion, betwixt my soule and thy Judgement, now and in the hour of my death. And vouchsafe to grant unto me thy grace and mercie, remission and rest; To the Church, peace, and concord; to us sinners, life, and glory everlasting; who livest and raignest with the Father, in the unitie of the Holy Ghost, one God, world without end: Amen.

Richard Crashaw, *Steps to the Temple* (1648), p. 14

O eternal God, I implore your help, that on account of Your pity You deem worthy to give me true discretion, and perfect charity, to whom

---

15 This is a great mystery.

is the glory and the power with the Father and the Holy Spirit for ever. Amen.

O merciful Lord, who has conceded such favours to me, grant to me to have true faith to hold with all humility, to preserve complete charity with all men, to serve you my Lord with a pure heart and with a chaste body, let me toil earnestly all the way to the end of life, so that after the toil I may be able to hear that longed for voice; Well done good servant, enter into the joy of your Lord. Amen.

> William Laud, translated from *A Summarie of Devotions* (1667), in *Works*, Vol. 3 (1853), p. 86

Advice concerning Confession.

I.

That besides this Examination of your Conscience (which may be done in secret between God and your own Soul) there is great use of Holy Confession: which though it be not generally in all Cases, and peremptorily commanded, as if without it no Salvation could possibly be had; yet you are advised by the Church under whose discipline you live, that before you are to receive the Holy Sacrament, or when you are visited with any dangerous sickness, if you finde any one particular sin or more that lies heavy upon you, to disburthen your self of it into the Bosome of your Confessour, who not only stands between God and you to pray for you, but hath the power of the Keys committed to him, upon your true Repentance to Absolve you in Christs Name from those sins which you have confessed to him.

II.

You are to remember that you bring along with you to Confession not only unfeigned Sorrow and Remorse of Conscience for sins past, but setled Resolutions for the time to come never to offend in the same kinde again: for without this, Confession is but a mere Pageant, and rather a mockery of God, then any effectual means to reconcile you to him.

III.

That having made choice of such a Confessor who is every way qualified that you may trust your Soul with him, you are advised plainly and sincerely to open your heart to him; and that laying aside all consideration of any personal weakness in him, you are to look upon him only as he is a Trustee from God, and commissioned by him as his Ministerial Deputy to hear, and judge, and absolve you.

IV.

That the Manner of your Confession be in an humble posture on your knees, as being made to God rather then man: and for the Matter of it, let it be severe and serious; but yet so as it may be without any inordinate Anxiety and unnecessary Scruples, which serve only to entangle the Soul, and in stead of setting you free (which is the benefit to be looked for by Confession) perplex you the more.

V.

That for the frequency of doing this, you are to consult with your own necessities: and as your Physician is not sent for upon every small distemper, which your own care may rectifie; so neither are you obliged upon every failing to be overscrupulous, or to think it a point of Necessity presently to confess it: For the Confessor cannot be always present, but your God is, to whom if you apply your self with Prayers and Penitence, confessing in his ears alone whatever you have done amiss, and stedfastly believing that through the merits of your Saviour they shall never be imputed to you, you may be confident that your Absolution is at that time sealed in Heaven, but the comfortable Declaration of it you are to look for from the Priest.

Brian Duppa, *A Guide for the Penitent* (1660), pp. 4–7

Of Burial.

When they come to the Grave, while the corps is made ready to be laid into the grave, *the Priest shall say or sing, Man that is born of a Woman,* &c. closing with a most devout prayer for grace and assistance in our last hour; a prayer very suitable to such a time, and such a spectacle before us.

Then they commit the body to the earth, (not as a lost and perished carcasse, but as having in it a seed of eternity) *in sure and certain hope of the resurrection to eternall life.* This is to bury it Christianly; the hope of the resurrection, being the proper hope of Christians. Such was the Christians burial of old, that it was accounted both an evident argument and presage of the resurrection; and an honour done to that body, which the holy Ghost had once made his Temple for the Offices of piety. *Aug.* de *Civit.* l.1. c.13.

After follows another Triumphant Hymn. Then a Lesson out of *S. Paul* to the same purpose; Then a Thanksgiving for that our brothers safe delivery out of misery; lastly a Prayer for his and our consummation in Glory, and joyfull Absolution at the last day. By all which prayers, praises, and holy lessons, and decent solemnities, we do glorifie God, Honour the dead, and comfort the living.

Take away these prayers, praises, and holy lessons, which were ordained to shew at Burials, the peculiar hope of the Church of the Resurrection of the dead, and in the manner of the dumbe funerals, what one thing is there, whereby the world may perceive that we are Christians? *HOOKER* l.5. *Eccl. Pol.* §75. there being in those dumb shews nothing but what heathens and pagans do, How can any *unlearned or unbeliever* be convinced by them, that either we who are present at them do, or that he ought to beleeve any part of Christian Religion? but when the unlearned or unbeleever hears us sing triumphant songs to God for our victory over death, when he hears holy Lessons and discourses of the Resurrection, when he hears us praying for a happy and joyful Resurrection to Glory: by all these he must be convinc'd, that we do beleeve the Resurrection, which is a principal Article of Christian faith, and the same may be the means to convince him also, and make him believe the same, *and so fall down and worship God*. And this is according to S. *Pauls* rule, 1 *Cor.* 14.23, 24, 25. who thence concludes, that all our publick religious services ought to be done, that the *unlearned or unbeleever may be convinced, and brought to worship God.*

Anthony Sparrow, *A Rationale upon the Book of Common-Prayer* (1657), pp. 352–5

Conclusion

Venat. Well master! these Verses be worthy to keep a room in every mans memory. I thank you for them; and I thank you for your many instructions, which (God willing) I will not forget: and as St. *Austin*, in his Confessions (book 4. chap. 3.) commemorates the kindness of his friend *Verecundus*, for lending him and his companion a *Country-house*, because there they rested and enjoyed themselves free from the troubles of the world; so, having had the like advantage, both by your conversation, and the Art you have taught me, I ought ever to do the like: for indeed, your company and discourse have been so useful and pleasant, that I may truly say, *I have only lived since I enjoyed them, and turned Angler, and not before.* Nevertheless, here I must part with you, here in this now sad place where I was so happy at first to meet you: But I shall long for the ninth of *May*, for then I hope again to enjoy your beloved company at the appointed time and place. And now I wish for some *somniferous potion*, that might force me to sleep away the intermitted time, which will pass away with me as tediously, as it does with men in sorrow; nevertheless I will make it as short as I can by my *hopes* and *wishes*. And my good Master, I will not forget the doctrine which you told me *Socrates* taught his Scholars, *That they should not think to be honoured so much for being* Philosophers, *as to honour* Philosophy *by their vertuous lives.* You advised me to the like concerning *Angling*, and I will endeavour to do so, and to live like those many *worthy men*, of which you made mention in the former part of your discourse. This is my firm resolution; and as a pious man advised his friend, *That to beget* Mortification *he should frequent* Churches; *and view* Monuments, *and* Charnel-houses, *and then and there consider, how many dead bones time had pil'd up at the gates of death.* So when I would beget *content*, and increase confidence in the *Power*, and *Wisdom*, and *Providence* of Almighty God, I will walk the *Meadows* by some gliding stream, and there contemplate the *Lillies* that take no care,[1] and those very many other various living

---

[1] Matthew 6.28; Luke 12.27.

creatures, that are not only created but fed (man knows not how) by the goodness of the God of *Nature*, and therefore trust in him. This is my purpose: and so, *Let everything that hath breath praise the Lord.*[2] And let the blessing of *St. Peters* Master be with mine.

Pisc. And upon all that are lovers of *Vertue*; and dare trust in his *providence*, and be *quiet*, and go a *Angling*.

Study to be quiet, 1 Thes. 4.11.

FINIS.

Izaak Walton, *The Compleat Angler* (1676), pp. 274–5

---

[2] Psalm 150.6.

Recommended Reading

The following is not intended to be exhaustive, but to provide readers with a solid basis for further study.

Primary sources

One should begin with Cicero, *On Duties*, and Aristotle, *Nicomachean Ethics*, available in a variety of editions. Charles I, *Eikon Basilike*, edited by Jim Daems and Holly Faith Nelson (Broadview, 2006), is an accessible edition of the great Caroline work. Izaak Walton, *The Compleat Angler*, is also available in any number of editions. Those interested in Herbert, Traherne, Andrewes and Taylor should peruse the individual volumes of their writings in the present series.

Secondary sources

Background

Marc Bloch, *The Royal Touch: Monarchy and Miracles in England and France*, trans. J. E. Anderson (Routledge, 1989), is the classic study of the royal miracle. Pierre Hadot, *What is Ancient Philosophy?*. trans. Michael Chase (Harvard University Press, 2002), will illuminate the classical background of seventeenth-century concerns. Gregory D. Dodds, *Exploiting Erasmus: The Erasmus Legacy and Religious Change in Early Modern England* (University of Toronto Press, 2009), surveys the foundational place occupied by Erasmus in early Anglican history.

W. B. Patterson, *King James VI and I and the Reunion of Christendom* (Cambridge University Press, 1997) and Alister McGrath, *In the Beginning: The Story of the King James Bible and How It Changed a Nation, a Language, and a Culture* (Doubleday, 2001), offer much insight into the Jacobean foundations of the Caroline era. Peter Marshall, *Reformation England 1480–1642* (Hodder Arnold, 2003), will bring readers up to date on both the Reformation and current historical debates.

Devotion

Elizabeth Clarke, *Theory and Theology in George Herbert's Poetry: 'Divinitie, and Poesie, Met'* (Clarendon Press, 1997), is perhaps the most important volume on Herbert in the last quarter-century. Philip West, *Henry Vaughan's* Silex Scintillans: *Scripture Uses* (Oxford University Press, 2001), focuses on Vaughan's biblical imagination. Both studies delineate major trends in seventeenth-century Anglican poetry.

Thomas Corns (ed.), *The Royal Image: Representations of Charles I* (Cambridge University Press, 1999), contains essays on a wide variety of literary and visual sources pertaining to the royal saint. Andrew Lacey, *The Cult of King Charles the Martyr* (Boydell Press, 2003), is the place to begin studying the royal saint and his influence.

Liturgy

David Cressy, *Birth, Marriage & Death: Ritual, Religion, and the Life-Cycle in Tudor and Stuart England* (Oxford University Press, 1997) and *Bonfires & Bells: National Memory and the Protestant Calendar in Elizabethan and Stuart England* (Sutton, 2004), look at the personal and national elements of Anglican and dissenting practice.

Judith Maltby, *Prayer Book and People in Elizabethan and Early Stuart England* (Cambridge University Press, 1998) is a delightful study of popular devotion to the Prayer Book. Graham Parry, *The Arts of the Anglican Counter-Reformation: Glory, Laud and Honour* (Boydell Press, 2006), sets a host of changes, from architecture to literature, within the context of the 1630s.

Nigel Yates, *Buildings, Faith, and Worship: The Liturgical Arrangement of Anglican Churches 1600–1900*, revised ed. (Oxford University Press, 2000) and *Liturgical Space: Christian Worship and Church Buildings in Western Europe 1500–2000* (Ashgate, 2008), offer much comparative context for understanding Caroline-era churches.

Politics

Kevin Sharpe, *Criticism and Compliment: The Politics of Literature in the England of Charles I* (Cambridge, 1987) and *The Personal Rule of Charles I* (Yale University Press, 1992) remain groundbreaking and are required reading for anyone interested in the period. Richard Cust, *Charles I: A Political Life* (Pearson Longman, 2007), is a solid and well-rounded biography.

Conrad Russell, *The Causes of the English Civil War* (Clarendon Press, 1990) and John Adamson, *The Noble Revolt: The Overthrow of Charles I* (Weidenfield & Nicolson, 2007), are key monographs of the breakdown between 1637 and 1642.

Diane Purkiss, *The English Civil War: Papists, Gentlewomen, Soldiers, and Witchfinders in the Birth of Modern Britain* (Basic Books, 2006) and Michael Braddick, *God's Fury, England's Fire* (Penguin, 2008), touch upon everything from popular providentialism to military history.

N. H. Keeble, *The Restoration: England in the 1660s* (Blackwell, 2002), offers a broad portrait of the first decade of Restoration. Anna Keay, *The Magnificent Monarch: Charles II and the Ceremonies of Power* (Hambledon Continuum, 2008), is the premier study of the Restoration court and the development of royal ritual.

Science/The New Philosophy

Keith Thomas, *Man and the Natural World: Changing Attitudes in England 1500–1800* (Pantheon, 1984), and Lorraine Daston and Katharine Park, *Wonders and the Order of Nature 1150–1750* (Zone Books, 1998), provide insightful overviews of conceptions of nature in late-medieval and early-modern Europe.

Jan W. Wojcik, *Robert Boyle and the Limits of Reason* (Cambridge University Press, 1997) and Peter Harrison, *The Fall of Man and the Foundations of Science* (Cambridge University Press, 2007), are fascinating surveys of the rise of science amid theological debate and the doctrine of original sin.

Theology

Iain M. MacKenzie, *God's Order and Natural Law: The Works of the Laudian Divines* (Ashgate, 2002), is an expansive study of Caroline conceptions of order in creation, law and theology.

Peter White, *Predestination, Policy and Polemic: Conflict and Consensus in the English Church from the Reformation to the Civil War* (Cambridge University Press, 1992), is the most subtle analysis of predestinarian controversy in the pre-Civil War Church of England. Richard A. Muller, *God, Creation, and Providence in the Thought of*

Jacob Arminius: Sources and Directions of Protestant Scholasticism in the Era of Early Orthodoxy (Revell Books, 1991), sets predestinarian debate in its historic context, drawing especial attention to scholasticism.

H. R. McAdoo, *The Structure of Caroline Moral Theology* (Longmans, Green & Co., 1949), although dated, remains a fine study that may be read with great profit.

Anthony Milton, *Catholic and Reformed: The Roman and Protestant Churches in English Protestant Thought, 1600–1640* (Cambridge University Press, 1995), and Jean-Louis Quantin, *The Church of England and Christian Antiquity: The Construction of a Confessional Identity in the 17th Century* (Oxford University Press, 2009), are sustained by immense learning and cover what we now term ecclesiology.

www.ingramcontent.com/pod-product-compliance
Lightning Source LLC
Chambersburg PA
CBHW071340080526
44587CB00017B/2911